This is number two hundred and thirteen in the
second numbered series of the
Miegunyah Volumes
made possible by the
Miegunyah Fund
established by bequests
under the wills of
Sir Russell and Lady Grimwade.

'Miegunyah' was Russell Grimwade's home
from 1911 to 1955
and Mab Grimwade's home
from 1911 to 1973.

By the Same Author

The Land Boomers (1966) (expanded and revised, 1995, 2013)
Who's Master, Who's Man? (1971)
Land Boom and Bust (1972)
An Australian Camera (1973)
Lola Montes (1973)
Life in the Country (1973)
Life in the Cities (1975)
That Damned Democrat: John Norton (1981)
Australia: A History in Photographs (1983)
The Long Last Summer (1985)
Australia: Spirit of a Nation (1985)
The Exploration of Australia (1987)
Who Killed the Koories? (1990)
Old Melbourne Town: Before the Gold Rush (1991)
Melbourne after the Gold Rush (1993)
The Woman as Murderer (1994)
Perilous Voyages to the New Land (1995)
The Human Face of the Great Depression (1996)
That Disreputable Firm: Slater & Gordon (1998)
Living in the Clouds (2004)

Books Introduced and Edited

The Vagabond Papers (1969) (expanded and reprinted in 2016)
Australasian Sketcher 1880 (1970)
Australasian Sketcher 1873 (1973)
Famous News Pages in Modern Australian History (1973)
The Australian Thunderer (1973)
Australasian Sketcher 1874 (1975)
Police News (1976)
The Chronicles of Early Melbourne (1976)
Vagabond Country (1981)
Historical Records of Victoria (1981–91)
The Victorian Gold Fields, 1852–3: by S. T. Gill (1982)
Forty Years in the Wilderness (1990)
Vagabond Adventures in Asia and the Pacific (2018)
Vagabond Voyager: The Untold Story (2019)
The Vagabond as Social Reformer (2020)
Vagabond Days on the Queensland Frontier (2021)

Michael Cannon was the founding editor of *Historical Records of Victoria* and an award-winning journalist, newspaper editor and historian. He wrote and edited more than thirty books, including bestseller *The Land Boomers*, which caused a sensation in Australia in the 1960s.

CANNON FIRE

A LIFE IN PRINT

Michael Cannon

THE MIEGUNYAH PRESS

Written for the next generation—
Paul, Sarah (Za), James and Patrick Cannon.

THE MIEGUNYAH PRESS
An imprint of Melbourne University Publishing Limited
Level 1, 715 Swanston Street, Carlton, Victoria 3053, Australia
mup-contact@unimelb.edu.au
www.mup.com.au

First published 2022

Cover design by Sandy Cull
Typeset in 11.5/15.5pt Adobe Caslon Pro by Cannon Typesetting
Printed in Australia by McPherson's Printing Group

NATIONAL LIBRARY OF AUSTRALIA
A catalogue record for this book is available from the National Library of Australia

9780522878721 (paperback)
9780522878738 (ebook)

Contents

Author's Note viii

PART I AN AUSTRALIAN BOYHOOD

1 The Village: Childhood 3
2 The Town: Adolescence 43
3 The City: Youth 66

PART II JUMPING INTO LIFE

4 Early Days in Melbourne and Sydney 87
5 Adventures Overseas 112
6 Work, Love and Death 123

PART III LIFE REVISITED

7 Reckless Rupert and Other High-Flyers 165
8 Back to Old Melbourne Town 177
9 Books *Are* Different 204

PART IV LAST EFFORTS

10 All Dreams Must Fade 235

Postscript 238
Index 239

Author's Note

Ambition was a dull pain, like a continually broken heart.

Enid Shomer, *The Twelve Rooms of the Nile*

It is only too easy to forget the mistakes and humiliations of the past. The ageing brain, as it slowly closes down its functions, recalls fewer of its earlier traumas, takes satisfaction in its protective solutions, and dies with a smile on its hidden face. That is why, before it is too late, I have tried to remember accurately what life was like for me so long ago, in order that my descendants and others may know that they are not alone in this sad and joyous world.

PART I

AN AUSTRALIAN BOYHOOD

CHAPTER 1

The Village: Childhood

> Youth is a wonderful thing. What a pity to waste it on children.
>
> George Bernard Shaw

I'M TOLD THAT when my mother's labour pains started on a warm Queensland night in 1929, Dad ran out and flagged down the local milkman. The two of them helped her onto the dray, drawn by a horse which clip-clopped off to the hospital where I would soon be born.

In the earliest recollections I can call my own, it is always summer. The rain pelts down, but I cannot remember ever getting wet. At mid-year, the night temperature would fall so low that washing left on the line would snap-freeze, but I never felt cold. The sky was always red-hot, the birds were always singing. The people, who owned almost nothing, joked about simple events. That is what I most remember about the Great Depression of the early 1930s, which I spent in the town of Cobden.

Thinking about how we got from Queensland to that small Victorian settlement, I recall how, as a small child, I took most things about my family for granted—as though my relations were trees, rooted in one place, yet able to be replanted. Not until much later did I discover, to my mother's consternation, that our first Australian ancestor, an Irishman named Peter McGuire, had been transported after an unsuccessful career as a highwayman. His floggings ceased in Van Diemen's Land, where he became a supervisor of convict labour gangs, was granted 60 acres of land as a reward, and began to grow crops and children. One of those offspring sailed to Melbourne a couple of years after John Batman, opening the Red Lion Hotel in Lonsdale Street. When he suddenly dropped dead in 1844, his widow took over the licence—at that time she was probably the only female publican operating in Melbourne. I would have liked to know more about her but she left no letters, no diaries—always too busy making a living, I suppose.

This wild Irish family began to yearn for respectability. One of the publicans' twin daughters duly married an Old Etonian named Harry Ehret Grover, the younger son of an English military and legal family that could trace its coat of arms back six centuries. He had travelled to Australia as a remittance man in 1851, in search of adventure and wealth at the dawn of the Victorian gold rush. This first Australian Grover served as a cadet officer in the gold escort, which galloped from the diggings to Melbourne—on one occasion his troop had to fight off a gang of Chinese bushrangers. Then he invested in mining companies and soon accrued the wealth he sought. Thereafter his occupation was always given as 'gentleman'.

The Grovers' only child was Montague, who became a leader in Australia's newspaper world. The first of Monty's two marriages was to Ada Goldberg, a Jewess of striking beauty whose family had fled the pogroms of Eastern Europe for the comparative safety of colonial Australia. One of their children was Dorothy, my mother.

As for my father's family, from what little is known of it, it seems Arthur was the result of a shipboard entanglement between Agnes Marie Booth of Edinburgh and Henry John Cannon, a Cockney seaman. They made love on their way to Australia in the summer of

1899 (those tropical nights!) and married in Brisbane; my father was born six months later. After an elementary education he became a piano tuner, and despite the lack of any formal tuition, on Saturday nights he played mood music to accompany silent movies being shown up and down the Queensland coast. During the 1920s he completed a course in wireless telegraphy and managed to get a job as radio operator on board the luxury liner RMS *Niagara*.

In Melbourne, meanwhile, Monty Grover, with a remarkable newspaper career already behind him, now had a second wife, Regina Varley—Ada had become fed up with Monty sleeping on a camp stretcher in his office while his newspapers went to press. The newlyweds decided to take a sea voyage to America and took Dorothy with them. Such chance decisions can yield unpredictable consequences. The tropical nights again worked their magic and Dorothy fell in love with the handsomely uniformed if rather astigmatic radio operator of the *Niagara*. On their return to Brisbane they married and set up business as newsagents.

A love of journalism ran strongly in my mother's veins. Her grandmother—the one who married the gold escort officer—had been one of Australia's first woman journalists, at a time when middle-class women who worked were often subjected to scorn and suspicion. With her convict origins well and truly suppressed, she became social editor of *Melbourne Punch* and the *Melbourne Bulletin* in the 1880s. Her only child, Monty Grover, would rise to become foundation editor of the Sydney *Sun* in 1910 and the Melbourne *Sun News-Pictorial* in 1922. Dorothy Grover herself had begun a newspaper career at the commencement of Melbourne's *Morning Post* in 1925. After marrying in 1928, was life as a working mother possible? She thought so.

In 1930, at which time most people believed that the recent economic 'slump' must soon end, my parents heard that a small weekly paper, the *Cobden Times*, was for sale in western Victoria. Monty loaned them £1000 to buy the title and printing plant, and they then made the long train journey from Queensland to Victoria, changing trains at each state border and capital city. Monty's first wife tried to get to Central Station in Sydney to see her new grandson (me) but collapsed on the way from a heart attack.

The newspaper my parents acquired had been established in a town that had expanded when many squatters' runs were compulsorily sold off in the 1860s and 1870s. Hundreds of selectors, including many former goldseekers, then moved into the district to take up dairy farming on its lush pastures. A handsome bluestone state school was built in the 1870s and a successful cooperative butter factory followed in the 1880s. Up to this time, the Calvinist pioneers, mostly Scots, had managed to prevent a hotel from being built in the district. But when the town grew to about 700 residents, the wowsers were finally outvoted and one pub was permitted.

The newspaper was initially produced using handset type and a hand-powered press. When the depression of the 1890s struck, the proprietor was glad to barter subscriptions and advertising for slabs of butter and other groceries, a practice my parents would continue. With a few pounds left over from the sale of their Brisbane newsagency, they were able to buy a little two-seater Morris runabout with a dicky seat, in which I slept happily while they bounced over gravel and corduroy roads in search of news items and subscribers.

~

I remember lying on my back in the only large room in my house, watching solar systems form and dissolve in the sunbeams streaming through the window. I was three years old. My left leg was propped up on cushions. There was a space below the calf muscle that had turned purple, yellow and crinkly brown—charred like a partly barbecued sausage. I had just used up the first of my lives, and Mother was still weeping with shock in the front bedroom.

Something like this had been bound to happen. To get to the printing works, you simply opened our sitting room door and walked into the adjoining room of the crumbling weatherboard structure in which we dwelt. In that space, rocking on greasy timber floorboards laid directly on the soil, were an Intertype typesetting machine, a big old Wharfedale printing press, and the donkey engine which now powered it. Like the rest of the building, the printery was heated by an open log fire. I would watch with delight when my father dowsed wet logs in kerosene to make them burn. So when I found myself alone in the pressroom and saw the fire wasn't burning too well, I knew how to make those magic flames curl up the chimney. I seized a kerosene bottle and started pouring the contents onto the fire. As I turned to flee, the flames leaped out and grabbed my leg. My screams brought both parents hurtling through the door, whereupon they extinguished the blaze, wrapped me in a blanket and ran for the town's only doctor.

So there I was, confined to bed for three months. I must have been in considerable pain, but somehow nature removes such memories. Instead, I recall staring at the sunbeams and then feeling myself slip easily out of my body, ascend to the ceiling, and hover in mid-air gazing downwards. Floating in this blissful state, I saw the entire room laid out below me as though on a map: the top of a half-open door; the entire pattern of the cheap carpet; the curved top of our primitive wireless receiver; the objects on top of a tall wardrobe that I could not possibly see from floor level. I felt no surprise at all at being able to watch the small figure lying supine on the couch, leg resting on cushions, apparently dozing. After a few ecstatic minutes, I slowly glided back into my body.

In later years, particularly when studying Sir Arthur Conan Doyle and spiritualism, I believed that I had been on some kind of astral voyage. But on my next encounter with death, when I had to be injected with morphine, I realised that the doctor must have given the three-year-old dreamer a needle to relieve the pain of his burned leg. The kindly old fellow had been through the Great War as a frontline medical officer and I suppose automatically used the drug for quick results in civilian life. I was sad to lose the illusion of a spiritual experience of extraordinary intensity. Yet the belief persisted that inside the demanding confines of everyday life there existed a shimmering, dazzling reality which embodied the true nature of everything in the universe—if only one could perceive it.

Electricity is at the heart of another memory from that time. I'd felt compelled to climb onto a chair and imitate my father in changing a faulty, low-hanging light globe. The current had thrown me clear across the room. The state's electricity grid had only recently arrived to transform life in Cobden, especially when streetlights were installed for the first time—in the supposedly backward 1930s, *that* was progress.

My hard-pressed father had spent one week at the Workingmen's College (later Victoria University) in Melbourne learning how to operate and repair a typesetting machine. Whenever the electricity failed, he was forced to return to the racks of well-worn loose type which had lain there since the 1890s. It was no joke for an untrained man to handset a whole forme in heavy lead and lift it onto the press without the type crashing to the floor, in which case it would have to be re-sorted and completely reset.

Small children such as I appreciated little of these everyday crises of olden times. We only knew that our parents usually had more urgent things to do than to talk or play with us. The loneliness of self-sufficiency descended too soon. I would take a flickering candle into the shadows of the stinking backyard dunny where spiders glared evilly from every crack. In the lean-to bathroom and laundry, an addition of the hygienic 1930s, I cleaned my teeth with salt because it was cheap and said to harden the gums. Surrounding me were such vivid night fears that I scarcely dared lower my head to the tin basin lest demons come creeping up from behind.

Soon, life again tightened its screws. My first sister, Jill, appeared from nowhere and my parents now had no time at all for me, or so it seemed. I watched that tiny new mouth clamp greedily around my mother's nipple, from which I'd been banished years before, and my childish heart filled with new emotions of jealousy and abandonment. Nonetheless, my leg had healed, although it would be permanently hairless, and at the age of four, suddenly it was time for me to start school.

The summer of 1933–34 was a scorcher. On 40-degree days, little kids mostly wore few clothes, not even nappies or pants, which just got dirty and would have to be changed. There was no mains water, and tank water was too scarce for unnecessary laundering. One day, wearing only a singlet, I somehow got out of the house and ventured into the fenced laneway that ran alongside it. For a few minutes I gravely studied an exhaust pipe that stuck out from the timber wall, puffing regular beats of smoke into the air from the donkey engine working the printing press. To me, the pipe was a rapid-firing gun, like the machine-guns in my father's illustrated volumes on World War I. I wondered how I could swivel it around to shoot at something. An experimental tug blistered both hands.

No use crawling back into the house: my parents would be too busy with the new baby or the next edition of the paper. Snivelling, I stumbled down the lane to a large yard where I discovered a group of men making shiny objects that resembled lengths of house guttering. The labourers were taciturn but kindly enough: a snot-nosed barefoot child without pants was an unremarkable sight. Beyond a gruff warning to 'Keep clear o' that there blowlamp', they didn't care if I watched or played with tin offcuts in the dirt.

After an hour or so I ambled towards the school, presenting myself in my undressed, rather dirty state, and with two blistered hands, to a scandalised teacher supervising a group of giggling children. She took me homewards, on the way running into two worried parents who had discovered my absence and begun searching the streets. An agreement must have been reached there and then. I would become the school's youngest pupil, attending in a clean shirt and shorts, and bringing a cheese sandwich each day; I would also be supplied with boots in the wintertime.

I loved that little bluestone school. Modern educators would probably be stunned by its filth, its rigid methods, its modest academic standards. But to me it was a revelation, a glimpse of what the world could offer. I was a thirsty sponge waiting to soak up knowledge.

~

Book learning was not highly valued in Australian country towns like ours in the 1930s. Fifty years earlier the community had hosted a mechanics' institute with a lending library of several hundred educational and literary volumes, but that had disappeared around World War I. Now, a tired old lady offered a few shelves of Western and romance novels in a small shop on the main street. I think she made more money out of selling packs of playing cards. People mostly seemed content to pore over lists of stock sales and council reports in our eight-page newspaper. One or two, like my father, erected tall timber masts with elaborate aerial wires to pull in broadcasts from the new metropolitan radio stations. I was stirred by much of the classical and popular music they played, but their information services seemed to consist of interminable descriptions of cricket and football matches. I could not understand why anyone would want to sit around listening to those when there were so many exciting books to read and things to do.

Needless to say, our village was largely cut off from the tremendous events occurring elsewhere in the world. Probably most residents preferred it that way. After all, it had only been twenty years since their sons had enlisted and marched away, some dying ghastly deaths, others returning home crippled in body and soul. In addition, these damaged, reserved people were proud of how they were surviving the Depression through local systems of barter and self-help, without experiencing the depths of misery that I later learned were destroying community spirit in larger towns and cities. So really, who needed that outside world, except as a fluctuating market for butter, meat and wool? Stoic self-reliance was the foundation of the townspeople's attitude to life, and you didn't need much book-learning for that. In fact, the more you knew about the rest of the world, the more discontented you might become with the real-life business of farming or shopkeeping. Contentment sprang from a determined ignorance which filtered out notions of social change. Even the town's few better-educated residents—clergymen, solicitors, schoolteachers—were preoccupied with preservation of the accepted way of life.

Fortunately, because of their urban background and occupations, my parents filled the knowledge gap before I even knew it existed. Books and journals were always lying around the house, partly because in those days, publishers were so desperate for free publicity that they even sent copies of their books to obscure newspapers like ours. My father had been converted to Labor's radicalism in Queensland and somehow found enough money to subscribe to the London-based Left Book Club. Its luminous pink-hued productions kept rolling in. I can still visualise the modernistic typefaces and feel the crinkly paper that marked my struggles with works like *The Socialist Sixth of the World*, when I understood perhaps one-tenth of what 'parlour pinks' of the time were saying.

More important still was my parents' sixth-birthday gift of a set of Arthur Mee's *Children's Encyclopaedia*: ten handsome volumes bound in blue buckram and reposing neatly in a varnished bookcase. The very shape of that bookcase is imprinted on my memory. Only a year or two earlier, I thought the world had opened right up when I found my way to school, saw that hundreds of other children existed, and started reciting with them the mystic formula 'A is for Apple, B is for Boy …' Now, because I had learned to read so young, I was able to make the leap into the mind of Mee, whose genius for popularising knowledge had reached out from London to this small boy in western Victoria.

Mee's aim, he wrote, was 'to tell the whole sum of human knowledge so that a child may understand'. His volumes were divided into dozens of sections on natural history, technology, legends and so on. So simple was the language used that the moon was described in one heading as 'The bit of the Earth that broke off long ago' (note the use of one-syllable words). Prehistoric paintings were 'The jolly pictures the cave men made'. Most of that information is now out-of-date, but so dramatic were the illustrations, and so easily absorbed was the text, that at the time the books formed a total educational system in themselves. The reader had to make an effort, of course. What exactly were the 'subterranean steam cavities' on the scary colour page entitled 'How the fires burst from the earth'? You needed a small dictionary, and from there it was but a step to discovering how to use the encyclopaedia's index.

The practical result for me was a prodigious input and output of schoolwork. Although two years younger than most of my classmates, I was always top of the class, with 100 per cent marks in every subject. Should the teacher mention Vasco da Gama's voyages during a geography lesson, at the age of six I would race home after school and prepare a project on the great navigator. There was always plenty of paper offcuts, staples and glue around the printery (no longer forbidden territory) with which to make small booklets. Most of the information I copied from the *Children's Encyclopaedia*, adding little drawings and proudly presenting the result to the teacher next morning. Wrongly regarded as a child prodigy, my ego swelled until I was in danger of being seen as insufferable by other children who didn't have my advantages. Yet they were, I now perceive, remarkably tolerant of this curious enthusiast who actually liked schoolwork.

In fact, the envy was mostly on my part. I admired my older playmates' prowess at outdoor activities and desperately tried to emulate them. Football and cricket suddenly seemed just as important as Vasco da Gama, and endless happy hours were spent learning to catch, kick and hit balls all over the grassy playgrounds. But the only 'sport' at which I excelled was marbles. Each year, every boy knew by instinct the exact Monday on which marble season began. Patient mothers were nagged into sewing up 'alley bags' in stout fabric with a drawstring at top. Into this, last year's marbles were carefully counted: agates, bottle-ohs, dribblers, glassies, milkies, slaters.

Two varieties of the game were played at my school. In the first, a large ring was scraped in the dirt by a boot-heel. Each player placed his least desirable marbles in the centre, and then, gripping his favourite 'stonker' between forefinger and bent thumb, each boy tried to knock an opponent's marble out of the ring. If he succeeded, the target became his property. The danger was that your best stonker would stay inside the ring and in turn become a target. The second type of game involved digging a series of small holes into which opponents' marbles were knocked and won. And while all this was going on, the girls simply stood around and watched, chattered or jeered—they were beneath our contempt.

For some reason I had unerring control over my stonker and usually went home after hours of play with a bulging marble-bag, as well as filthy knees and clothes. Losers had to find some way of earning sixpence so they could go to the newsagent and replenish their supplies.

What were we really learning from scrabbling in the dirt? It was that every game had logical rules, and if you stuck to the rules, the game went happily—even if you lost most of your marble collection. There was always another day to improve your technique, fight back and win. If you attempted to cheat, however, others would roar at you or even cuff you. If you blubbered, or kept on trying to cheat, in the end no-one would play with you.

The school practised a system of honour and discipline that kept it a relatively calm place—even on the day of the great apple raid. Alongside a house next door to the school grew a row of old but vigorous apple trees protected from intruders by an array of barbed-wire entanglements; tales of slavering watchdogs and shotguns also circulated. But as the apples ripened, we kept eyeing them eagerly from the schoolground, until my class evolved a cunning plan. The appointed desperadoes arrived at the school very early one morning. Someone had brought old chaff bags, and with our pocket knives we quickly cut out holes for a child's head and arms. Being by far the smallest, I was selected to don this protective gear and crawl through the barbed wire, suffering only a scratched and bleeding scalp. On reaching the nearest tree, I grabbed an armful of apples, threw them into the schoolground, and hastily crawled back to safety.

An hour or so later the neighbour arose, spotted the mangled branches, and complained to the headmaster. At general assembly, after we had saluted the Union Jack and sung 'God Save the King', the head announced that any boy who had stolen or eaten the neighbour's apples should report immediately to his office—he didn't mention the girls, as it was not within human possibility that any such had participated. The drums rattled, we marched inside, and a dozen of us peeled off to attend the headmaster's office. The reaction was instinctive, with no thought of concealment. The head had made it plain that a crime had been committed, we knew we were guilty, and now it was time to receive absolution through lawful punishment.

As we lined up, I saw the headmaster trying not to laugh when he looked down at the size of the midget (me) at one end of the line. 'Get Miss ... to put some iodine on your head,' he muttered gruffly. Then it was 'Put out your right hand' as he reached for the folded leather strap he always carried in his hip pocket. I was first, the strap barely stinging my hand as it came down six times. That was fair, I thought. It hurt just enough—I would never steal apples again. The 'cuts' got harder as the boys got bigger, but not a murmur nor a tear escaped those seven- and eight-year-olds. Through the hundreds of savage blows I saw inflicted on boys during my schooling, I never heard a whimper.

~

During school holidays, an uncle, a newspaper cartoonist, would come down from the city to stay, accompanied by his son who was a year older than me. Alex Gurney would gain renown during World War II for creating a comic strip depicting the adventures of two larrikin diggers. So perhaps in the mid-1930s he was already finding sardonic amusement in watching others get into trouble. Two young mischief-makers gave him the perfect opportunity for this.

With absentminded consent from my parents, he fitted us out with aprons, brushes and pots of crimson paint, and told us to spend the day painting the dunny at the bottom of the garden. He then went fishing. My cousin and I agreed that I should paint the smelly interior while he painted the outside. 'It's mostly your shit,' he pointed out. Within an hour we had splashed a fair amount of colour around, and I called my cousin's attention to the smooth effect I had achieved on the toilet seat and the bottle of phenyl disinfectant. We then decided that the neighbours would appreciate having their lavatories decorated in similar fashion. Two small crimson-stained figures then went wandering down laneways, through back gates and into dunnies, where the seat would be daubed with sticky red oil paint.

To our astonishment, the grocer, whose combined shop and dwelling was several doors away, shouted angrily when he saw what we were doing. He grabbed us painfully by the ears and marched us home, where he demanded that someone immediately scrub off the paint with turpentine so he could sit down to do his business in safety. Yet we were not severely punished. My father was the gentlest of souls. I think he had been knocked about a bit by his own father, and so not once in his life, despite great provocation, did he ever lift his hand against another person.

Revenge on the grocer was childish and sweet. We loved rummaging messily through his shelves, which displayed iron-mongery, balls of twine, cake tins and the like. One day, when we were doing our best to convert new stock into shop-soiled goods, he loomed over us. My cousin looked up at him innocently before exclaiming 'You big bastard!' and dashing for the door. The grocer turned to me and said, 'Michael, did you hear what he called me?' 'Yes,' I replied, 'and I think you're a big bastard too.' Somehow I got through his legs and went out the door like a rocket.

At about this time, the Duke of Gloucester toured the country to represent the royal family while Victoria celebrated a century of white settlement. We schoolchildren were rounded up by the thousands and taken to Colac by bus and train to 'see the Duke'. For hours we stood hatless in a line in the hot sun, buckling at the knees and waving our Union Jacks, waiting for the great man to arrive. Eventually his special train steamed into the station. We stared at the royal carriage, but not a curtain moved, not a door opened.

My mother, keen reporter that she was, discovered that the Duke was deep in alcoholic slumber and could not be disturbed. She sent the story to the city papers, which censored it considerably while hinting at the truth. As for the thousands of exhausted children, we simply boarded our transportation and returned home.

~

When I was about six, a major change took place in our family life. The local Church of England minister won approval to build and rent to us a new house and separate printing works on the church's disused tennis courts, just south of the town centre. Things were looking up for us economically. Once when I heard my parents talking, I learned that they were making about £2 a week profit out of the paper, and £1.10s out of the regular news reports written by my mother that were printed in city newspapers. That gave us a cash income roughly equivalent to that of a single labourer. But we achieved a higher standard of living through special deals with shopkeepers and occasional gifts from my mother's father.

Our new weatherboard house certainly seemed the height of luxury. It had two actual bedrooms, one of which became mine. A third room was a kind of sleep-out, with the window space covered by flywire and a large canvas roller-blind that kept out some of the frigid winter air—perhaps the money ran out at this point and a normal window couldn't be financed—and it was here that my small sister slept. The house also had a good kitchen, sitting room and bathroom.

The builders must have known their trade because when I revisited the house half a century later, every weatherboard was still accurately aligned, every original window still in place, and the chimneys still in perfect condition. All that had vanished was the 6-foot paling fence that had enclosed a wonderful private playing yard, half-grass and half-asphalt, perfect for ball games and tricycle races.

The former clubhouse beside the old tennis court had been converted into a garage for the vicar's car. My father reconverted it into a ham radio shack, erecting the timber mast and spending some nights getting in touch with other amateur radio enthusiasts throughout the world—a sort of forerunner of the internet. I remember, on the arrival of my second baby sister, Dina, that we had to engage a farm girl as temporary help for a few shillings a week, and I assisted in packing up the radio equipment and turning the shack into a maid's quarters. One of the items I found was what I later recognised as a medical battery kit. This widely advertised but fraudulent device consisted of two large dry cells in a wooden box fitted with meters, electrodes, a switch to reverse the current, and various massage rollers and brushes for application to troublesome parts of the body. At a time when electricity was still regarded as a marvel, such machines were believed to cure everything from baldness to impotence.

Behind the maid's quarters was the old tennis club lavatory, which was cleaned up—the exterior disguised with a rampant banana–passionfruit vine—and converted into the family toilet. Chamber-pots kept underneath our beds were tipped into the same repository each morning. To empty the large black dunny can, the nightman drove his one-horse cart up to our high fence before dawn, brought in a fresh can, and hoisted onto his shoulder the full can which, well patronised by fat blowflies, had been festering there since the previous week.

For years I laboured under the illusion that the nightman also filled up the milk billy, which we hung on the fence each evening. Later I realised that this job was done by an almost equally soiled dairyman who milked his cows in squalid conditions on the western side of town. Our billy of milk, taken straight from untested cows, would stay on the fence, gradually heating in the dawn sunlight, until someone rose and carried it into the kitchen. No-one owned a refrigerator, of course: we were lucky to have an ice chest cooled with blocks of ice made in the local butter factory and delivered in hessian bags.

The streets themselves had no kerbs or underground pipes, just deep gutters dug into the soil where household drainage accumulated into gobs of green scum, filled in summer with interesting tadpoles, blowflies and mosquito larvae. When rainstorms scoured out the gutters, our favourite sport was to race matchstick boats along with the current.

The new printery was basically a corrugated iron shed on the far side of the old tennis court, but to us it seemed impressively modern. The office frontage consisted of two tiers of red bricks with a large window and a part-glass door. The door led to a small reception counter where customers could discuss job printing and advertising. The walls and roof of the printery were made of unlined corrugated iron sheets, broiling in summer and freezing in winter. Before the last of these were nailed on, the printing press appeared in the road outside, drawn by a two-horse float borrowed from the butter factory and followed by a mob of excited small boys. Grunting men used crowbars and rollers to manipulate the dead weight through the open wall onto a concrete slab. The donkey engine was connected up with its exhaust pipe through the back wall, and we were back in business. The paper never missed an issue.

Dina arrived soon after we settled into the new house. I had not even been conscious of my mother's growing weight and fatigue. All I knew was that one day she walked off to the bush nursing hospital which formed part of the doctor's large house, and came back a few days later with a tiny blonde bundle who lived in a cot in my older sister's freezing room. It was at that time that my grandfather came down from Melbourne to put the newspaper together. I doubt if the townsfolk knew or cared that Australia's greatest editor of the day was producing the local rag—what counted was that he got the stock prices and sports results right.

I came to love our new girl baby, the first thing outside myself for which I can recall a generous outgoing feeling. When she developed the usual childhood ailments, I was the one who stood by her cot for hours at night, stroking her brow, applying dampened cloths and persuading her not to cry. About three years later, when a long yellow tapeworm slid down her leg after she had been to the dunny, I was the one she came to for help. I never thought of telling my parents about such trivia.

Earlier, before the diminishment of my stupid jealousy of younger children in the house, that self-pitying feeling of being unfairly displaced, I had considered drastic action. Late one afternoon, a swagman, a victim of hard times, came to the kitchen door and asked for food. My mother gave two eggs to this bearded, smelly, cheerful-looking cove. I followed him to the local football ground and stood there in the glowing sunset, watching a real adventurer build a small fire, unroll his swag on the ground, and crack the eggs into a blackened frying pan. This was obviously an exciting life. I asked the rover if I could travel and live with him. 'Sonny,' he said, 'you don't know what it's like. Go home to your Mum and Dad and stay there.' I had been told that swaggies knew a secret mark which they put on the gatepost of charitable people, but I could never find it on ours.

The next area of shame developed when I began to steal money from my parents. I had discovered the delights of the town's three milk bars, how you could exchange coins for an endless cavalcade of gobstoppers, sherbet bombs, chewing gum, chocolate frogs, licorice allsorts, and an aerated drink—foul only in retrospect—called creamy soda. The problem grew even worse when Peters ('The Health Food of a Nation') introduced the first chocolate-coated 'two-in-one' ice-cream sticks, followed by an even more enticing caramel-coated variety. In desperation, my parents introduced weekly pocket-money payments, threepence every Saturday, which was pretty generous for those days. I spent the first threepence immediately, applied for more, and was stunned to learn that I had to wait seven days for the next instalment. The problem was that you had to have sixpence to buy anything really good, or to be able to grandly tell your mates that you would 'shout' for them—never anything for the sisters, of course. My parents put a lock on their bedroom door to prevent me from taking more money, and when I began climbing through the bedroom window, they locked that, too. They each gave me serious talks—which I rather enjoyed—warning that boys who stole were sent off to places called reformatories. I am not sure what would have happened if they had inflicted the more conventional punishment of a severe thrashing: either complete alienation or an instant cure, I suppose.

I found a solution that got me through this bad period. I had noted that, when the school needed money, the mothers made cakes and sweets to be sold at local bazaars. In our extensive backyard, I set up a stall, instructed my sisters to make toffee and cordials, repaired a few toys I no longer played with, and invited family members and friends of all ages. Many were so amused by this juvenile enterprise that they felt impelled to buy something—although when subsequent bazaars were announced, their interest seemed to wane. Still, I now had a few shillings ('bob'), most of which I managed to save, endlessly counting it into neat heaps of halfpennies, pennies, threepences ('treys') and sixpences ('zacks'). My sisters received a zack and a bob for their efforts as cooks and the business went into liquidation.

Rummaging through my parents' bedroom during my short career as a burglar had one curious result. At the back of my mother's side of the wardrobe, which I could just reach by standing on a chair, I discovered a large pink rubber syringe. Its function puzzled me for years until, in a second-hand bookshop, I discovered a copy of Bessie Smyth's pamphlet 'Limitation of Offspring', published in North Melbourne in 1893. The purpose of the syringe, I found, was to inject a chemical substance such as alum or even soapy water before or after intercourse, to wash out the male semen and help prevent conception. Now I knew how my parents had avoided having more than three children, and those neatly spaced several years apart, while other couples in town bred like rabbits.

Some families I remember with awful clarity, such as Billy and his many brothers and sisters. One day a younger brother asked Billy to show him how to chop kindling. 'For a start, don't leave your hand on the block,' said Billy. The brother naturally put his hand on the chopping block, so when Billy brought down the axe, he neatly sliced off his brother's fingers. Billy finished up as an incorrigible jailbird.

Households in those days consumed enormous quantities of sweet stuff. Tea wasn't tea unless it was hot, strong, usually a deep red-black colour, and contained at least two heaped spoons of sugar. Treacle or golden syrup made from sugar cane was a common spread on bread and toast, and often used on porridge in addition to sprinkled sugar. Dinner wasn't a meal without some kind of sugary pudding. Nestle's sweetened condensed milk was often used as well as cream—I once ate a whole tin of the thick fluid then vomited it up. Afternoon tea and supper comprised sweet biscuits, cake and more sugary tea. For her frequent Saturday night card parties, my mother made sponge cakes filled with thickened cream and heavily iced with a white sugar mixture sprinkled with passionfruit. Slices were always left for us to eat on Sunday morning, along with cream-filled meringues and vanilla slices, in preparation for the midday dinner of lamb roasted in rancid dripping.

From a 1939 edition of the *Commonwealth Year Book*, I learned that every Australian man, woman and child supported the Queensland sugar industry by consuming 110 pounds of refined sugar and 114 pounds of raw sugar each year—slightly more than 4 pounds per person each per week. Add to all that my illegal consumption of sweets and ice cream and it was obvious why my teeth, like most other people's, soon began to rot. In those days we didn't appreciate the cause or the cure, but the penalty was frightening. Off we trooped to an itinerant dentist who installed himself for a few days each month in the manager's office at the front of the picture theatre. Pain-killing injections were unknown: the dentist simply jammed your mouth open, started pedalling on his foot-operated drill, and gouged great hunks out of several teeth at each sitting, while his patient sat there suffering the maximum pain and terror.

My flirtation with crime temporarily intensified when my cousin returned to town, bringing with him from 'the big smoke' a money-making scheme whose audacity startled me. In brief, we would manufacture small booklets of duplicate numbered tickets for what he called a 'raffle'. We would sell the tickets for threepence each, announcing the prize as a fountain pen and pencil set we had seen on sale at the newsagent for 10 shillings. What would happen if customers wanted to see the prize? We only had to sell forty tickets to get enough cash to buy it. Every ticket over that would be pure profit. What charity would the raffle assist? Our private code was 'The SRF', which sounded like it was part of the local swimming pool appeal but actually stood for our own 'Stomach Relief Fund'.

Such juvenile cunning did not keep us out of trouble for long. We were doing well, with about thirty tickets sold from going door to door, when I reached the local police station. The constable was a decent bloke, whose son I often played cops-and-bushrangers with in the empty stables at the back of the station. But he also had a good police nose and he smelt a rat in the threepenny raffle affair. He knew very well that no permit had been issued for such a venture. So I was marched home along the entire main street to my long-suffering parents. It was one of the worst walks of my life. So fearful was I of the consequences that my bowels voided and shit flowed down both legs to my toes. It looked like a spell in the reformatory at last.

While I cleaned myself up, constable and parents reached a compromise. My parents would purchase the prize and the constable would issue an official permit in the name of a swimming pool appeal. The money we had collected would be donated to that appeal and we would sell the remainder of the tickets without hope of personal reward. That is how our names finally appeared as donors in the list of contributions printed in the paper a few weeks later.

The Anglican Church probably came to regret providing finance for my family's new house and printery. The parson had a son and daughter similar in ages to me and my sisters, and I suppose he thought that newspaper-bred children would make suitable playmates for his offspring, enabling them to avoid the riffraff who ran shouting through the streets. How wrong he was. The minister's children were repressed and supervised to the stage of primness, but we weren't.

One day, when we were mucking around at the back of the parsonage, the son politely warned me to stop sitting on a concrete step. If I didn't, he whispered, I would be sure to get 'piles'. What were piles? He couldn't bring himself to describe the affliction. A few days later, he called out some other warning to me through the high palings and wire fence dividing our blocks. Without thinking I bent down and picked up a fair-sized stone. With a Zen-like motion, disdain flowing through my arm, I propelled the stone unerringly into the little toad's face, smashing one lens in his spectacles. After that we were never again allowed to play together, which suited me fine.

Mum and Dad decided I had better go to Sunday school, in the hope that moral precepts would infiltrate my hide, so reluctantly I trudged up the hill to the small wooden Presbyterian church that had been erected by descendants of the first Scottish immigrants. There, I was bored silly by the preacher's unctuous talk of his travels through Palestine, accompanied by incomprehensible quotations from the Bible. Once was enough. The world held far more enticing things to do on a Sunday morning.

My parents themselves did not set a good example in churchgoing. Attendance at a few weddings and funerals was the extent of their devotion. But the town seemed to accept these atheistic near-socialists in their midst calmly enough. My father went so far as to join other tradesmen in the local Freemasons lodge. One day, I was puzzled to find, on his side of the wardrobe, a flat leather case containing a richly embroidered apron and a handbook explaining masonic beliefs. This dealt with the movement's alleged origins in ancient Egypt and its development in the Middle Ages as a secret society of skilled artisans, as well as detailing the secret signs and handshakes that enabled the 'brothers' to recognise one another. The complex rituals outlined in this book mystified and even frightened me: did grown men really behave in this manner?

The mystery deepened one summer evening as I wended my way homeward past the windowless, squat, red-brick Masonic Hall in Cobden's main street. It usually had the air of being sealed tight as a mummy's tomb, but by chance the heavy wooden doors were now ajar. I could see into a blaze of electric light, and there, to my astonishment, was my own father wearing the little apron over his best suit. The ways of God were certainly enigmatic. The possibility that some kind of shame was involved in the arcane rites prevented me from ever asking him for an explanation, but I did observe one practical result: during a particularly severe drought, when our household tanks ran dry, my father was able to carry home buckets of water from the Masonic Hall tanks so that we could drink, wash, and clean our teeth.

~

How does one convey the wild, free, kaleidoscopic nature of a boy's life in a country town of the 1930s? We wandered along the little-used railway, placing halfpennies on the tracks in the hope they would be flattened by the next goods train and transformed into pennies. Pieces of black coal rescued from between the sleepers were invaluable for keeping alight a secret camp fire, sparked by focusing the sun's rays through a piece of broken glass onto a dry gumleaf and wisps of grass. We investigated salmon spawning boxes installed by some enthusiast on the banks of a bush stream, and probably killed most of the tiny eggs.

We went to the delicious-smelling town bakery, where customers could watch the owner using a long paddle to draw new loaves from an immense wood-fired oven. From white milled flour, he made high-tin loaves for ordinary use, square loaves for sandwiches, and

Boston buns covered with sticky coconut icing. Housewives baked almost everything else, although a few varieties of packaged biscuits were available from the grocer. With threepence we could buy a large brown-paper bag of 'broken biscuits', which tasted just as good as the unbroken ones, and stuck just as satisfactorily between our teeth. 'Teddy bears' and 'cream-betweens' were firm favourites. But I hated having to go into the fruit shop, where the fecund smell of rotting fruit, rarely discarded, mingled heavily with the body stenches of the sharp-tongued old Irish woman who owned it and her bold-eyed twenty-year-old daughter. I overheard one man tell another that the fruit shop was the place to go if you wanted a good root, but it was not until years later that I understood what he meant.

One time, a craze for lead soldiers swept the town's juvenile population. Soon, my family's front lawn had been honeycombed to accommodate the brightly lacquered lead figures in opposing trenches and mud fortresses. It had occurred to me that my father had plenty of molten lead intended for the Intertype machine. But my interest quickly shifted to stamp collecting. By one means or another, mainly birthday presents and swaps, I finally accumulated full sets of all the Australian stamps up to 1939—kangaroos, Sydney Bridge, and so on—plus a number of colonial issues. Then I lost interest and sold the lot for a few shillings.

At Christmas, the local traders banded together to string coloured lights along their verandah posts and on small trees. On hot summer evenings the main street became a magic space, with people strolling, window-shopping, exchanging gossip, smoking and drinking, and us children laughing, leaping and running under the lights from pavement to gutter and back again—there were no speeding cars, no kidnappers, no assaults on the innocent that we ever heard of.

We looked forward to the annual gymkhanas at the football ground, where we could take part in three-legged races and egg-and-spoon contests. Under marquees, amazing machines might return two pennies for one, if you were able to shoot a small metal ball into the correct slot. We attended juvenile fancy-dress parties, where I might wear a red tunic cut down from an old winter dress of my mother's, plus a borrowed Scout hat and toy pistol, so as to be transformed into Sergeant Lionheart Logan of the Mounties, famed for 'always getting his man'. At birthday parties we consumed huge quantities of sausage rolls, bread slices covered with hundreds-and-thousands, meringues and pastry horns filled with whipped vanilla-flavoured cream.

I became friendly with the son of the manager of the local National Bank. After riffling through boxes of cancelled cheques kept in a supposedly locked outhouse, and recognising familiar names, we crept upstairs to his parents' bedroom. Opening a drawer, he took out his father's automatic pistol, heavy with its load of bullets. I was allowed to hold it for a moment and say 'Stick 'em up!' But not with my finger on the trigger—for once I obeyed.

I felt it was essential to have a hut of my own in our backyard. The far corner of a high timber fence provided two walls. Someone gave me a corner post and a few old wooden scraps to build a framework, to which I nailed hessian bags that the saddler had given away for nothing. The roof and door were simply wooden pallets on which reams of newsprint had been transported to the printery. When the roof leaked, I cemented it over, and was then surprised to find it continued to leak. Despite this, I insisted on sleeping in my damp hideaway on fine nights, like a dog in its kennel. As I look back now on that nine-year-old boy, I sense that he was attempting to build up a separate personality not entirely dependent on family, school or social life.

Life could be rich in fantasy. On occasional visits to Melbourne, my cousin let me look at his copies of American science-fiction magazines like *Amazing Stories*. I fell in love with their gaudy, surreal illustrations and the thick pulpy paper on which they were printed. Soon, the first issues of *Buck Rogers in the 25th Century*, a comic-strip magazine, came to our town. Every copy must have had at least twenty juvenile readers, each passed from hand to hand for gradually lessening sums: twopence for a second-hand copy in good condition, a halfpenny for a tattered copy. The bizarre adventures of Buck and his bird-brained girlfriend Wilma Deering accustomed us to the conquest of space long before it became a scientific possibility, besides reinforcing the truth, never to be denied, that females were inferior to males.

On a more realistic level, we dreamed ourselves into the role of a courageous fighter pilot. The origins of this fantasy lay in the adventures of Rockfist Rogan, Royal Air Force ace of World War I, which we knew better as 'the Great War'. These stories, published every week in an English boys' paper called *Champion*, found a hungry audience in our town. I was allowed a regular subscription and soon found myself drawing warplanes all over my exercise books at school. During the lunch hour, ordinary sports were abandoned in favour of 'buzzing' other boys by running straight at them with outstretched arms and emitting loud 'rat-a-tat-tat' noises. The political world in the mid-1930s might have been promoting appeasement with Germany, but we were hoping for war.

The newsagent's son and I discovered some loose boards in a usually locked timber shed behind his shop where unsold magazines were kept, awaiting a return to the distributors. Regularly we crept in there and devoured periodicals too expensive to buy, including *Triumph* (which seemed to be a copy of *Champion*, or perhaps it was the other way around), *Film Fun* and *Hotspur*. Girls' magazines like the romantic *Peg's Paper* we glanced at, then kicked aside. Who could be bothered with such trash?

When a barnstorming biplane landed in a cow paddock near the town and the pilot announced that he would demonstrate daredevil stunts, practically every resident turned out to buy tickets for short joyrides. A few months later, when my family was visiting Melbourne and a plane flew overhead, I nearly unscrewed my head watching it while yelling 'Look—look!' My minder for the day, an elderly relative, was embarrassed by such enthusiasm. 'Don't point at it, boy,' she commanded. 'Everyone will know you're from the bush.'

Another important source of fantasy was the local picture theatre. This was a long, tall, solid structure that had been erected in the main street after the advent of sound in movies. Products of the American and English dream factories percolated through the rigid Australian censorship, finally trickling out from the cities to villages like ours. My Saturdays always concluded with picture night. Our parents had a contra arrangement with the exhibitor: in part-exchange for a large weekly advertisement, two aisle seats were always reserved for my family. My parents often did not want to go, so I was free to take a friend—or, reluctantly, my elder sister Jill if a Shirley Temple film was showing.

Once inside, illusions took over. The long program consisted of shorts, some B-grade film (usually a Western), an interval—dominated by advertising slides typed by my mother on special squares of transparent material inserted into her Remington portable typewriter—followed by the main feature. We laughed ourselves to tears over the early Walt Disney film *Silly Symphonies*. We wondered about curiosities of history during John Nesbitt's *Passing Parade*. We quivered under the portentous impact of *The March of Time*, and were glad to get back to good old Australia with the *Cinesound Newsreel*. We galloped over the prairie with Hopalong Cassidy, swearing to save enough money to buy a white Stetson and a bigger cap gun to duplicate his feats with the six-shooter. We identified with the original *Tarzan the Ape Man*, convincingly played by champion swimmer Johnny Weissmuller.

The interval itself was a big event. By this time I had learned that threepences were not to be squandered on instant pleasure but saved for later and greater satisfaction. Carefully knotted in the corner of a snotty handkerchief, the little silver coin would be produced as hordes of shouting children descended on the milk bar across the road, all demanding meat pies with tomato sauce. The pie of those days was not the pallid, factory-made object of today. It was home-baked with hand-rolled pastry, filled with first-class chunks of beef and rich gravy, injected with blood-red tomato sauce, and handed out piping hot in a brown-paper bag. Then it was back to the cinema, still slurping hot gravy and sauce, anxious for the main film to begin.

The feature movies of those days were totally convincing to our unsophisticated minds. For some years I believed that the roaring lion which heralded MGM films was real, kept backstage and shown through a circular hole in the screen. So complete was the suspension of reality that when we watched Leslie Howard in *Of Human Bondage*, or Clark Gable in *Mutiny on the Bounty*, or Spencer Tracy in *San Francisco*—classics which appear so stilted and slow-moving today—we were filled with belief in the accuracy and significance of what we were seeing. By midnight we were dizzy with revelations of the outside world and its wonders.

I pleaded long and loud for an air rifle, so that I could duplicate the feats of the cowboys I saw who pulled a rifle out of its sheath and potted half-a-dozen vile Indians at the gallop. My mother resisted hardest, for one of her elder brothers had shot himself with a rifle while climbing through a barbed-wire fence, and the memory still gave her great pain. Eventually, my parents gave in. On that proud birthday morning, I cocked the lever of my new Daisy airgun, slipped in a lead slug, and aimed at a sparrow perched on a power line. With awful conviction, my intention flew out with the slug and hit the sparrow in the chest. I walked over and watched in awe as it trembled and died on the asphalt. I have not shot a living thing since that day, not even a rabbit, and I hope I never have to. Some cowboy.

The picture theatre doubled as a public hall. The seats, joined together in packs of five, could be swiftly swept against the walls to clear a large area suitable for everything from indoor bazaars to dances. Us kids often helped to spread wax on the boards, then sat on a chaff bag to be pulled around by adults and polish the floor for dancing. One Irish family exhibited real talent on the harmonica, jew's harp and piano accordion, and served as the mainstay of concerts and socials, where the classics of World War I were played over and over—people didn't want too many new songs, just the repetition of emotions already savoured. We unconsciously absorbed the bitter-sweet significance of 'Roses of Picardy', 'Pack up Your Troubles in Your Old Kit-Bag' and 'Take Me Back to Dear Old Blighty'. Eighty years later, such songs still call to mind those innocent gatherings, lamplight casting blocks of yellow and black on friendly faces, most of them long since perished, in the days when people still made many of their own amusements.

More solemn, more puzzling, were the Anzac Day services. Beforehand, returned soldiers conducted an almost private mourning around a granite war memorial, which bore in brass letters the names of all the men of the district who had 'fallen'—I assumed their bodies had been buried in a deep hole underneath the monument. When the service proper was to begin, all children of school age would troop into the hall. In front of the silver screen, temporarily vacant of Hollywood phantoms, stood a speaker who tried to convey to us something of what had been endured less than twenty years earlier.

The effort didn't work very well: I for one could not reconcile the gnarled, taciturn, haggard, sometimes coughing, often gloomy returned soldiers seen around town, with the deeds of valour they were said to have performed. Now, if they had looked heroic, like Gary Cooper ... What did make a lasting impact on my mind were the mournful trumpet notes of 'The Last Post', played by a uniformed Light Horse trooper with an emu feather waving from his slouch hat, and the singing every year of Kipling's 'Recessional': 'Lest we forget—lest we forget!' As intended, these raised visions of dusty plains where tumult and shouting died. When Captains and Kings departed, 'Lo, all our pomp of yesterday Is one with Nineveh and Tyre!' On hearing these words, a cold tightness gripped my childish heart and the hair on the back of my neck rose. I knew from my reading what had happened to Nineveh and Tyre, and for the first time I wondered why people bothered to do anything when we were all bound to die.

Outside the dark interior of the cinema-cum-public-hall, there was football. Our local team, made up mostly of hefty farmers' sons and town tradesmen, played on the home ground near the Catholic church every second Saturday afternoon. My father took time off from his eternal typesetting duties to report the matches. He would sit in the press box—a little tin shed near the perimeter of the ground—gravely recording every good kick and player. Each man wore a large white number on his jersey, so that despite his poor eyesight, Dad simply had to consult his lists to see who had done what. In this way, the sports page was soon filled and the readers kept happy.

When I grew big enough, I was given the job of changing the scoreboard. This was a high timber structure behind the press box where I sat in all weather. When a goal or point was scored, it was simply a matter of jumping up to remove one large numbered plate from the nails on which they all hung and substituting another. One dared not make a mistake.

Our team didn't often win against teams from the bigger centres. When we did manage to reach the finals, a cavalcade of buses, tin lizzies, and one or two larger Dodge or Chevrolet sedans would set off, full of enthusiasts intent on supporting their local boys. As representatives of the press, my father and I travelled in the team bus, where the smell of eucalyptus oil and the glowing, open faces of these cheerful, beefy men prompted a desire in me to grow up quickly and become like them.

After victory or defeat, there was surprisingly little drinking at the pub dinner which often followed. I suppose none of them could afford to spend too much, even on cheap beer. Then came the bliss of a night-time drive home, with me wedged between Dad and a hero figure from the team, watching the stars overhead or the sleet outside, the rickety bus lurching over potholes in the gravel roads, its headlights cutting through the darkness, the occasional flare of a match lighting pipe or cigarette, bursts of reminiscence or song, the long, long trail a-winding into the land of the past … exhausted, I slept on my father's broad shoulder.

Summertime sometimes meant sizzling days at the beach. How could Sunday school or church expect to win us when the sun was blazing in a cloudless sky, and when we were able to drag our parents out of bed for the long bumpy drive to the seaside? A few doorstopper sandwiches and thermoses full of black sweetened tea were the only other necessities. We got to the beach only once or twice a month, but in retrospect it seems that almost every Sunday meant piling into the car with a couple of friends and setting off—no seatbelts, no speeding laws, no limitation on the number of people crammed together.

Our family eventually graduated to a second-hand, four-seater Morris Cowley tourer, an indication of more prosperous times. The car had a soft top which could be folded back, and mica windows which could be removed to let in even more breeze. It also had a broken windscreen wiper which had to be operated by hand. Usually we took it to Peterborough or Port Campbell. We took the scenic wonders more or less for granted, for it was difficult to explore such areas as Loch Ard Gorge until later when timber steps were installed on the steep cliff. Our greatest adventure was to drive east to Lorne along the recently opened Great Ocean Road, which had been hacked out of the hillsides by 'susso' (sustenance) workers during the Depression. Once, we drove over a large snake coiled up in the middle of the gravel road, then stopped to check whether it had wound itself around the axle—here was food for nightmares, with slit-eyed serpents coming at me through the floorboards.

Beaches and rivers were our main joy. At Peterborough, the Curdies River estuary formed a shallow lake with sandy shores, ideal for learning to swim and sail. On the far side of a sandy point, where the gold-rush clipper *Schomberg* and many other ships had been pounded to pieces against shallow reefs, the undertow was too powerful for children to be allowed into the surf. But on the other side, the rocks protruded several feet above the water, forming (in those days) enclosed ocean pools where one could swim and dive in reasonable safety. Desperate to imitate the feats of pearl divers described in books on northern Australia, us kids cut holes in old kerosene tins and inserted pieces of garden hose, one end of which was kept above the water by wooden floats. This experiment didn't work very well because we didn't realise that we also needed a pump, but we spluttered on in hope.

Port Campbell was a little more civilised than Peterborough, with a main street lined with shops and boarding houses, and a 'comfort station' built across the best view of the bay. At one end of the beach, Campbell's Creek formed a wide, shallow estuary full of brackish water in which small fish teemed. In earlier days, someone had built a timber-and-wire suspension bridge across it, and we delighted in rocking back and forth while hanging onto the suspension cables until one of us slipped and fell into the warm water below. High limestone cliffs nearby contained a deep cave where the sea had torn out part of the weaker structure. Of course, it had to contain hidden treasure, but dig as we might, we never found it. Today, a section of the cliff has fallen and blocked the tunnel entrance: people who now stroll on the paths above do not know what childhood fantasies are buried underneath.

On the beach, we endlessly built sand castles, tunnels, trenches and walls to keep out the incoming tide. No-one thought much about protective creams in those days, and in any case, we wouldn't have been able to afford them. So our backs would blister in the fierce sun, until we had to be smothered in calamine lotion and forced to wear shirts. Cuts from sharp rocks or broken bottles were doused in iodine or hydrogen peroxide, the latter also used by many women for blonding their hair in the accepted Hollywood style.

When we learned to swim overarm, the great challenge was to make it from the shore about a hundred yards through surf to the pier, which jutted from one headland. Somehow, with no thought of sharks or other perils, we always got there, dodging the hooks of amateur fishermen, and racing back barefoot along the roughly built roadway to again get the blood circulating in our frozen limbs.

Almost as dangerous were expeditions to fish for sweep and leatherjackets from the tops of high cliffs to the east, such as the now-collapsed London Bridge. First we helped the adults to dig up sandworms as the tide receded. Then we drove out to the cliffs and peered gingerly over the edge to make sure there was a reasonably calm sea with the tide about to turn. Hundreds of feet of line and a large float were necessary. We watched in admiration as an adult cast their line far out to sea, listening to the delicate 'swish' as it snaked through the air. As fish came in to feed, the worms on multiple hooks would take their fancy and the catch would be reeled all the way up the sheer bluff. River fishing seemed tame after such thrills.

Some friends owned a beach house where we were sometimes able to stay. It was tightly sealed against winter gales, then opened up for spring and summer. But no matter how briskly the summer breezes blew, a thick, cloying odour never seemed to leave some of the rooms. A mixture of salt, sweat, stale food and heavy dust must have been impregnated in the mattresses, old blankets, and lengths of carpet discarded from the main house. I would recognise traces of that smell every time I went to stay at certain seaside resorts.

~

Cobden's main hotel, built about the time of Federation, was a two-storey red-brick structure incongruously decorated with cast-iron lace. Here, the district's 'upper class' drank, and dined on the mandatory diet of roast lamb spiced with mint sauce. The town's one remaining saddlery abutted the hotel's old stables, now used as a shelter for visitors' cars. A few farmers still drove horse-and-buggy rigs into town, but by the late 1930s most had changed to motor transport of one kind or another. In his shop full of the incomparable odours of dressed leather and oils, and humming with little machines, the old saddler survived for a few years yet by repairing our shoes while we waited, and good-humouredly cutting new leather sprigs for our second-hand football boots.

The town's second hotel was directly across from our new house. It had been built there because the stockyards occupied the corner diagonally opposite us. Although this was a gathering place for stockmen, rouseabouts and workmen, and occasionally a drunk could be seen asleep on the footpath, no-one ever bothered us. Six o'clock closing was strictly enforced: licensed premises were dark and silent soon afterwards. During the day, Jill and I might take a sackful of empties—mainly lemonade bottles—to the second pub's back entrance and sell them for a few pence. The stockyards did become odoriferous on sale days, when sheep and cattle were penned there for buyers' inspection and the wind blew from the south, but we grew up in acceptance of nature's smells and the clouds of dust kicked up in summer.

From the saleyards it was only a few hundred yards to another favourite playground: the town's rubbish tip. This dumping ground was simply a deep ravine behind the stockyards where the land fell away sharply. Clambering down the steep sides was dangerous, but small boys think they can go anywhere. Besides, the expedition was worth it for you never knew what treasures would turn up—spring beds, building materials for huts, old Coolgardie safes, household rubbish of all kinds. In one hand we would carry a heavy stick with which to chase rats through the rotting piles of garbage. That done, the remaining entertainment involved setting up a cracked chamber-pot on a post and heaving stones at it. Later, we graduated to catapults made from the stout Y-shaped fork of a eucalypt branch and pieces of inner tube begged from the garageman. These dangerous devices, also called shanghais, were prohibited by police, parents and school, but most boys had one hidden somewhere.

Opposite the tip, on an otherwise vacant allotment, was a small hut not much sturdier or more comfortable than the lean-to I had built at home. Here lived a family of Aboriginal people who were not so much ostracised as ignored by most of the other townspeople. I had no idea that these individuals were descendants of tribes who had once freely roamed the grasslands and forests of the district. There was something a little scary about their faces, and usually I kept well away, but I saw inside their home once. My mother, hearing about this family from the hospital matron, had filled up our old pram with bread, sugar, potatoes and cast-off clothing and told me to help her push it down the unmade road to the humpy. Within the dark interior was a dirt floor and a few broken pieces of furniture which looked as though they had been salvaged from the tip; there was no bathroom that I could see. A new baby was squalling in a rough crib made from a wooden fruit box. We left the food and clothes with the taciturn parents and never returned.

In 1937 a frightful poliomyelitis epidemic reached the district. It was called infantile paralysis because it affected mainly infants and children, who had little natural immunity. The border between New South Wales and Victoria was closed in an attempt to prevent the disease from spreading. Nobody knew who brought the infection to our town, but it spread quickly in the insanitary conditions. Soon, a dozen or so children were stricken. The first we knew of it was when an ambulance pulled up opposite our house and took a playmate of one of my sisters to the isolation ward at Colac Hospital. Then my sister Jill herself fell ill, complaining of headaches, a high temperature and leg pains. The doctor, frantic from overwork, came as soon as he could. By this time I had also developed aches and pains—whether real or imaginary, I do not remember. Our mother was in tears and our father grey-faced, but our symptoms eased after a few days in bed.

The town was practically sealed off, the school shut down for three months and all children quarantined inside their homes. Jill and I spent most of that time hanging over our high wooden fence, trying to see what was happening outside our prison.

When the panic was over, my mother conducted an appeal through the newspaper for money and toys to give to our little friends who were lying paralysed in hospital. On two successive Christmases, she took a busload of children, party treats and presents to the row of sufferers who would never rise from their white enamelled beds or iron lungs. I wonder what they thought as we healthy children, reluctant and half-ashamed of that reluctance, tentatively handed our gifts to those who had once been able to run and jostle with us.

How could they avoid feeling sorry for themselves? In their position, I would have been bitter and resentful at being robbed of life. Yet they did not seem to be, instead smiling and apparently grateful for this interruption to the hospital routine.

The polio epidemic was just the start of that time of troubles. In mid-January 1939, some of the worst bushfires in memory set practically the whole of Victoria alight. On Friday 13 January, known thereafter as Black Friday, north winds whipped up the flames into a horrifying fireball effect, when the very air caught fire and exploded. All told, seventy-one people and millions of sheep and cattle perished as they tried to escape. Some towns in timbered areas simply vanished.

Our village was fairly safe, because the land for miles around had been cleared for dairy farms and sheep pastures—the fires seemed to underscore the wisdom of farmers who believed in removing every tree from their properties. Still, when the nearby Heytesbury Forest caught fire, vast clouds of smoke and ash obliterated the sun. Flying cinders caused spot fires wherever pasture grass was long and dry. Local volunteer brigades dashed around dowsing small fires with knapsack pumps and attempted to burn new fire breaks. That was about all they could do. The flames roared on until the wind changed, driving the fires back into areas already burned out.

My mother, active journalist that she was, drove all over the devastated countryside, sometimes taking us children with her. Once or twice she tried to drive along bush roads where the fire had passed, before being forced back. Huge gum trees incandescent on the ground, or standing like black chimneys and emitting showers of red and orange sparks, still glow in my memory. On the charred paddocks, thousands of bloated sheep lay with legs rigidly sticking into the air.

Mother sent many fine reports to the city papers. A piece of hers in the Melbourne *Herald* said:

> I have given lifts to men, women and children, who, worn out after terrifying experiences, were seeking safety away from the blackened

> ruins … they just collapsed into the car … They have, poor things, lost everything and their outlook is as black as the blackened waste … I have seen toddlers, too young to understand the meaning of this upheaval, looking for lost pets, and seen the grateful look on a mother's face when I refrained from telling the awful truth …

My mother really was a remarkable woman. She crackled with obsessive energy, which kept her working long hours until her eighties. When she could find no-one else to look after us, she simply loaded us into the car and took us on her rounds. So we came to see more things within a 50-mile radius of home than most children, even though I was only aged about ten, and Jill and Dina seven and four, respectively.

The bluestone homesteads and mansions of Western District squatters particularly intrigued me. I could not quite believe that real people lived in such places. Some mansions, particularly the ones with baronial entrances where we were sometimes allowed to study the stuffed animals lining the walls, seemed more suited to legends of knights in armour and damsels in distress—which I knew all about from reading Beatrice Clay's romantic *King Arthur and His Round Table*, mother's English prize of 1920 from Hampton Beach College. One stately two-storey mansion we visited had been inherited by the widow of a famous pioneer's offspring. On his death, the remainder of the family had told the widow she must be sure to keep every furnishing, every painting, every carpet exactly as it was. Later, she grew so tired of their nagging that one day she got in touch with Whelan the Wrecker, who came down from Melbourne and demolished the entire structure stone by stone, leaving only a bare paddock for her inheritors.

Our family developed close friendships with a few grazier families who lived in more modest but still spacious single-storey homesteads. Although we were poor by comparison, I suppose we represented a breath of the wider world compared with the usual fairly stolid run of farmers and town citizens.

One family took me in for week-long summer periods. Their large homestead, with its red-painted iron roof, was built on a hilltop overlooking a deep river valley. The family owned an ancient mariner's brass telescope, through which they could see on far hillsides any sheep which had fallen down through disease and needed assistance or burial. The grazier and his one farmhand taught me how to cut down trees in comparative safety, milk the household cows, extract the cream in a hand-operated Laval separator, and feed the skim milk to calves. The property generated its own flickering electricity from a donkey engine turning a dynamo housed inside a small tin shed. What impressed me even more was their lavatory, erected over a deep pitch-black hole that may have been an old mine shaft. When you 'did' something, several seconds seemed to elapse before you heard it hit the bottom. My sisters were terrified of falling into the hole: it would have been impossible to climb out.

My body was now preparing itself for the changes of adolescence. When I was about eleven, I found a Western novelette on the farmhouse bookshelves. It had a brightly coloured cover showing a 'Red Indian' lying spread-eagled on the ground, his arms and legs tied to stakes; and apart from headdress, patterned necklace and loincloth, he was naked. I stared at the picture in fascination without knowing why it impressed me so vividly. A day or two later, I happened to see the grazier's wife bending over her sewing machine in a room set aside for odd jobs. She was wearing a loose sleeveless dress to suit the summer heat, and as she leaned forward I could see a bare breast through the large armhole. I stood in the doorway silent and amazed, desperately wanting to touch her, with a warm feeling beginning to suffuse my body. A few minutes later she noticed me standing there and told me to call the men to tea.

A few months later, a tragedy occurred that rocked the district. The grazier's wife, it appeared, had been engaged in a secret affair with one of the neighbouring squatters. The husband, that handsome, broad-shouldered man who had shown me so many things, who seemed to have everything to live for, picked up his gun and loaded it. But he didn't go forth to shoot the errant wife or her lover. He went into one of the paddocks, placed the gun in his mouth, and shot himself dead.

Why did he do it, I kept on asking myself obsessively, as though he had been my own father. How frail that poor man's ego must have been, beneath a heroic exterior that in the last days of his life revealed nothing of the moral cataclysm that had struck him. Perhaps he foresaw that some people would snigger at his misfortune, never quite forgetting it no matter how many years passed. Or perhaps he blamed himself for not being able to keep his beautiful wife faithful. How does anyone know, particularly in a repressive society, what goes on inside other people's relationships?

~

Another friendly family owned a glorious property of about 2000 acres at the end of a rough gravel road cut through the bush. It had been established in the distant past, when shepherds were employed to tend the flocks. On Sundays they were forced to attend religious services, and a cedar-lined 'church' had been built on the property for this purpose. Now the building was deserted, had become a repository for unwanted furniture, dust, spiders, and broken household appliances still awaiting spare parts fifty years later. It was a perfect hiding place in which a child could experiment with inventions, hurl stones at mice, or simply dream away the long days as tinted sunlight streamed through the ancient cypresses surrounding the outbuildings.

The owner of the property was a rarity among Australian graziers: a man of Jewish descent. With a two-horse Clydesdale team, he ploughed and harrowed the compressed pastures with their sparse native grasses. He planted subterranean clover, rye grass and cocksfoot seed, spreading large quantities of the newfangled superphosphate to encourage their growth. Soon, the sour old pastures were green, pulsating with life. On them he grazed large Romney and Southdown sheep, better able than merino and other fine-wool animals to withstand footrot and worm infestation in that damp country. One year he achieved the state's highest price for fat lambs—the fleeces, hacked off by itinerant shearers in a tumbledown, greasy, dimly lit shed, were of secondary importance.

All these things I absorbed unconsciously as I helped to chase sheep from one paddock to another, or—joy of joys—was given the responsibility of operating a drafting gate. As a matter of course, I watched sheep being slaughtered for the table: the animal thrown on its back, a sharpened knife inserted and drawn quickly across its throat with no apparent effect, then, a second later, a great gout of blood, welling out on the grass.

I don't suppose a town boy ever owed a greater debt to a friendly farmer. He handed me my first real rifle, with which I nearly shot off my foot while learning how to extract a live bullet from the breech. 'Don't tell your mother,' was his only comment. He showed me how windmills drew summer water supplies from underground sources. He chopped off a hen's head, slit her open, and showed me the succession of egglets glowing like pearls inside her ovaries. He demonstrated how to net the escape holes in a rabbit warren and send in a sharp-toothed ferret to chase the animals into the nets—perhaps he was disappointed when I could not join him in the task of twisting each rabbit's neck. He took me spotlight-shooting in the bush at night, when he and other men slaughtered foxes and kangaroos by the score. He took me to visit nearby sharefarmer properties, where rural poverty seemed more bearable than town poverty. He understood when I just wanted to go off alone and moon among the giant trees that lined the long driveway, or race downhill to the small stream on the mushroom-rich river flats.

Inside the old homestead, the large sitting room was lit by a pressurised acetylene lamp which cast a light of dazzling purity. The other rooms were illuminated only by candles: one night we nearly burned the place down when a curtain blown by the night breeze touched a candle flame and caught fire. At the dining table, we seemed to live on prime cuts of lamb and roast vegetables, cooked in a large wood-fire stove in the antique kitchen. At night, us kids snuggled into corners of a supremely comfortable leather lounge in front of a huge log fire, while the adults grouped themselves around a card table for interminable games of poker.

One Sunday early in September 1939, the routine changed. Word had gone out over the single party-line telephone wire which linked homesteads that the prime minister, Robert Menzies, would make an important broadcast that evening. Many guessed what he would say but still wanted to hear him. After an early dinner, we sat around the crackling radio receiver to listen to Menzies's voice: 'Fellow Australians, it is my melancholy duty to inform you officially that, in consequence of the persistence by Germany in her invasion of Poland, Great Britain has declared war upon her, and that, as a result, Australia is also at war.'

As the words continued—'No harder task can fall to the lot of a democratic leader …'—I felt cheerful, buoyant. War to me was a glorious, manly affair. So when I looked around at the adults, I could scarcely believe what I saw. Tears were rolling silently down their faces, women and men alike. Never before had I seen grown men cry. I hadn't known they *could* cry. But they had realised what I had not: that the happy times were over.

CHAPTER 2

The Town: Adolescence

NOT MANY LOCAL men joined the armed forces during the so-called 'phoney war', the six-month period at the beginning of World War II when little actual fighting took place. After pictures of the September 1939 bombing of Warsaw were shown at my school, masters and older boys did make sporadic attempts to dig slit trenches around the place. These soon filled with water: a bombing raid would at least have caused a few drownings. Otherwise, life seemed to go on much as usual. Most people believed that France's 'impregnable' Maginot Line would hold back the German invaders forever. We boys were entranced by the detailed drawings, published in newspapers and magazines, depicting the vast underground railways and storage systems of the French fortresses. We tried to imitate them in the garden with our lead soldiers, model trains, and forts made from empty treacle tins. The opposing villains, like Red Indians, were always soundly defeated.

Then, in the European autumn of 1940, came the German blitzkrieg, the sudden collapse of Belgium, Holland and France, and the British Army's narrow escape from the beaches of Dunkirk. The news electrified our district, as it must have done everywhere.

The loyalty to the British Empire that had been drummed into generations of Australian schoolchildren bloomed.

As for me, now aged ten, I was old enough to help in the printery. The business had progressed a little. Dad had been able to engage a first-year apprentice, a lanky youth who slept behind a canvas blind on the front porch of an old single-fronted timber cottage in the main street. Together, we experimented with locking handset type and brass rules into a chase, and printing the result on a foot-powered Chandler & Price platen machine. Printing held a hypnotic fascination for me: I loved the idea of producing repetitive copies of one's own creations, whatever they were. Soon, we could produce respectable-enough receipt books and advertising leaflets for local shopkeepers. My birthday present that year was an American book called *The Art and Practice of Printing*. I pored eagerly over its luxurious art-paper pages and detailed illustrations—and continued to do so until it disappeared in one of too many moves to different dwellings. The world lost one of its noblest crafts when computers and lithography took over from traditional letterpress printing.

Sometimes, when weekly press day came around, the old donkey engine that powered the big cylinder press would break down. On these occasions Dad called on the assistance of the local milkman. He came willingly enough, as long as the evening milking was not due. A powerful man, his task was to turn the heavy iron flywheel using a handle fixed to its outer rim. This action spread tacky black ink from the inking table via long composition rollers onto the flat pages of type clamped inside the machine. At the same time, my father fed large sheets of newsprint into a set of grippers, after which the heavy cylinder pressed the paper against the inked type. Because the machine was rotating so slowly under these conditions, it would not automatically 'fly' the printed sheets along a set of long thin sticks onto the delivery pile. So my job was to stand on a raised platform, lean forward and grasp the edge of each printed sheet as it came off the cylinder, flicking a cushion of air underneath, to float it safely and squarely onto the stack. I felt very important, and delighted to earn another sixpence.

Being the printer's son yielded another benefit. When Victorian and federal elections came around, the town's solicitor engaged me on market days to place dodgers (small handbills) under the windscreen wipers of the cars parked in the main street; I shared the balance among local shopkeepers, who often used the reverse side as scrap paper to tot up amounts owed by customers. This simple task earned me a shiny 2-shilling coin bearing the image of King George VI. Only later did I realise the solicitor's little joke: he knew my father's socialist views, and the dodgers always promoted the winning conservative candidate.

One day I found my father practising Morse code on the feed-board of the big press. He had unpacked his old radio apparatus and was wondering aloud whether his wrist was as supple as before. 'I'm joining up,' he said simply. There was no legal need for him to do so. As a man of forty with several children, he would not have been conscripted for years. He may secretly have been glad to find a way of escaping the seventy-hours-a-week drudgery of producing a local newspaper, and to embark on his life's last adventure; I have no idea what my mother thought of all this. The RAAF snapped Dad up as a six-bob-a-day aircraftman, rapidly promoting him through the ranks to flight lieutenant, responsible for helping to train thousands of wireless air gunners in the Empire Air Training Scheme.

My parents arranged to sell the newspaper to a larger press in nearby Camperdown that was owned by descendants of squatting pioneers. My mother agreed to act as editor of both papers, which meant she had to work harder than ever, travelling long distances at all hours and typing until well after midnight to fill the columns.

We stayed in the same house for another few months, where our live-in maid sulkily prepared our meals when mother did not appear. Apart from that, we kids pretty much looked after ourselves. The printery now lay deserted, but I still spent hours fiddling with the old type, admiring its classical lines and setting it around electros of masonic symbols and the like, or dragging out the yellowing bound files of newspapers dating back to the 1890s to read them in the dusty sunlight. The new owners took the typesetting machine and lead ingots but didn't want the rest of the worn-out junk. I have no idea of its final fate; possibly it was melted down as scrap metal.

My father gave me some parting advice before he went to the RAAF training camp. 'Never be beholden to anyone,' he told me gravely. This meant, he said, that you should never accept favours or assistance from anyone if you could possibly avoid it. In other words, you had to learn to stand on your own feet. This was the longest personal talk I ever had with him. Aged eleven, I would mull over his words and eventually agree that they formed a sensible philosophy for life.

In a rather embarrassed fashion, Dad had also handed me a booklet entitled 'Advice to Boys' and recommended I read it carefully. Produced by a Melbourne organisation called The Fathers and Sons Movement, the booklet's main aim was to ensure that, at all costs, young boys should beware of falling into the habit of something called 'self-abuse'. It explained that, in early adolescence, boys would begin to have 'peculiar feelings' involving the opposite sex. The author nerved himself to add that boys, when asleep, might experience vivid dreams accompanied by 'nocturnal emissions'. These awful experiences were to be avoided, because a growing boy needed all his strength. 'Immoral urges' could be overcome, in time, through lots of physical exercise during the day, cold showers, and constant prayer if afflicted at night. With indignation, the writer described a class of boys who actually produced emissions at will by 'manipulation'. The harmful effect of this vile practice upon the body was proven by the feelings of 'weakness' and 'lassitude' which occurred after such discharges. Its disgusting practitioners could easily be identified by their pale faces, nervous gestures, and inability to look other people straight in the eye. Parents were advised to watch out for these symptoms and when necessary take severe disciplinary measures.

All this was interesting, if not a bit frightening, but it didn't mean much to me at the time. It was true that I had begun to dream obsessively, but mostly about the war. The apocalyptic drama of *The March of Time* films and newsreels of Japanese bombardments in China had the greatest effect on my thoughts. I began to be haunted by Technicolor dreams of Japanese planes, easily identified by their distinctive red roundels, bombing the streets of our town—this more than a year before Japan embarked on the war in the Pacific. In my imagination, my family cowered under the household tank-stand while foreign fiends firing vivid yellow flashes dived towards our bedrooms. Each time, I woke up shaking and bathed in sweat just as they were about to kill us all.

Another repetitive dream in bright colour must have originated from Buck Rogers comics and Flash Gordon cinema serials. Usually I was crouched behind a low stone wall, paralysed with fear, while invaders from space moved remorselessly across the countryside in mobile cupolas, obliterating buildings and people with flashing purple death rays, leaving only a flat smoking wasteland behind them. In my hand was a loaded six-shooter, but every time I aimed it and tried to pull the trigger, my hand refused to obey the mind's command. I always woke knowing the humiliation of helplessness and defeat.

In another frightening dream, I was a tiny figure crouched behind the printery. The typesetting machine, angrily clicking its levers, broke through a wall and towered over me. Its intention, I knew, was to immolate me in molten lead, and I was powerless to move my legs and flee.

~

Amidst the fears of my dreams, it was with delight that I discovered the Boy Scout movement. I had once been to a meeting of Wolf Cubs in the church hall near our back fence. Their cries of 'a-ké-la' and 'dib-dib-dib' seemed childish and I never returned. But a friend who was about a year older than me explained that Scouts dealt with more grown-up matters. For instance, you could get boxing lessons there, and in a personal world growing more uncertain by the minute, that seemed like a good idea.

Robert Baden-Powell developed the idea of scouting as an army colonel during the Boer War, when his forces were besieged in Mafeking. After the war, he worked out exactly how to exploit the gang instinct among boys by organising them into 'patrols' and 'troops' within a tight system of leadership, reinforced by badges for proficiency in woodcraft, camping, signalling, first aid, knotting, tracking and so on. His book *Scouting for Boys* became the bible of practically every twelve-year-old boy in Cobden. Some even tried to live up to the ideals of the Scout Law and Promise, which enjoined us, among other things, to be 'pure in thought, word, and deed'.

The most attractive thing about scouting, especially in a rural district, was the wide range of physical activities it offered. Our fathers built a Scout Hall behind the town swimming pool, on a steep rise covered with long grass and low bushes. Here at night we played 'spotlighting', trying to avoid the brief flashes of a torch while crawling from bush to bush to reach the top of the hill unobserved. In those extensive grounds, we could also practise axemanship and fire-lighting to our heart's content.

For our scoutmaster, we were lucky enough to have the knowledgeable shire engineer. 'Skipper' showed us how to fell and skin suitable trees, then bind them with ropes and special knots to make a marvellous flying fox, on which we flew across the creek. He took us camping beside quiet rivers in the dense bush and taught us how to navigate by compass, pitch tents so they would stay up in a storm, light safe fires without using matches, cook our meat and damper in camp ovens, play tunes on gumleaves, and identify bush animals by their tracks. He arranged for a shire truck to take us to the site of underground caves in the lava plains, which nobody else seemed to know about. On sunset journeys home, he taught us traditional ballads like 'Green Grow the Rushes-o'. Around camp fires, an older boy might produce a mouth organ and lead us into 'Waltzing Matilda' or 'Click Go the Shears'. Ghostly figures of pioneer heroes seemed to appear in the flickering shadows—especially after my parents gave me a large red volume containing the immortal prose of Henry Lawson.

A scoutmaster who could be bothered to lead us into all these adventures was bound to become a substitute father to some of the boys. I certainly felt that way. Hence my sense of betrayal when I was elected leader of the Eagle Patrol but Skipper insisted on a 'best of three' ballot among all the boys. He made no secret of his opinion that the newsagent's son should get the position, and only eventually gave way to my appointment, with poor grace. Perhaps he opposed me because I was getting too big for my boots. Or perhaps one of my mother's comprehensive reports of shire council activities had reflected adversely upon him. Whatever his reasons, I was wounded more deeply than I could admit to anyone. It was as though my own father had suddenly said that he disliked me.

My spirits lifted considerably when my real father came home on leave in his smart new uniform and offered to teach the boys how to interpret and transmit Morse code. This skill was worth another proficiency badge, to be sewn on khaki shirts already laden with symbols of achievement. The whole troop turned up to these lessons: I was never so proud as when my father set up his Morse key to demonstrate the technique of sending clear messages through the ether. A craze began in the town for stringing lengths of copper wire from one cubby house to another and trying to send battery-powered messages along it.

A more practical result was the enlistment of Scouts who'd qualified for the signaller's badge in the communications arm of the local Volunteer Defence Corps. Occasionally we turned out with this 'Dad's Army' for Saturday afternoon drills. The adults were well armed, for almost every man left in country districts possessed a rifle or shotgun and sufficient ammunition. And the district's Light Horse reserve troop still had its own World War I Vickers heavy machine-gun, which could be dismantled and fastened into special saddle packs to be galloped to new positions. I was sure that, as a guerrilla army, they would have caused serious trouble (with juvenile assistance) to any invader. However, when an army officer came up from Melbourne to supervise some mock battles, he told us afterwards that every semaphore signaller—that is, my mates and I—had been shot dead because we had jumped up from cover to send messages.

Still, these events only made me determined that the Eagle Patrol would become the best in the world. I decided that we should hold weekly patrol meetings in addition to the troop meetings, to expand our knowledge of scouting lore. The deserted printery seemed the ideal place for these get-togethers, so after school we nestled into the bags of waste that littered the building and talked about the brave things we were going to do—or rather, I talked and the others listened. At the height of this juvenile idealism, it occurred to me that if only the whole world would follow Scout law, mankind's problems would disappear. The 'truths' that Baden-Powell propounded, based largely on a mixture of Christian and military ethics, seemed so obvious that they only needed to be disseminated to convert people on the spot. I therefore proposed that we should start a news-sheet which would be sold cheaply to the unsuspecting townsfolk. It would consist largely of lighthearted gossip about young people's activities, the sugar-coating that would sweeten Baden-Powell's messianic message.

My Scouts gathered whatever printable jokes and 'news items' they could think of, while I added the more portentous contents—which is why I am glad that no copy seems to survive today. The shire clerk agreed to run off a hundred copies of the journal's eight pages on his Roneo machine. I slowly pecked out the stencils on my mother's typewriter, filling up the machine with wax fragments which had to be winkled out with an old toothbrush. I also came up with the journal's title, the *Fly Paper*, which could be taken to refer either to the Eagle Patrol or to the sticky brown tape which most people hung from their ceilings to trap blowflies. The childish pun was made worse by the journal's motto: 'Our readers stick to it.'

After copies had been printed and stapled, we put on our Scout uniforms, picked up long wooden staves with which to beat off aggressive dogs, and set off on sales expeditions. We offered copies to households at threepence each, calculating that this would enable us to pay the shire office for the costs of paper and ink. We had no trouble getting rid of the first hundred copies, with many people seemingly amused by the venture—the Sydney *Bulletin* even published an item drawing attention to this threat to the established media. Then the going got harder, with some boys resenting my attempts to organise their leisure time so we could publish regularly. After half-a-dozen issues, the *Fly Paper* no longer buzzed in the land.

As part of the war effort, my mob of Scouts clung to the back of the council truck on runs to collect piles of rotting newspapers and battered aluminium utensils. We were told that the newsprint would be converted into brown wrapping paper and the aluminium into fighter planes. In fact, these materials for years lay in a deserted timber shed halfway between our house and the rubbish tip. When my friends and I had nothing better to do, we would creep in among the damp bundles of newsprint, cut them open and read anything that took our interest. The *Australian Women's Weekly* seemed to stand the dampness best, and it contained large pictures of our cinema heroes and the comic strip *Mandrake the Magician*, who could foil villains with one hypnotic gesture.

Outside the shed was a huge peppercorn tree that became fragrant when heated by the summer sun, and which provided green peppercorns of exactly the right size to fire through 6-inch lengths of glass tubing thoughtfully sold to us by the local chemist. A great test of daring was to take the peashooter to school concealed in one's sock, wait for the teacher to turn to the blackboard, and fire a peppercorn at the neck of a child in front of you. The resulting cuts from the teacher's strap and confiscation of said peashooter were almost worth it.

~

Even before I finished primary school, soon after the outbreak of war, I was looking forward to the experience of secondary education in Camperdown, where my mother now spent most of her time. As I waited at the bus stop on that first morning, resplendent in a pair of long grey worsted trousers, a man lounging there said, 'Off to high school, are you?'

'That's right,' said I.

'No you're not,' he replied. 'The school burned down last night.'

And so it had. Some local clod, infuriated by teachers' attempts to penetrate his brain cells, had carried out the traditional revenge.

Under wartime conditions, it would take more than two years to build a brick replacement for the old weatherboard high school. But within a few days of the fire, arrangements had been made for the large building that comprised the primary school in Camperdown to also accommodate me and my secondary peers. Sufficient desks were crammed together so that classes of up to sixty could be taught by the staff. I haven't much memory of what knowledge they tried to pass on to us in these circumstances. But still vivid is the astonishment I felt on seeing the hinged lid of a desk occupied by an older boy begin to rise into the air, even though his hands were resting on top of it. A tremor of amusement spread through the other boys and girls, and a neighbour whispered the incomprehensible words, 'Gee, he's horny.'

A highlight of that first week, as far as I was concerned, was the afternoon when the boys of our class were instructed in the finer points of carpentry, which was called sloyd after its Swedish origins. In a workshop crunchy with shavings and filled with the odour of heated animal glue, a patient artisan taught us what he knew. Some boys progressed as far as cutting dovetail joints for various items of furniture, but most of us concentrated on making simple walking sticks for wounded soldiers. I loved the long straight grain and silken feel of mountain ash as I carefully tapered each stick with a plane and spokeshave, then fitted a handle which had been cut with a special saw to a standard pattern. We endlessly smoothed each stick with glasspaper before applying several coats of French polish. We must have manufactured enough walking sticks to supply every wounded soldier in the world—perhaps they still lie in some forgotten army warehouse.

Not so successful was the task of knitting squares for soldiers. These pieces of wool, we were assured, would be sewn together into comforting blankets for our troops. The female teacher in charge of the project insisted that boys as well as girls should knit the squares. I received instructions at home on how to cast the wool onto needles and knit purl and plain, but it was no use: my fingers, normally so nimble, refused to make the stitches. I tried to persevere, only to burst into rare sobs of frustration. At school I skulked around the outskirts of the playground, hoping for the bell to ring quickly and diving behind trees whenever the teacher in charge of knitting appeared. I was consumed with guilt at letting down the men who were freezing during desert nights in the Middle East. Then I discovered that practically none of the other boys had completed their knitted squares either.

One day I overheard two people talking about potential winners of the upcoming Melbourne Cup. 'Well, if you put your money on Old Rowley,' one concluded, 'you'd make a fortune.' That sounded good, so I persuaded one of them to 'invest' 2 shillings on my behalf with the local SP bookie. When that horse came home at odds of 100 to one, I found myself in possession of the unprecedented sum of £10 in crisp, green £1 notes. A few weeks later, I was still bragging about my extraordinary fortune. I must have become quite objectionable to the other boys, who scarcely ever saw a spare sixpence. While waiting for the bus after school one day, a boy clenched his fist and without warning hit me hard in the lower gut. I collapsed like a burst balloon, writhing on the footpath and struggling to breathe. On the way home I sat sore and subdued on the bus, brooding over the incident. Mostly I was ashamed of being too paralysed to get up and hit back. I said nothing to anyone about the incident.

I remained sore for the next few days. The pain diminished, but I was gradually overcome by a lassitude that made it difficult even to get out of bed. Mother asked the doctor to come, but he was too busy to call on someone suffering from vague symptoms of tiredness. Instead, he sent over the nursing sister who supervised his small private hospital. She prodded my stomach and diagnosed that I had 'eaten too many green apples'. I feebly denied the charge, but she was used to children's fibs.

My mother had already driven off to work, but she'd asked a friendly neighbour to call in around lunchtime to check on me. This simple action saved my life. The neighbour found me pale, clammy, almost fainting, and decided we had to go straight to the hospital, located only a short distance away. I'd staggered about thirty paces, my arm around the neighbour's neck, when I blacked out. I half woke up as I was being wheeled into a primitive operating theatre, where I obeyed a command to start counting as drops of ether were squirted onto a pad covering my nose. I slid down a long tunnel into blackness. When I regained consciousness, I was lying on my back in a ward, unable to move a limb. The doctor was at the end of the bed talking to my mother. 'I think he'll pull through,' I heard him say. Then he noticed my eyelids were flickering and fetched his needle. Once again I experienced the incomparable comfort of morphine circulating in my veins. I soared on rainbows through jet-black skies.

Later, I learned that my appendix had burst, causing infection to swarm into the adjoining organs. The doctor had operated immediately, leaving a long incision from which a drainage tube now extended. He had then telephoned Melbourne and pleaded with the army authorities to send him a new drug called sulphanilamide. This had been invented in Germany some years earlier but was extremely difficult to obtain because of wartime demands. Nevertheless, a supply was found and sent down by train and then bus. What a difference that drug would have made to the shattered men doctors had tried to patch up during World War I. My case must have seemed routine by comparison.

The air force gave my father compassionate leave. He came to see me every day, often bearing a fresh bundle of novels from the lending library. He would've had to clean out the libraries in nearby towns as well, because as I recovered, my consumption of books became enormous. I sometimes read up to three a day, including every Western novel available, especially those written by the master, Zane Grey. After three weeks in hospital, family friends took me on a long holiday to Lorne, where I recuperated with walks beginning at a few yards and slowly extending all round the beach and nearby hills.

While my sisters returned to school after the summer holidays, I was not quite well enough to resume my education, and for several weeks I was left alone in our house. One day, searching through the highest bookshelf in the sitting room for any tomes I had not yet consumed, I came across a singular publication. It had a soft cover and a stapled back, and was so thin it might easily have been missed between two large volumes. About half the contents consisted of text and half were drawings by a Sydney artist named Brodie Mack. The title was something like *The Adventures of Maisie*. The booklet described how a buxom young woman had laundered her only pair of panties and hung them on a line to dry. A vagrant breeze had snatched the garment from the line and blown it through adjoining flats and houses. The woman chased it everywhere, becoming involved in embarrassing incidents and explanations. As she was wearing only a brief summer dress, the artist took the opportunity of depicting in some detail almost every part of her anatomy. On reading this book, I became sexually aroused.

Up to now I had vaguely believed, on the rare occasions when I thought about it at all, that a man had sex with a woman through her navel. I don't know the origin of this belief: possibly seeing a pregnant woman with a swollen belly. No-one at school or at home ever attempted to explain human anatomy to me. If they had, I would have been shocked by the idea that the 'dirty' parts of the body were also used for copulation and childbirth. Farm observations had in no way prepared me for the reality.

Led on by the increasing tension in my trousers, I walked with difficulty into my sisters' room and found a discarded rag doll which had been thrown to the back of the wardrobe. I compared its anatomy to the crude drawings of the girl in the magazine. If I wanted to hold and kiss that girl, while thrusting my penis somewhere into her body, then the entrance had to be well below the navel. Instinct completed the rest, and the following rapture, but I concluded that my body had got rid of some of its 'badness'. It looked too much like the matter which came out of boils on the necks of some children at school. No-one, not even the editor of the *Children's Encyclopaedia*, told me that it contained the very stuff of life.

Meanwhile, a feeling of vast contentment and lethargy had stolen over my body. Dreamily, my thoughts drifted on. Then, out of memory, came the words of The Fathers and Sons booklet: those who practised the abominable crime were dissipating their bodily strength, as shown by the weakness they felt afterwards. Yes, I felt weak, so these thrilling sensations and activities were the unnamed sin! I began to feel guilty, full of shamed regret, and swore I would never do it again. That was the extent of my education in human relations, circa 1941.

Girls en masse were a pain in the neck, a gaggle of giggling, useless, plump creatures who couldn't run fast, swim any distance, build forts, or even throw straight. They gathered in gossiping groups, remote from the boys but always at hand to tell on anyone who broke real or imaginary rules. One girl, though, seemed different from the others. At school she was just a unit in the anonymous mob, but one afternoon, while walking home, I saw her sitting on the front porch of her house. The low sun illuminated the young woman's face that was beginning to emerge from the puppy fat, and reflected from her startlingly clear violet eyes. Thick coils of blonde hair lay golden on her shoulders. She smiled. I smiled back, and was smitten.

How, I wondered at home that night, could I summon up the nerve to talk to her? It would not be as simple as going up to her and saying hello. It was not just a matter of my own sudden shyness: if any other boy saw me, my life would be made a misery, and the feelings developing in my overheated imagination seemed too special and private to risk that. So I posted her a kind of love letter, saying I would leave further notes in a hole under the brickwork at the side of the chemist's shop. The notes always vanished, although I never saw anyone pick them up. This childish, yearning correspondence continued with increasing ardour, until she was sent away to boarding school.

Quite by chance, I saw the same girl years later in a Melbourne suburb. She was pushing a pram containing a squalling baby, and scowling while she muttered at it. Her delicious curves had gone, and the soft contours of her face and neck were covered with blotches. Ah the memories of youth.

~

The effects of the Pacific War soon began to trickle home. Petrol became harder to obtain, even in country areas where primary producers were dependent on it. Seaside and city trips almost stopped completely. Every road sign in the district was taken down, in order to baffle potential Japanese invasion forces. Cars were fitted with clumsy 'gas producers' which burned charcoal instead of petrol. A family we knew, who lived in the bush a few miles out of town, built a giant kiln to produce charcoal for local use. I watched as they split large logs and stacked them inside the kiln, then sealed it up to encourage the slow combustion that produced fine charcoal. They were glad of the extra income.

The authorities recruited a Volunteer Air Observers Corps, to report any enemy planes flying overhead. I applied and was allotted the Saturday morning shift from 8 a.m. to noon, which nobody else wanted. Corps members were given exclusive use of the golf clubhouse and its hand-crank telephone, which enabled us to report to regional headquarters. Posters tacked on the walls showed us the silhouettes of all Allied and Japanese aircraft. Week after week I studied them eagerly—if a squadron of Jap bombers and fighters suddenly appeared from over the horizon, I wanted to be able to identify them immediately and accurately, thus saving nearby townships from annihilation, and of course becoming a local hero. Invasion seemed near. Unbelievable rumours spread of spies signalling to Japanese submarines from high coastal cliffs. But during my two years of duty, only one plane flew overhead: a noisy little Tiger Moth, Australia's answer to the enemy's might.

Most of those solitary hours I spent putting together the Scouts magazine. I also wrote letters and paragraphs about local events. I had discovered that the Sydney *Bulletin*, still in its old-style format, would occasionally supply a half-crown for such contributions. Fortunately they didn't have to be of high literary quality. I even wrote a radio play which was broadcast by 3UZ in Melbourne.

Despite the wartime shortages, my parents managed to get hold of a new Malvern Star bicycle for my thirteenth birthday. I was overjoyed. The bicycle was surely the world's greatest invention for youngsters. In one stroke my universe expanded from the townships and school bus route to a radius of 20 miles or so, wherever tracks existed. As my cycling strength grew, I left the flat pasture lands for more adventurous rides through hilly country, even going as far as Port Campbell, where I arrived with numb legs and a sense of triumph. A favourite short trip was to a place called Devil's Gully, where a river had cut deep gorges on its way to the ocean. Here and there I came across the remnants of old corduroy roads, built by farmers in the days before the shire could afford a mechanised road-making plant. The roads were formed simply by laying large logs together at right angles across muddy patches, and on steep inclines. Cars had a rough time using them, and bicycles were useless on such tracks.

I loved that heavy pushbike. I was constantly oiling it, adjusting its mechanisms, fussing over it. Past the dairy farms I flew, their houses often crumbling into decay but their sheds and fencing well cared for. I laughed at their sardonic names: Gunna-doo, Upsandowns, Thistle-doo, Emoh Ruo, Dunroamin. Past abandoned road-making machinery I sped, antique steam traction engines and road rollers turning to rust. A stop here to gaze at an abandoned oil-drilling rig erected by some optimist in the 1920s. A brief halt there in the scented shade of a large gum tree to eat a cheese and jam sandwich, which tasted much better than the same meal eaten at school. Sweat soaking my shirt and the broad brim of my hat. Lying down at the first clear stream and sucking up copious draughts of water, unconcerned about any pollution from animals upstream. The days were still young, everlasting, golden.

Main roads and transport facilities had improved so much by this time that smaller outlying creameries and milk-processing factories were closing down, their production now centralised—I poked among their disused boilers and vats, not appreciating the pride with which dairy farmers of the 1880s had formed these cooperative enterprises. When our local butter and cheese factories installed modern pasteurising equipment, they became focal points for most of the district's milk production. I never tired of watching the Reo and Dodge lorries (and the last few horse-drawn wagons) reverse into the loading ramps, where burly men seized the tapered milk churns and emptied them into shining vats. They didn't seem to mind if I wandered inside to watch the large cream-separating and pasteurising plant, where the rich, viscous fluid formed a shimmering waterfall as it tumbled over a series of cooling fins. Even better was the packing room, where huge cubes of golden butter were encased in square wooden boxes stencilled with blue trademarks. I could watch for hours as an employee in white coveralls seized a wide wooden roller bearing lettering embossed in reverse, dipped it into clean water, and carefully impressed the factory's name and trademark into the flat upper surface of the butter.

Scout camps had taught me how to survive in the bush with minimum food and equipment. And there was some other message underneath, something I couldn't quite perceive beyond the noisy games and nightly sing-songs. It seemed to come nearest when we were silently tracking through the tall gums, or when everyone else was asleep in the tents and I was staring through the open flap at the night sky. A few weeks after the best of these camps, I rode back to the site on my pushbike. Little sign of occupation remained, merely a small cleared area near the stream where we had leaned over—and fallen in, laughing and spluttering—to get billies of water. With no human disturbance, the weird spirit of the bush had closed in again. My quiet arrival barely rippled the opaque atmosphere. I was puzzled: this was exactly the same place physically, but it was now quite different because I was there alone. Why did it feel so? The tall trees dressed in grey and green, the silently flowing stream, they just … existed, endured.

I was seized by the desire to be alone, to gaze at the world and try to understand it intuitively. One weekend I borrowed a small tent, packed my knapsack, and rode beyond the town cemetery to an unexplored patch of bush. I told only my best friend where I was going, but he must have told his father, the doctor who had saved my life when my appendix burst, or his mother, the shy French woman who returned with him from the Great War, and they must have told my mother. Late that afternoon she appeared at the spot where I had pitched the tent.

'Are you all right?'

'Yes, fine.'

'Why did you come here?'

'I wanted to be alone.'

'Have you got enough to eat?'

'Yes.'

I could see that she was puzzled by this extraordinary urge to sleep on the ground—or rather, on piles of fragrant gumleaves, with a hip-hole dug into the hard earth with my sheath-knife. As she drove away, no doubt wondering what kind of strange creature she had bred, the bush closed in once more. A couple of sausages, a hunk of bread, a billy of tea by the lone campfire—that was really living. Later that night, lying on my back watching the blazing stars in their familiar constellations, I felt my skin tighten and my hair begin to prickle, as my soul once again soared and dipped through the universe. If that is what Aboriginal people feel in their Dreaming, then they are the luckiest people on earth.

I wrote to my father at his air force base, trying to tell him about some of the things I had been experiencing, and posing all kinds of unanswerable questions on the nature of the universe and the purpose of life, if any. Poor Dad was baffled. He wrote back saying that he had not expected to be asked such questions by someone my age. He never did try to discuss them with me, and I only felt more peculiar than ever.

By this time, a smart new high school building had been erected in Camperdown. Although the classrooms were now less crowded, each containing about forty boys and girls, we were still taught by the old system of rote, rod and rule. One teacher was responsible for practically every subject taught in our form. The only breaks in this routine, during which teachers and pupils became heartily fed up with each other, came with occasional sessions in the combination music and art room. Almost every hour spent at school was remote from any conceivable future activities of the healthy adolescents trapped within its walls. No wonder most of them hated it, and escaped into real life as soon as they reached the minimum legal age of fourteen.

My mother had by now moved permanently to Camperdown, where she occupied a suite in the town's best hotel. At first my sisters and I were boarded out with a kindly red-haired woman, Scottish I think, who also gave piano lessons. The girls continued to walk to the state school while I caught the daily bus to the high school. Being male, I was given the best bedroom, while my sisters occupied the sleep-out. I suppose they helped with the household chores, too, which males were not expected to do. After dinner, I usually went straight to my room to read or study, trying to disregard the clanging sounds of piano scales emerging from the parlour. What else was there to do, except ride around on my pushbike? Boys didn't learn to play the piano in our town.

At the start of my last year at high school, my mother put me in a smaller room in the hotel where she lived. My sisters were left in the village. Our family was now well and truly split up.

~

The men in the printery at the large newspaper office were extremely helpful. Some afternoons I would stand around watching their professional approach to jobbing and newspaper printing. On press days I was hypnotised by the stream of printed papers travelling along the delivery tapes of their big machine, much faster than I had thought possible. To multiply one's words and broadcast them to the waiting world seemed an ever more desirable activity.

About this time, early in 1943, my mother's father died. Writing in the *Journalist*, fellow reporter Creighton Burns called Monty Grover 'the greatest and most lovable editor I have known'. Mother prepared a two-column obituary for her newspaper, no doubt puzzling bucolic readers unused to such items. 'There is not a newspaper office where his influence has not been felt,' she wrote.

What do I remember of him? A pathetic figure felled by a stroke which paralysed him down one side, confined to bed in his South Yarra home, still trying bravely to grin at me from a twisted mouth. To his bedside came lifelong friends: Charles Bean, the great war correspondent; Alfred Foster, the reformist Arbitration Court judge; and many others whose names meant little to a fourteen-year-old boy visiting the city. Media mogul Sir Keith Murdoch came once but never returned.

Back in Camperdown, we saved the type from Monty's obituary notice. The men in the printery checked my work in making it up into smaller pages and running it off on the platen machine as an eight-page booklet. They found some spare sheets of embossed purple cover paper, on which I printed the title 'Montague Grover.

He Brightened the Inky Way'. They showed me how to apply a tacky light ink and then rub gold dust over it. When it dried, I folded and stapled the pages, and my first printed book lay glowing before me. It was a premonition of what I would do with my life.

Most schoolwork, meanwhile, was still drummed into reluctant heads by repetition and punishment, although the principal made some attempts to vary the Education Department's traditional system. One of his ideas was that any pupil who had some special interest, hobby or knowledge should be encouraged to talk about it before the whole school, which would assemble in the art room. Which is why, aged fourteen, I volunteered to analyse the world's economic systems and their faults.

I had just finished reading an exciting book written by my grandfather and published a few years earlier under the title *The Time Is Now Ripe*. Like most other Australian radicals of the 1930s, Monty Grover had been impressed by the apparent success of Soviet Russia, which was thought to have weathered the Depression much better than capitalist nations. To such writers, it seemed obvious that state monopolisation of all productive activities would be more efficient than cut-throat competition between privately owned companies and newspapers. Monty thought that this would become apparent even to conservative politicians. I copied some of these ideas, learned a rousing five-minute speech by heart, and delivered it at breakneck speed to the assembled students and teachers.

It converted no-one: the applause was meagre, and all the principal could manage to say was that he had been 'interested'. My mother, of course, was convinced that a national leader was budding. She reprinted much of my address in her two newspapers, no doubt freshly astonishing her farmer and squatter readers.

Then I made a serious mistake. I started preparing a little handwritten 'newspaper' called the *Red Ragger* that included criticism of some of the school's teaching methods, and began circulating it surreptitiously in class. My form master caught one of the pupils reading the *Red Ragger* and glanced through its inflammatory comments.

'Who is responsible for this trash?' he demanded. Of course, he already knew.

'I am, sir,' said I.

'Out here, boy,' said he.

I dumbly marched out and automatically held out my right hand. Six tremendous blows descended on it. My hand became so paralysed that I felt only the first three or four. Not another sound could be heard but the flick-crack of that heavy strap—to have whimpered or cried was out of the question. For an hour after returning to my seat, I could barely hold my pen to dip it into the inkwell, and instead of writing could only make jagged lines and blotches on the page.

I was subsequently transferred to the front row of desks where sat other habitual criminals. Their misbehaviour consisted of not completing homework (regardless of the number of cows that had to be milked the previous evening), talking in class, glancing out the window for a few seconds, shuffling feet, or asking too often to go to the toilet. When the need arose, offences such as glancing up at the ceiling were easily invented. It was impossible for me to avoid being trapped in this network of paranoia. At least once a week, I took my turn with other incorrigibles to be severely strapped. In winter time, when the blood would scarcely return to one mangled hand, my form teacher alternated that punishment by strapping the left hand. For some reason this seemed a lesser penalty: one felt vaguely grateful for it and learned to cope with the torture.

I never dreamed of telling my parents what was happening. In fact, after a while it just seemed like a normal part of school routine. One day, when it was my turn to read aloud to the class from a history of tribal wars in South Africa, I mispronounced an unfamiliar name. The class laughed. 'Out here, Cannon.' Another six of the best. After that, when talking or reading aloud, I began to stammer slightly. It got worse, and despair began to fill my heart. Barely a fragment of schoolwork remained in my mind.

At my parents' behest, and with a last convulsive effort, I sat for a special examination and managed to win a scholarship to

Geelong College, a major Presbyterian school which accepted boarders. With reductions given to the children of servicemen, and further reductions allowed because my sisters were to become boarders at the associated Morongo Girls' College, we quit town life forever. The city now called.

CHAPTER 3

The City: Youth

CHILDHOOD, A GENERALLY happy time for me, springs into focus with crystal clarity. Boarding school, a hateful time, is blurred, half-buried. My sensitivity in not being able to cope with comparatively trivial hardships remains a scar which never heals.

Mother was thrilled at the idea that her son would be attending one of the leading 'public' schools. This was success: a triumph of upward mobility over the static life of a bush town, back towards the position she had known when her father was king of newspaperdom. She took a rare holiday to indulge in a shopping spree for me and my sisters, at least as far as wartime clothes rationing would allow. Hundreds of name tags were ordered, to be sewn into sets of singlets, underpants, socks and shirts. I looked in dismay at the shirts with their separate stiff collars, fastened by uncomfortable brass studs at back and front, to be worn every day with school tie and blazer. I think every boy at Geelong College came to hate them. As our bodies and necks grew, the starched collars became stranglers, inside which we chafed and sweated the summers away. Yet to remove them was considered a major crime. They were a constant reminder of subservience to middle-class values, transported from the chilly schools of Britain to the often sweltering regions of colonial Australia.

We changed those collars daily, to enable grime to be removed and fresh starch to be applied. Our remaining clothes were changed twice weekly: by the third or fourth day they would be in a ripe state and need heavy laundering. Such tasks, and any mending necessary, were handled by 'Matron', a stout soul who in the days before the general use of deodorants must have become hardened to the stench of generations of schoolboys. Indeed, we were surrounded by an atmosphere of mustiness, or worse. We called it 'cheesy', but like old men we got used to it—we forgot the gum-scented freshness of the bush after rain, or the bone-tinging cleanliness of southern winds coming off the sea.

On the first evening of the first term, senior boys passed the word to all new boys that they must gather on the upper floor of the quadrangle block for the traditional initiation ceremony. Masters wisely disappeared for several hours, while fearful rumours spread about the nature of the ceremony. In previous years, it was whispered, some boys had been carried away with broken limbs. In fact, it wasn't as bad as that—only our fears had made it so.

Every new boy was lined up outside the largest classroom and instructed to strip down to their underpants. Older hands sloshed crude designs on our faces and chests using pots of red and blue paint. Each 'fresher' in turn was then pushed through the door of the classroom, where the more senior boarders were cheering and whistling. The bewildered recruit was ordered to climb up a rickety stack of tables and chairs. Swaying precariously on top of the pile, he had to shout out his name, where he came from, and what his father did for a living. This could prompt roars of acclaim or derision. I could not comprehend why boys would want to do this to newcomers already bewildered by their circumstances. I got off fairly lightly because my father was in the air force. Farmers' and graziers' sons were similarly approved. One unlucky boy, whose father was a Jewish estate agent, never quite recovered from the booing his confession produced, leaving after one miserable term.

After the initiation, us new boys were given three days to learn the school song. Then the senior prefects lined us up against the lockers in the change room. This time we were fully naked, for a reason which soon became obvious. In turn, each boy had to sing the school song, word-perfect, to the tune of 'British Grenadiers'. At any mistake, no matter how small, one of the prefects would flick the culprit painfully in the groin with the end of a wet towel, cracking it in stockwhip fashion. I had a good memory and escaped punishment. The poor devils who faltered, or whose memory was paralysed by fear, were given another three days before going through the same ordeal. All this was to ensure that at sporting events we could roar out the trivial, boastful words in unison. The hidden sexual motivation was never admitted.

The Year 11 boarders were put into a decrepit seventy-year-old weatherboard building on the outskirts of the school grounds. Several rooms had been opened up with the aid of girders and differing floor levels to make a large, draughty, L-shaped dormitory, crammed with boys ranging in age from fourteen to sixteen. The housemaster was a gruff but friendly enough old Scot who had seen better days. I soon discovered that some of the older boys were prone to conducting public masturbation contests. Luckily the floors were varnished timber, so the mess was easily cleaned up with paper from the toilets. I refused to take part, not just through moral objection, but because these competitions reduced to mere entertainment and physical release an activity which seemed to me far more meaningful if accompanied by imaginative private fantasies. And perhaps I was still suffering from feelings of guilt dating back to my Boy Scout days.

Each night we were sent in pairs to the shower cubicles to make the most of the limited supply of hot water. We stood back to back and soaped ourselves all over as quickly as possible while sharing the meagre stream of water. One boy, the son of strict Presbyterian parents, confided to me that he tried to wait until he was last in line, as sometimes he was able to have a longer shower that way. More importantly, he often made an odd number and so was able to shower alone. When that happened, he said, he could wash himself properly. When he was forced to shower with another boy, he felt unable to touch 'those' parts of his body. I didn't have the first problem because I had been circumcised as a baby, but I agreed with him about the second problem.

One of my dormitory mates was a pale, lank-haired youth who had a set of conjuring tricks. Sometimes he entertained us at night with feats such as joining apparently solid metal rings together, or producing endless coloured handkerchiefs from an empty tube. He soon won the ambiguous nickname 'Tricky'. Well, a few weeks into first term, Tricky was found underneath a staircase of the junior boarding house, engaged in some form of erotic activity with another boy. I suppose the poor devils were trying to forge an emotional bond as well as gain physical satisfaction. We never learned the full details, but with prompting from some of the more knowledgeable older boys, we assumed the worst: that they had been engaged in a mysterious thing called 'homosexuality'. Such were our colonic repressions—we were all so constipated that our stools were usually stiff and tacky—that the idea seemed incredible.

Within an hour of their discovery, both boys' parents had been contacted, their belongings packed, and the boys kept in seclusion until transport was arranged. We never saw them again.

~

The religious nature of our education was emphasised on Sundays, when we were twice forced to endure full church services. Each Sunday morning we donned clean clothes and marched in a long crocodile to a church about a mile away. The service was dreary, for there was no way of challenging the preacher's often nonsensical propositions as enunciated from the pulpit. The only relief from the monotony was that boarders from the girls' school had been shepherded into the church before we arrived. They were hidden behind their large hats, but occasionally one dared to half-turn her head and you might glimpse softly curved rosy cheeks partly veiled by long hair.

The normal run of school lessons was another exercise in tedium, based largely on rote learning. What value was it to anyone to be able to recite the chief exports of Canada? Yet you had to know such things to pass the old-style Leaving Certificate and matriculation examinations. Only the French master made any attempt to humanise his subject. He took us to any French cargo ship that happened to be in port picking up bales of wool, so that we could try to converse with the officers. As a result of his methods, much French vocab and grammar would remain in my mind decades later.

English literature classes largely consisted of attempting to memorise slabs of Shakespeare and Milton. The master, bored and waspish after a lifetime of trying to cram great works into cloddish minds, made desultory attempts to analyse the significance of obscure passages. We noted that, when in *Hamlet* he came to 'the rank sweat of an ensem'd bed' and 'That's a fair thought to lie between maids' legs', he hurried on lest anyone dare ask him to explain the precise meaning.

We studied only the history of nations in the Northern Hemisphere. Australia and the Pacific region were thought to have no traditions worthy of academic attention. Even the enthralling events of the American and French revolutions were made safe and dull. The stupidities of British monarchs, politicians and generals of that era were somehow changed into virtues. Naturally, I thought I knew better. With an egotism which endeared me neither to masters nor boys, I persisted in writing essays which did not match the accepted textbooks at all. I earned a bare pass in History with the admonition: 'Has a liking for startling views.' To me, they seemed commonsense deductions.

Some classes were conducted in the school's so-called library, a small room fitted with ornately carved timber bookcases but containing only a couple of hundred volumes. These were kept behind glass doors, and apparently were never accessed because they weren't on the prescribed list. I found several masterpieces in there by HG Wells, including his *Outline of History* and *Science of Life*. What unconventional schoolmaster of the past had persuaded the authorities to part with scarce shillings for these books? The school probably had not recognised what radical thoughts lay buried in its collection. In *The Outline of History*, for instance, the author pays tribute to the 'inimitable greatness' of Jesus Christ, but attacks the Church authorities who exploit and pervert his teachings. And in *The Science of Life*, Wells gives full and frank details of human reproduction—information not easily available to adolescents in those days.

Not content with filling our days with the tyranny of rote learning, the school imposed compulsory study every weekday evening. For Year 11 pupils, this was conducted in a sub-basement classroom. We trooped dispiritedly downstairs as darkness fell, still wearing our wilting collars and ties, to sit there and try to complete assignments that had been set during the day. Talking was forbidden.

We were supervised by one of the final-year prefects, who inevitably had his own work and exam results to worry about, and was not patient in dealing with interruptions from boys who had already been sitting at a desk for too long. Prefects were not allowed to use the cane, so our supervisor had come up with a simple but effective remedy for quelling disturbances. The perpetrators were brought out in front of the class, ordered to stand with their backs to the prefect, and given a powerful 'kick up the jack'. Those who experienced the punishment never risked a second kick, for it was painful to sit down for some days until the damage healed.

The severest punishment for talking bullshit was to be 'bockered', which consisted of a sharp blow with a closed fist, second joint of the second finger slightly extended to make a solid protrusion, delivered on the muscle of the upper arm where it was close to the bone. Properly aimed, a bocker temporarily paralysed the arm and hurt for several days. Yet no-one dreamed of complaining to the authorities or even mentioning such matters in letters home.

Boarders ate their meals in the school dining hall, a spacious construction of Hawthorn brick donated by old boys in the 1920s. We sat in appointed places at long tables under the supervision of masters and prefects. After grace, we eagerly gulped down everything, no matter how badly cooked or congealed. For breakfast, we slurped stout oatmeal porridge, milk, sugar, toast, jam and tea. Lunch often consisted of cold meat, a boiled potato and a leaf of lettuce, accompanied by ample white bread and milk. Dinner almost invariably comprised hot meat and vegetables in various guises, ranging from roast beef to lamb's fry, followed by a sturdy pudding such as jam roly-poly with custard. Fruit was rarely served.

The only dishes not avidly consumed were a foul custardy mess allegedly scrambled from dried eggs, and a 'cold collation' served on the Sabbath and consisting of a dried-out piece of meat (sometimes merely a slice of tinned spam) and a lump of mashed potato. To help us deal with such dietary emergencies, we were permitted to keep private food stocks in a series of battered wooden lockers near the masters' common room. Fruit cake and similar luxuries sent from home often saved us from Sunday starvation. Everyone kept their supplies in tins, but the locker area was pervaded by the mephitic smell of the generations of boarders who'd dropped crumbs as they wolfed down food, and the bright-eyed rats which scratched and scavenged behind the woodwork.

Instead of adopting a self-service layout, which would have spared a good deal of hired labour, the school insisted on retaining the pre-war system in which every table was waited on by a uniformed maid. Behind that, I imagine, was a desire that all food should be brought to the table simultaneously, so the tradition could be preserved that the senior master present led prayers for grace before eating began. The maids ranged from rather severe-looking local housewives, doing part-time work, to younger, often good-looking girls who were full-time servers and dishwashers. As randy youths, it was simply torture to have these girls waiting on us.

Cold showers or vigorous athletics didn't solve this problem. The preferred place for senior boys to masturbate away their desires was in a combined toilet–washroom block close to the classrooms. The cubicles had doors, of course, but the catches had been removed so that boys could not lock themselves in. However, by stretching out one's feet against the door, it was possible to maintain some degree of privacy while sitting uncomfortably on the toilet seat.

Some boys amused themselves by climbing up the cubicle partitions, which were open at the top, and peering down to spot anyone engaged in forbidden activities. A few precious copies of the Sydney magazine *Man* had been smuggled into the school: even individual pages torn from these, showing shapely girls, could be sold for a couple of shillings. On seeing someone studying such a page, the watcher might signal to friends at floor level, who would suddenly kick open the cubicle door and shout that an individual was 'pulling himself!' Everyone in the vicinity would run over to jeer at the unfortunate lad.

~

The school's repressive outlook was reinforced by its emphasis on military training. In happier days, I had found that scouting developed individual initiative. Cadet training was exactly the opposite. It attempted to mould boys through rigidly disciplined British Army routines, so that they would obey orders without question. Generations of genuine diggers could have told them better, had they been willing to listen. Our school cadet corps certainly took its work seriously. This was wartime, after all, and while the threat of invasion had receded, old collegians just a year or two older than us were fighting and dying in New Guinea and Borneo. If the Japanese clung to their conquered territories for a couple more years, we, too, would face the task of 'cleaning them out'.

Our first year of cadet training had its comic elements. We were issued with musty worsted uniforms bearing the colours of pre-Federation colonial forces. Men of those days must have been tiny: their old jackets left our bums exposed and freezing. Our rifles were single-shot Martini–Henry carbines. Only one fat cartridge at a time could be inserted by hand into the firing chamber, and so worn was the rifling after sixty years of use that you could almost see the bullet emerge from the muzzle and arc 100 yards into the air before falling to the ground—it was simply impossible for anyone to score a bullseye with such weapons. The bayonet was a long round piece of pointed steel, rather like a large meat skewer.

These antiques had to be kept spotlessly clean at all times. Much of our elementary 'training' consisted of the boring job of polishing rifles, belts and boots. For the rest of the time, we were formed into ranks and marched up and down, back and forth, until we achieved some semblance of a disciplined unit.

The process of breaking the individual will of recruits was continued at training camps held at the Watsonia Army Camp, located in Melbourne's northern suburbs, and at the Puckapunyal base in central Victoria, during what would normally have been term vacations. Here, experienced army NCOs (non-commissioned officers) gave us a foretaste of what life in the forces would be like when we reached eighteen and enlisted for active service. And yet, even though we had to live in large bell tents, use freezing outside latrines and showers, and struggle through mud while sarcastic red-faced men bellowed incomprehensible orders, I still preferred it to boarding school. At least in wartime there seemed a definite point to it all.

Cadet training improved considerably during my final year. We passed on our laughable unwashed colonial uniforms to the next intake of freshers and were issued with proper army uniforms and slouch hats. They were probably militia cast-offs, but we didn't mind. We were equipped with lethal Lee–Enfield .303 repeating rifles and shown how to load magazines quickly with clips of ten long metal-jacket bullets. Rapid-fire practice on a nearby rifle range—with the inevitable tins of spam for lunch—turned us into a force with considerable firepower. At the final Puckapunyal camp, we were taught how to strip, reassemble and fire Bren machine-guns at moving targets.

Many of my fellows were now seventeen, nearly eighteen. They could already see themselves at war, performing heroic deeds in the Anzac tradition.

~

By early 1945, my mother had moved to Melbourne, where she had been appointed social editor of the *Argus*, a leading morning newspaper of the time. With other relatives, she shared two blocks of maisonettes at numbers 89 and 95 Alexandra Avenue in South Yarra. These had been built by her father in pre-war days, when his socialist convictions had not prevented him from becoming a landlord and hence marked for extermination when the revolution came.

Another cousin and I made friends with a family in Williams Road, at that time regarded as a rather 'low' area of Toorak. They lived in one of a row of broken-down terrace houses. Our friend's father spent most of his time in a foetid back room, coughing endlessly with deep racking heaves of a tortured chest, and glowering at strangers. He had been gassed on the Western Front thirty years before, defending the British Empire, and had not long to live.

That summer, my cousin and I decided to ride through the Goulburn Valley to make some money picking fruit. We loaded a tent, blankets, a billy and frypan on our bikes and blithely set off. After three days of hard pushing against hot northerly winds, we got as far as Kyabram. Plenty of jobs were available here helping Australian Women's Land Army girls to harvest apricots. The work itself was not too hard, involving the use of ladders to strip the tops of the trees, before dropping the fruit into a bag strapped to neck and waist. Sticky juice from overripe apricots continually dribbled down our legs, but at the lunch break and after work we cleaned up by swimming in the irrigation canals along with yabbies and the occasional snake.

I made the mistake of wearing shorts and open sandals to work. After a few days, my legs and feet became so sunburned they swelled up like sausages on an overheated barbecue. I managed to get a new job working inside the local canning factory. For a further week, I simply shifted empty and full jam tins on pallets from one place to another, or in and out of rail wagons at the factory siding. As empty cans rattled noisily along a conveyor belt inside the factory, I soon learned how to pick up the maximum number of cans with two hands at a time.

I enjoyed the work, the friendliness of the place, the outgoing girls in their large aprons and headscarves, the sense of people cooperating for a shared objective—even if it was just to fill, seal and ship tins of apricots. Too soon it was time to leave and pedal our bicycles back to Melbourne. Such minor adventures, the freedom of wandering the land at will, made it even harder to return to the disciplines of boarding school.

The following summer we became much more ambitious, cycling most of the 350 miles to Mildura through increasingly arid country. A week's hard pedalling along mediocre roads got us as far as Ouyen, where heat and temporary exhaustion got the better of us and we put our bikes on a train for the remaining distance. In Mildura, descendants of the pioneering Chaffey family, friends of my aunt, put us up in a back room. They had built a new brick house close to Rio Vista, the original homestead (later a museum) and at the time still occupied by the matriarch of the family. But since we looked more like vagabonds than schoolboys, we were not allowed in her house. We were, however, taken to see the old irrigation pumphouse installed by the Chaffey pioneers during the booming 1880s, and Bob Chaffey even took us for a beer in what was originally the teetotal Mildura Coffee Palace.

Within a day we had recovered sufficiently to begin picking oranges. The orange plantations, assisted by ample irrigation and rich soil not yet affected by salination, had grown into massive bushy groves yielding large amounts of fruit. When you tried to penetrate each tree to strip it, the spiky branches tore at your clothes and flesh. With our long thin bodies (I had grown to just on 6 feet), we did better than most, but I would not like to depend on the work for a living.

~

During that final year at school, I steadily became unhappier. Boarders in their matriculation year were transferred into the senior house, which occupied most of the second storey of the original school quadrangle. Here, in large dormitories, we were under the close supervision of masters and prefects. Their rooms were grouped around the top of the only staircase, to prevent us from wandering at night. The only other way out was to tie sheets to a bedstead and scramble down the outside brickwork. Three of us tried it one night, simply for the pleasure of knowing we could escape.

Under such controls, life inside the dormitories was usually humdrum. Due to a shortage of domestic servants, we made our own beds in tight hospital style, and underwent occasional spot checks on our general tidiness and cleanliness. The nightly showers were often cold by the time we got to them; prefects stood by to ensure that boys soaped themselves and stood under the freezing jets for at least thirty seconds. A hairdresser visited the school every fortnight to shear the hair of all boarders down to the regulation short back and sides.

My stammer had now become much worse, at least in class. We took it in turns to read and explain some essay or grammatical conundrum, and panic would grip me when my go approached. Sometimes I stumbled through with barely a pause, but sometimes I could not even get out the first word. If one of the other boys tittered or even grinned, my cheeks burned with shame and I was completely nonplussed. Most of them must have felt something of my agony, for they generally remained quiet, at least until the master lost patience and called up the next boy. Never was there any realisation that I needed treatment.

A past benefactor had given the school a rambling old homestead opposite the main grounds. This was converted into a series of workrooms where boys could pursue any approved hobby, ranging from carpentry to making model aeroplanes. For us boarders, the place was a godsend, taking us away from the monotony of school under a loose kind of supervision. The school was even more uncharacteristic in selecting a master to manage the house. He was a notable British mountain climber who had become involved in Antarctic expeditions and written several books. Almost uniquely in those days, he sported a bushy greying beard and a free-ranging outlook. His eyes constantly twinkled with good humour.

We admired and even loved this unusual mentor, eagerly assisting him to set up new departments, such as a small print shop. After that I moved on to photography and was chosen as the committee member in charge of processing and exhibitions. For the first time at Geelong College, I felt the enthusiasm of devoting one's energies to a group effort, namely assisting dozens of younger boys to become proficient in elementary photography. In fact, at committee meetings my stammer completely disappeared. I felt as though a steel casing had been briefly lifted from my mind.

This paternalistic master even devoted some of his own term holidays to expeditions involving a dozen or so of the keenest boys. The most memorable for me was a winter hike across snow-covered Mount Buffalo in north-eastern Victoria. We made the long trip by steam train to Myrtleford, camping that night on the grassy banks of the Ovens River. The next morning we loaded ourselves with knapsacks stretched tight with food, balanced by tent and blanket roll carried against our chests, and festooned about with cooking utensils. We kept as close as we could to the route beside the icy-cold Buffalo River, and soon we were trudging ankle-deep in snow along cattle trails leading to the heights. Our army boots and gaiters could not keep out the mush, and it was with damp socks and frozen feet that we reached a flat snow-plain by late afternoon. Here, we built huge camp fires with damp snow gums to thaw our bodies and cook our rations. Groundsheets had been sewn into the tents before we'd left. Exhausted, we crept inside at dusk without removing our clothes, and spent a miserable night trying to sleep on a mattress of snow.

The next day we trudged on, finally reaching a ranger's hut where we were able to dry out and regain our spirits. From there on it was comparatively easy to settle into snowfields life. We borrowed skis from Mount Buffalo Chalet and skimmed over flat areas and down hills with amateurish enthusiasm. We climbed Cathedral Rock and other landmarks, watching in admiration as our leader chimneyed himself up narrow crevices and clambered down swinging ropes. School was never like this—we could have gone on forever. But finally the morning arrived when we loaded our belongings once more and then completed a 25-mile trek back to the railway line in one remorseless day. Toughened a little by now, hunger, thirst and blisters meant little to us. For the group's sake, one marched on, refusing to be thought the weakest.

Having tasted freedom once more, my relations with the remainder of the school got worse and worse, and the standard of my work steadily deteriorated. I took every chance available to get away from the hateful place. Officially, leave was limited to those few Saturdays when there were no important sporting events, and to Sunday afternoons for approved activities. To obtain leave you had to present yourself in full school uniform, including tie and cap, at the door of the masters' common room and announce your purpose. 'C-c-cannon, sir,' I would stammer, then a deep breath. 'Requesting p-p-permission for four hours' leave.' Then a halting explanation of purpose and movements. The master on duty gravely noted these details in the leave book, and if the case met regulations he might grant the temporary escape.

The expedition could be as simple as walking to the nearest shops to buy a postcard or look through a bookshop. Needless to say, our behaviour in public had to be impeccable. Once, an alert citizen reported that he had seen a boy in school uniform eating an ice-cream cone in the street. At assembly the next morning, the headmaster warned that any further offence would lead to the suspension of all leave privileges.

My mother came to see me only once. This was not unusual: mothers were an uncommon sight around the school. My father, meanwhile, had been transferred to an air force base in another state and could not get home very often. Besides which, most of his rare leave periods were spent travelling. He sacrificed an occasional day to take me to 'lunch and the pictures'. I would try to tell him some of my troubles, but in comparison to a world at war they must have seemed utterly trivial. On the last occasion, sitting on a bench in a park, I begged him to take me away from the college, to let me go back to high school, to let me live 'at home', wherever that was. Then I shocked both him and myself by bursting into uncontrollable sobs. Flustered, he asked me, for everyone's sake, to try to stick it out until the end of the year. With my guts churning, I said unhappily that I would. But that was the last time I ever confided in him.

As though all this emotional turmoil wasn't enough, I managed to fall in love. Occasionally on Sunday afternoons I would obtain permission to depart, mount my old pushbike and pedal out to see my sisters. Entertainment at their almost equally supervised school consisted of sitting politely on the front lawn and trying to make conversation. Still, somehow, emotions broke through. Our little group, seemingly so acceptable to any schoolmistress glancing through a window, was joined one day by an attractive senior girl. She was a prefect, a day-girl who lived in town. I could scarcely keep my gaze off her softly waving hair, her open friendly face, her cool grey eyes.

God knows what she saw in me: a stammering fool, voted most unlikely to succeed in all the things which public schools hold dear, sinking in stormy seas of doubt and self-hatred. Nevertheless, we 'fell in love' and somehow arranged to meet the following Sunday afternoon. For her it was simple: the only rules at the weekend were those imposed by her parents. For me it was a matter of telling a lie or two. I should have trembled and stammered as I approached the master on duty, but the words came out without hesitation: 'I would like to go and see my sisters again.' Instead, I cycled to my girlfriend's home, was introduced to her parents, and authorised to spend an hour or two strolling along the riverbank before returning for afternoon tea.

Dreams of early love may be fleeting but are never forgotten. Sunlight sparkled on the water and reflected on her face. Sometimes she seemed thoughtful but usually she was laughing, responsive to every random thought which tumbled from my brain through a tongue no longer caught in a vice. Hands touched as we walked through long spring grasses. My heart pounded, slowed and speeded again.

Nearing her home again, she led me through the back gate and into a dark garage lit only by stray sunbeams. This was the moment, the last chance. We fell into each other's arms and kissed not amateurishly but passionately, bodies straining against each other, as though we were long-practised lovers instead of virginal boy and girl. It was the first time I had ever kissed anyone that way. The feeling was abandoned yet innocent. Even if her house had been empty instead of occupied, I doubt whether we would have gone any further. To kiss was an end in itself, a discovery of mutual enchantment so satisfying that it needed none of the vile point-scoring with which older boys tallied their alleged conquests. This was not a conquest. It had nothing in common with the sexual fantasies that preoccupied us in the isolation of an all-male school. It was complete in its own nature.

And yet, like all dreams, it vanished on impact with the real world. So lacking was I in self-confidence that I would or could not make any further move towards adult love. Before that could happen, I somehow had to glue together the fragments of my personality into a facsimile of normality.

~

Due to the swirling mixture of my emotions, I began to violate many of the rules and traditions which my school held sacred. Where the others sang hymns in church or assembly, I remained silent. When my name was listed for athletics or swimming—the only sports at which I was moderately competent—I failed to turn out. On boat race day, I attended to sneer, not cheer. At boxing practice in the gym, I was suspended for hitting below the belt. At cadet training, the despairing master in charge asked sarcastically if I considered myself to be the only person in step.

In class, I committed the unheard-of sin of being rude to one of the masters. Such an attack on the sanctity of their position was intolerable. I was ordered to attend the office of the vice-principal after school for punishment. The boys were delighted: a thrashing applied to another person's posterior proved that someone else could be worse off than themselves. With calculated malice, one advised me to insert an exercise book inside my underpants, and like a fool I followed his advice. The master must have seen the outline of the book beneath my trousers. As I bent over at his command, he swished the pliable cane through the air in a practice swing. Then he hit me what felt like a tremendous blow across the muscles of my upper legs, just below the line of the exercise book. Five more crashing blows followed before I was released. Rigidly controlled, I uttered no sound at all, just limped out the door.

Unprotected by the pliable tissues of the gluteus maximus, the flesh of my legs had been torn by every stroke. As I removed the exercise book, blood seeped through my underpants and trousers. Within a short time, black horizontal stripes and scabs appeared. For once I was a hero to the other boys. But it was extremely painful to sit still in class, and the weals took several weeks to disappear.

Later, I wondered why I had not just knocked the master to the floor after the first blow. I was a good 6 inches taller than him, and at least as strong. But he had all constituted authority behind him, all the psychological dominance the old system gave to adults, through which they could do practically everything they wished to in the name of discipline. I only knew that if I met him in later life, I would belt him in the guts, knock him into the gutter, kick his face in, and preferably kill him. For now, though, instead of carrying out such fantasies, I became more uncooperative than ever. I completed the bare minimum of work necessary to scrape through the matriculation examination. I refused to turn out for any sport at all. Moodily, I sat through prayers and church services, reflecting on the charming hypocrisies of Christian gentlemen.

One evening, when all was quiet, I arose, put on my clothes, and crept out of the dormitory on stockinged feet, shoes in hand, past the housemaster's guardroom, down the stairs, and out into the freedom of a starry night. I had a vague notion of thumbing a ride to a warm fruit-picking area, where I would live anonymously beyond the reach of my tormentors. Then they would all be sorry! I slept that night in a band rotunda in one of the public parks. At first light, half-frozen and hungry, my resolution cracked. I walked quickly back to school and knocked, trembling all over, on the housemaster's door. He was already up and dressed, and speaking on the telephone, I suppose to the local police. 'Do what you like to me,' I said to him. 'I don't care what you do.'

The matter was beyond a mere caning. It went to the saintly old headmaster in his private quarters, far removed from the trivia of boarding-school life. He interviewed me fairly calmly, asking for no explanations but telling me how disappointed everyone was in the erratic behaviour of a scholarship boy. For his part, he could see no alternative to expulsion.

My parents were notified. My poor father came all the way from his interstate airfield and saw the headmaster and vice-principal. I don't know what he said, or how he may have begged. In the end they agreed to keep me until the end of the year, as long as I conformed to their rules in every respect. Shaken to the core, Dad took me out for the rest of the day and begged me in turn to stay the course, for his sake, for my own sake, for the family's sake. Sitting on a park bench, his voice trembling, he told me that his relations with my mother were not good, but that when the war was over, he would do everything he could to re-establish a solid home where we would all live together in happiness. That was all he lived for.

As we sat together under the trees, I looked with new eyes on this large man in a blue officer's uniform who had seemed stolid, unchanging, throughout the years. For the first time I realised that he, too, could suffer internal tortures from the world's slings and arrows. Perhaps they could be as bad as my own. Of course I would try harder to conform. And it was with me in this frame of mind that the rock-like year slowly wore away, one dreary day at a time, until it was all over and the headmaster could write on my final report: 'He has imagination, and if he could regain the enthusiasm of childhood and keep it through the experiences of manhood, he might have success as a writer.'

My first free act was to throw my school cap into an incinerator and buy a bright red shirt with which to greet the revolution.

PART II

JUMPING INTO LIFE

CHAPTER 4

Early Days in Melbourne and Sydney

It is but once that we can know our worst sorrows.

George Eliot, *Romola*

DURING THE NIHILISTIC years of war, my mother and father had drifted far apart. But when the conflict ended, they attempted to get together again—at least partly, they maintained, 'for the sake of the children'.

On my father's side, he had become part of a disciplined chain of command, not unlike boarding school, where formal regulations and unquestioning obedience were supposed to set up sturdy defences against fate and the future. He thrived in that atmosphere. Once, in exciting secrecy, he took me to Frognall, a Victorian-era mansion in Mont Albert whose spacious rooms were filled with desks and conveyor belts transferring urgent messages from one communications section to another, while impossibly smart-uniformed young women known as WAAAFs (members of the Women's Auxiliary Australian Air Force) glided about on mysterious errands. But as soon as World War II ended, Dad had to descend from this highly regarded, even glamorous, life to the only job he could get: being in charge of the mailroom at Amalgamated Wireless Australasia. There, his docility and fondness for scheduled routine kept him occupied in apparent contentment while the rest of the world ambitiously pressed on.

My mother, however, was once again savouring the frenetic world of daily newspaper production. After years spent buried in country towns, it must have seemed like a rebirth, a return to the giddy days of the 1920s when she had quit university to win her first job as a twenty-year-old reporter on the short-lived *Morning Post*. Now, in the mid-1940s, as a prominent journalist, and the mother of three almost-grown children, she blossomed again. Reporters who once manned the vanished daily *Argus* told me that they never saw anything quite like the striking forty-year-old 'Dolly' Cannon emerging from her office, snappily dressed, notebook in hand, off to report on some gathering of social notables—just as her father's mother had done in the booming 1880s. Melbourne might no longer be marvellous, but to my mother it was better than the bush.

At this time my two younger sisters Jill and Dina remained at boarding school, while the rest of my relations still lived in the Spanish-style maisonettes in South Yarra. I could ride my bicycle in comparative safety around most of the local suburban streets, but one day I took a risk too many and was knocked down by a tram in Chapel Street. I crawled dizzily to the edge of the road and managed to haul myself upright, leaning against a verandah post. I clung there with head spinning while people gathered around, muttering suggestions. As I slithered to the ground again, I vaguely heard one old digger say, 'Pull yourself together, son—be a man!' Curiously, that helped. I ended up in the Alfred Hospital, being prodded all over to make sure my bones were still connected.

Up the hill behind the maisonettes was a no-man's-land occupied partly by the Methodist Babies' Home. Here, in one of the few alternatives to illegal backyard abortions, unmarried mothers were able to leave the products of their liaisons. Further south towards Toorak Road were narrow streets containing small factories and rows of workers' cottages. Today, these houses are prized assets of the middle class, but in the 1940s we feared the larrikins and thieves who infested them. They practised their own form of democratic socialism by stealing anything that wasn't nailed down—even laundry off our clothesline. My padlocked bike even disappeared, and that was, I lamented, the end of my cycling days.

At least my cousin and I managed to save £12 to buy a two-man kayak that didn't leak too badly. The boat was light enough to carry across the road for launching in the Yarra. We spent fine days paddling upstream to Herring Island, and further to secret parts of the river where the banks were steep, leafy branches dangled in the ripples, and large allotments—the backyards of barely visible Toorak mansions—ran down to the water. Nothing disturbed the river: you could drift quietly under foliage to within a few feet of dozing waterbirds.

My mother rarely returned home before midnight, so Dad did his best to feed us, but his culinary skills were limited to boiling eggs or heating a tin of dreadful gunk called M&V (meat and vegetables). Such tucker required a liberal coat of tomato sauce, made mainly from pumpkins in an odoriferous Rosella factory across the river in the slums of Richmond.

Most of the domestic burden fell on my mother's younger sister, Aunty Bea, who lived in one of the family maisonettes with her two sons. Bea's cuisine seemed limited to grilled chops, mashed vegetables and rice pudding. She would spend endless days in the outside laundry, where she sombrely poked the clothes in the gas copper with a wooden stick, and, no doubt, wondered what her pharmacist ex-husband was up to. One day she absentmindedly ran her hand along with the sheets through a new-fangled electric wringer and, fainting, had to be taken away to hospital. We were forced to begin looking after ourselves.

My middle-aged father, sweat-stained grey Akubra planted squarely on his head, pipe clamped in his mouth, remained at heart a simple country bloke. He invested most of his deferred pay in a little Austin tourer, and the remainder as a deposit on a bush block at Kinglake, in heavily timbered, hilly country to the north-east of Melbourne. Here, we spent satisfying weekends felling enough trees for a camp site, exploring bush trails and spying on lyrebirds. On one occasion we discovered an abandoned tramway with its wooden rails and bridges still intact—timber getters had once used this infrastructure to haul giant logs out of the mountain ash forest.

My mother came with us only once, and spent most of the day dozing on a rug by the camp fire. The mystery and sublime peace of the bush were not for her.

~

While enjoying the last months of my non-working life, my lust for books became almost insatiable. I exhausted the resources of the family bookshelves, including hundreds of Monty Grover's old books, all of Dickens, five volumes of journalist John Stanley James's *The Vagabond Papers*, and endless tracts on socialism.

HG Wells remained my hero, and in Robertson & Mullens's city bookshop I discovered a delicious series of Wells's early fiction: *Mr. Polly*, *Tono-Bungay* and all the rest, bound in maroon leatherette. I could just afford half a crown for one of them. The next day I went back and slipped another under my jumper. A couple of days later I tried it again. Halfway down Elizabeth Street, I felt the firm hand of the floor manager on my shoulder. He steered me back into the shop, into an antique lift, and up to the office of the boss, Captain Charles Peters, MC and bar, who made a show of preparing to call the police. Instead, he rang my father. Poor Dad had to hurry down from Queen Street and beg on behalf of his now-tearful son not to have the young criminal sent to a reformatory.

At the beginning of 1946, it seemed imperative that I should find 'real' work. Aged only a few months over sixteen, I was too young to apply for a newspaper cadetship. However, my mother was able to get me a job on the *Argus* as a copyboy. This was said to be the first step on the ladder to journalistic success. In reality, copyboys were slaves to executives and subeditors. For 30 shillings a week, we started work at 2 p.m. and went through until midnight or later, which meant catching one of the all-night trams to get home. We made cups of tea, delivered messages, fetched galley proofs from the composing room, and ran to answer cries of 'Copy, boy!', grabbing the latest edited material and stuffing it into a vacuum tube for instant transmission to the typesetters.

At that time the *Argus* was still the conservative voice of Victoria's squattocracy and mercantile community, represented by the large shareholding of Colonel Allan Spowers. To manage the initially radical paper, Spowers engaged men with appropriate wartime records. The managing director, Errol Knox, was a short, rotund fellow of pleasant demeanour who had risen from being an Australian Imperial Force private in France to a major in the Royal Air Force, then to a barracks brigadier during World War II. The chief of staff, Brigadier Ted Rasmussen, was precisely the opposite: tall, cadaverous and brusque. Editor Ted Doyle seemed to me kind and avuncular, until one night I forgot to collect his galley proofs and was angrily lectured on the necessity of regarding The Editor as being equivalent to God.

On the same floor at the *Argus* were the hot-shot reporters: my aunt Helen Seager, Laurie Kerr (a league footballer and protégé of John Wren, who would become a key force in international public relations), Peter Knox, Ron Testro and Tom Farrell, among others. Upstairs, Bruce Kneale edited the colour-printed *Weekend Magazine*, which used a few of my outpourings. Sitting in a cramped, tiny office, former war correspondent George Johnston was wasting his unique writing talent wrestling with the editorial and circulation problems of the long-established *Australasian Post*.

The life of a messenger boy soon palled for me, but as I approached seventeen, Brigadier Rasmussen remained adamant in his refusal to consider me for a cadetship—perhaps he resented my mother's influence in getting me even a copyboy's job. So I quit, the first of many times when an employer's ways failed to match my desires.

I decided that if I couldn't get a job as a trainee reporter, the best way to learn the business was to attempt to support myself as a freelance writer. The essential thing was to start writing, and to keep on producing a thousand words a day until it became second nature. Fortunately, there were quite a few publications, even in paper-rationed 1946, which needed to fill their pages but didn't want the bother and expense of supporting staff journalists. My first little success was with a radical monthly journal named *Tomorrow*. This began as an exercise in left-wing idealism by a jovial journalist named Jack Bellew, brother of the better-known Pierre Bellew, who graduated from the editorship of *Art in Australia* to a senior position with the United Nations Educational, Scientific and Cultural Organization in Europe. Jack used to regale me with stories of how, working for Monty Grover in the 1930s as foreign editor of the Sydney-based *World*, he would simply 'invent' news from Manchuria and other remote areas if cabled stories failed to turn up by deadline.

Tomorrow was produced from a corner of the Queen Street office of the publishers Reed & Harris, where piles of unsold books and art magazines took up much of the available space. For some reason, Jack Bellew appreciated my puerile attempts to satirise political and economic beliefs of the day. He published them intermittently, and even paid for them. Through his Labor Party connections, Jack managed to obtain a licence to import Russian newsprint, and profits from the resale of this high-grade paper kept his little journal afloat. Even so, Jack drifted from one printer to another in search of better terms, finishing up with the *Radio Times* printery in King Street before going bust.

Meanwhile, I had decided to specialise in writing about movies. At that time, the *Age* was publishing a weekly children's supplement called *Junior Age*. Its editor, Mac Gordon, was good enough to commission from me a nine-part series on the history and techniques of the film industry. That gave me the first continuous income

I ever earned from writing, and set me on the path to survival as a freelancer.

About this time, Clive Turnbull was writing a superb column in the *Herald* called 'Free Speech'—although managing director Sir Keith Murdoch employed Turnbull more for his knowledge of which artworks to purchase than for his journalistic ability, no doubt viewing his radical opinions on daily events with amused tolerance. Nonetheless, Turnbull managed to score hits against the establishment while avoiding libel writs. One of his paragraphs extolled the activities of several young people who styled themselves the Realist Film Makers. Turnbull told me how to contact them and I enthusiastically joined the group.

We attended every film session held at the communist-run New Theatre in Flinders Street near the *Herald* office, gripped by deep emotion during flickering scenes in *Battleship Potemkin*, *Ten Days that Shook the World*, and some of John Grierson's documentaries. Privately, we reckoned we could do as well with Australian subjects. We had a 16-millimetre camera but no projector, and no scripts but plenty of caffeine-driven ideas. When the group decided to emigrate to Sydney to make brilliant films and start a film-lovers' magazine on the side, I went along. My mother staged a tearful farewell as we caught the train from Spencer Street Station.

In Sydney, I found cheap lodgings on an enclosed verandah in the lower-middle-class suburb of Arncliffe and began planning the magazine, while the others rented a broken-down, leaking mansion on the North Shore. We never made a single film. The need to earn enough money for rent and food ultimately paralysed all our fine thoughts.

~

Sydney in those days was reminiscent in some ways of Melbourne: comparatively cheap to live in, and filled with charming, if cockroach-ridden, low-rise Georgian and Victorian buildings. Antique toast-rack electric trams trundled the main streets and clattered into nearby suburbs; a reliable train service took you further afield if necessary. The greatest joys were simple ones: even a leisurely ferry trip on an uncrowded harbour could bring peace to an unquiet heart.

In 1946–47, further satisfactions were in store on weekends. One of my mother's sisters had settled in Mosman and her two sons kept an 18-foot yacht at The Spit, which lies between North Sydney and Manly. On sunny days we would sail all around Middle Harbour, past Chinamans Beach and Middle Head, and even dared the shark-infested ocean. Occasional capsizes in a southerly buster didn't seem to matter: someone always sailed up and rescued us. Not once did my older cousin refer to his wartime experiences, when, as a commando, he had fought the Japanese on Timor. Nowadays, he just wanted to forget, and enjoy life. On sunny weekdays I would sometimes make the long bus trip to Bilgola Beach, then totally uninhabited, and scribble thoughts and verses on a pad between occasional swims. Youth, the rolling ocean, a disdain for sunburn, and mild creative exercise make an exquisite combination, for the brief time we are able to enjoy it.

By now almost penniless, I cobbled together some articles about the film industry for the *Sydney Morning Herald*. In this, I was assisted by the fact that another aunt on my father's side owned the Sesqui Cinema in Crows Nest, where her son-in-law worked as manager. He gave me all the airmailed Hollywood publicity about forthcoming epics, eventually converting me from the gritty ideals of realist filmmaking to the more acceptable products of American dream factories. Anything the *SMH* didn't want I sent to other papers, and soon found my articles featured in *New Idea* and the *Western Mail*.

I contributed several articles to a venture by Syd Nichols, the artist who had invented *Fatty Finn*, a newspaper cartoon which also became the first comic book published in Australia. Now, in the newsprint-starved postwar period, Syd was trying to repeat this early success with a children's tabloid. Syd paid me well, but his paper, printed only in black and white, didn't last long.

I also tried to get a full-time job, intending to write in the evenings. Oswald 'Ossie' Mingay, who ran a chain of electrical and radio trade journals from his printery in the slums of Surry Hills, engaged me as an editorial assistant. A week later, my first *SMH* article appeared, spread all over the first of their broadsheet Saturday magazine pages. The result of about two days' work, it was paid for at almost double the minuscule weekly salary which Mingay offered. First thing Monday morning, Mingay called me into his office and asked if I had written the article. 'Yes,' I replied proudly, expecting praise. Instead, he said: 'Everyone who works here has to give his complete loyalty to me and my firm ... you've got to make up your mind whether to do one thing or the other.' Five minutes later I was back to freelancing.

Then, a stroke of luck. Arthur Thorn, who sported an Errol Flynn moustache and worked from his home at Kyeemagh, not far from where I was boarding, started a magazine called *Sports Novels*. His journal consisted mainly of fiction with a sporting theme, but for December 1946 he wanted to produce a non-fiction Davis Cup issue for the first challenge round to be held since Australia had won the cup in 1939. The assignment was a wonderful opportunity for a learner, involving my first stint of historical research at Mitchell Library, and interviews with the Australian players then training at White City in Rushcutters Bay. Jack Crawford, Adrian Quist and John Bromwich were especially enthusiastic about the project, which would form the first comprehensive printed history of Australia's participation in the Davis Cup.

A short time later I moved to an apartment in Elizabeth Bay, leased by the widow of noted Sydney poet and former *Bulletin* writer Arthur Adams. She was sweet to a struggling young writer, fed me as best she could, and was not surprised to have to wait for the rent during lean weeks. I am ashamed to say that much of the rent money was spent on endless cups of coffee during conversations about 'life' in the little cafes which thronged the city and Kings Cross.

I spent some time pestering *Bulletin* staff in their George Street office for a job, but they only wanted more freelance contributions—I didn't know they were on their last legs as an independent publisher. I had a couple of interviews further uptown at *Smith's Weekly* with editor Claude McKay, who had worked closely with my grandfather, but *Smith's*, too, was destined for early closure. Finally, I approached Brian Penton, editor of the *Daily Telegraph*, with an idea for a weekly children's supplement along the lines of *Junior Age*. He stared at me in his saturnine way and finally announced that 'even if Mr [Frank] Packer agreed, the job would be done by experienced staff journalists'. At least he was open about it.

I was forced to fall back on smaller journals. The one I liked most was *Pertinent*, published by a printer in Kent Street, no doubt to fill up vacant time on his presses. The editor for a while was Leon Batt, a consumptive poet whose book *Not for Fools* was, in my opinion, one of the great elitist works of that century—nobody else seems to have heard of it, and my copy has been lost. Leon gave me the task of reviewing the fringe movies from Europe and Russia that were beginning to sneak into Sydney, such as Mosfilm's *Stone Flower*, shown at the Maccabean Hall in Darlinghurst. But then Leon's printer obtained more commercial work and abandoned publication of *Pertinent* just as it seemed about to catch on.

It became apparent even to me that, at the age of seventeen or so, I hadn't exactly set Sydney on fire. I was barely supporting myself, no matter how many articles I sent around to editors. It was time to see what was happening back in Melbourne. Before leaving Sydney, however, I had a few drinks with the publisher Frank Johnston, at a pub opposite the *Bulletin* office, and arranged to supply Melbourne news for his monthly musical magazine, which was called *Tempo*. This was something of a leap into the unknown. I knew little of music, traditional or modern, and played no instrument, just 'knew what people liked'. But I was learning how to ask the right questions of the right people. It is easy enough to scoff at the easygoing, often sentimental music of that era, but at least it set out to make people feel relaxed and happy.

From early 1948, I filled the columns of *Tempo* with dozens of interviews with everyone from Dixieland jazz players to Melbourne's singing hairdresser, Joseph Schepsi, who once hired Melbourne Town Hall and secretly gave away hundreds of free tickets to make sure it was filled. One of the most satisfying conversations was with the 24-year-old Aboriginal tenor Harold Blair, who achieved fair success in what was then a white man's world. One of the worst was with the families of four musicians from the Storklub at Black Rock who had been killed in a single car smash one summer morning. Then there was Victoria's first female dance band, Mollie Byron's Offbeats, which caused a buzz at the Trocadero in their black skirts and red jackets. Even opera wasn't beyond my range: with the aid of free tickets, I reviewed the National Theatre Movement's 1948 inaugural opera season at the Princess Theatre, and attempts by Sir Robert Knox and Victorian premier Tom Hollway to form a permanent state opera.

However, I still thought I needed some full-time newspaper experience. I wrote to Sir Keith Murdoch, the guiding genius of the Herald & Weekly Times Ltd's fortunes, shamelessly pointing out how much he needed the ideas of Monty Grover's grandson. Murdoch's secretary soon informed me I had been selected from 300 applicants to be interviewed by the great man. Our brief talk took place in his spacious oak-panelled office overlooking the Jolimont railway yards. My stammer had more or less disappeared by then, but his seemed worse than reputed. 'I r-r-re-member your g-g-grand-father,' he ground out at last. (Was he recalling that, after his takeover of the *Sun News-Pictorial*, he had removed the inimitable Monty and put in his own safe nominee, Lloyd Dumas?)

'Thank you, sir,' I smiled.

Suddenly and firmly, Murdoch asked, 'Tell me, young man, are you a c-c-communist?'

Providence flew to my aid: 'I used to be, sir, but that was when I was young.'

Murdoch burst into laughter and said, 'Start on Monday—see Reg Leonard.' With my earnings doubled in an instant, I walked on air to the hatter at Flinders Street Station and bought a pork-pie hat, essential equipment for young reporters of the time.

After all my boasting, I don't think I did too well as one of Murdoch's bright young men. Thrown headfirst into the shipping round, my attempts to extract news items from passenger liners, tramp steamers and shipping agents didn't seem quite like the fantasy world of fame in which I usually dwelt. I got a few harmless stories ('Ship Shortage Is Worst for 30 Years', 'Melbourne Port among World's Best'), but it was really rather humdrum—except for the occasion when I was forcibly thrown out of the Seamen's Union office at the other end of Flinders Street because I represented 'the capitalist press'.

The cadet instructor was the lovable 38-year-old Osmar White, returned from an exciting life as a war correspondent in the Pacific to the thankless task of trying to instil elementary journalistic practice into know-it-all youngsters like myself. He insisted, for instance, that we learn Pitman shorthand. But I couldn't remember some of the basic outlines even when halfway through the manual, and instead developed a kind of internal tape recorder (the real thing had not yet been invented), a quirk of the brain that enabled me to repeat quite lengthy conversations almost verbatim. That said, practically all I can remember now of 'Ossie' White's lectures is the 'law of the inverted pyramid': put the main facts in your first paragraph, put the next most important facts in the second paragraph, and so on, with the least important facts at the end. This enabled page make-up men to 'cut on the stone'—throw away the last slugs of linotype metal to fit a story into its allotted space, without ruining its beginning. This technique, well suited to the hustle of newspaper production, seemed the precise opposite of good storytelling, where the writer must slowly build up to a climax.

I was also earning a few pounds by freelancing for a monthly journal called the *Digest of World Reading*. This was a quite professional version of the American *Reader's Digest* and was published by Specialty Press at its printing works behind Georges Ltd in Little Collins Street. The editor was George Lee, who taught me a lot about skimming through the world's publications to pick up ideas and items that might interest Australian readers: adventure stories in the wilds seemed a particular favourite of city folks. As rarely as possible, and as cheaply as possible, George would buy the reprint rights, after which I would help cut the articles down to size and later check the galley proofs. The editor was under constant financial pressure from his skinflint printer bosses. Often enough, my payment consisted of a decent two-bob lunch in the Old Vienna cafe in Russell Street, near the venue where my favourite foreign films were shown, the Savoy Theatre (which would sadly be demolished in 1963 to make way for, of all things, a car park). In a good week, George would give me a real assignment—'Horrifying Vandalism in Our Cemeteries'—and squeeze a few pounds in real money from the recesses of his budget.

Knowing that I was impatient with seeming trivia on the *Herald*, George introduced me to Reg Chambers, sales manager of Holeproof Hosiery during the day and writer of sensitive short stories at night. Reg had an idea that was beginning to gain popularity in America: that if large companies published their own 'house magazine', this would somehow make lowlier employees feel part of a big happy family. Somebody should have told such dreamers that most workers simply wanted higher wages and shorter hours, and cared little about the rest. But many company executives were like writers: chockful of illusions about the real world. The result was that Holeproof offered me double my existing wage to create their house journal. I was to get an enormous salary of about £7 a week, and the freedom to convey management philosophy to a grateful staff.

Every morning I travelled by two trams to the industrial area of Brunswick and began planning elaborate dummies. I had just enough experience to be able to do it. Unfortunately, I also started poking about the extensive factory area, investigating the mysterious processes whereby rayon and nylon thread were converted into socks, stockings, men's ties and so on. This brought swift revenge from a dictatorial factory manager, who wasn't going to have any whippersnapper talking to his operatives and deflecting them from the primary task of maximising productivity. I was offered a substitute job on the advertising staff, but in my mind it had to be a news journal or nothing. I was out on the street again.

~

By the late 1940s, what people might now call 'the search for meaning' had been pressing on me for some years. While at boarding school I had been permitted to attend a series of lectures in the local mechanics' institute on comparative religions of the world. Although somewhat superficial and censored, these talks had at least revealed the range of beliefs possible beyond the narrow Presbyterianism practised at Geelong College. Now, in my late teens, I became convinced that all religious belief was a manifestation of a universe of the spirit that existed all around us. In other words, I discovered spiritualism. I searched Melbourne for mediums who could convincingly evoke spirits for true believers, but failed to find anything beyond ageing females of uncertain sanity.

The quest had one good effect, however: it led me to patronise what was then called the Melbourne Public Library (later to become the State Library Victoria). In dim greenish light under the great dome, I read everything the library possessed on this queer cult, which led me to pick from the shelves books and magazines on many other ideas about which I had never heard. While other young people were getting on in business or studying for degrees in specialised subjects, I was qualifying for my own doctorate as a generalist. Knowledge of all kinds poured daily into my starved brain cells. I even began to read through the *Encyclopaedia Britannica*, vainly attempting to copy George Bernard Shaw's boast that he had read the whole damn thing.

As part of this search for understanding, and reconciliation of real life with my earlier notions, I visited my old headmaster, by now retired and living in Camberwell. After one discussion I wrote to him about my mental struggles, and expressed a growing conviction that some people had been 'chosen' to show lesser breeds the way into the light. His reply is worth quoting:

> My dear Michael, I have very seldom received a letter as interesting as yours. It was gracious of you to think me in any way worthy of your confidence. I am often tempted to agree with you about democracy. And yet the alternative is to abandon what our finest rebels have thought and fought for—the liberty to choose. One has to remember that [the biblical] Peter was a fishmonger and not a very pleasant character: but he was able to love the highest when he saw it, and to serve it more loyally than H. G. Wells would have confessed he did. Teddy Rankin [employed at Geelong College] was a gardener but had his standards, and a month before the end had a remarkable vision that was real enough to him to take away any fear—and he was a very timid man. Still this does not prove that every one is able to catch the music of the spheres on his wireless set. You may be right about varying sets and that most can hear only the nearer 'stations'. And yet I wonder. Doesn't every one wonder sometimes, and wonder is close to awe. I lived very close to navvies in the front line in World War I, simple souls but volunteers all of them to what they felt was duty. They had no love of adventure, most of them: but they were loyal & loving to each other down to the gates of death. If only we could get the same brotherhood in peace—the same devotion to his men in the employer that a good officer showed to his men …
>
> Mrs Rolland sends you good wishes for your Odyssey.
>
> Very sincerely yours, F. W. Rolland.
>
> P.S. I did a wise thing in marrying my cook. You should come and try her specialties.

~

Having been forced back into freelance work, I turned to a small monthly magazine called *The Writer*. This was edited by a paraplegic author named Arthur Adams (not the Sydney poet), who lived at Berwick, and published by John Cronan, who ran a one-man printery on the rickety wooden floor of a dirty room at the back of the run-down old Eastern Market in Exhibition Street. Every month, Cronan sent material for *The Writer* to a linotype operator, printed the journal two pages at a time on a hand-fed platen, folded and stapled the pages, and sent Adams' words of advice out to a couple of hundred subscribers.

I contributed several articles to *The Writer*, proving perhaps that the blind can lead the blind. About once a month I climbed onto my tiny two-stroke, ex-army paratroop bike and putt-putted out to Berwick, at that time an attractive but isolated country village. On one occasion, Adams, who had known the insides of too many hospitals, gave me a sensational story about the way in which some psychiatrists were ordering prefrontal lobotomy operations for uncontrollable patients, even for intractable pain. The practice, which turned people into permanent zombies, was abandoned soon afterwards and buried in the cemetery of bizarre medical scandals.

Profitless labour on *The Writer* became too heavy for Cronan, however, and he decided to close it down. I couldn't afford to buy the journal, so I tried to negotiate a partnership arrangement. Cronan at first agreed, then changed his mind. Apart from an inference that he didn't want an energetic young partner, he couldn't give any reason, but Adams later explained that Cronan could not talk about the discovery that his wife was dying of cancer, one of the great unmentionables of the time. The little magazine died with her.

My swift changes of job and my attempts to survive by freelancing were frowned upon in the security-conscious 1940s. Most other young men were faithfully serving their time, notching up years in the slow-motion process of becoming dependable pillars of society.

But surely life held brighter goals than that? The more I read and pondered, the more I wanted. Enter an adventurous schoolmate who had also worked on the *Herald*, and who suggested that we should try to hitchhike around Australia. So in the autumn of 1948, we duly packed our swags, donned old army jackets, and managed to thumb our way from Melbourne to Murray Town in South Australia.

One evening, as we squatted on the outskirts of that dusty little place, a local vigilante told the police that two suspicious characters were camping outside town—although we didn't know it, two young men had apparently escaped from jail in the vicinity. As darkness fell, a Model T Ford tourer rolled up to our spot and suddenly braked. Out jumped two men in civilian clothes who both pointed automatic pistols at us. Without identifying themselves, they ordered us to fall flat on the ground and stretch out our arms. Bewildered, I began to obey, but my mate put his head down, butted one man in the stomach, and grabbed for his gun. 'There's people coming to help us!' I shouted—and indeed, most of the town's population seemed to be running towards this exciting scene, like a Hollywood film come to life. My mate continued to fight but was then borne down by two burly residents.

'Help us!' I cried.

'They're the police!' someone shouted back.

Only then did we realise that we were being arrested and could easily have been shot dead. When we produced our press passes, the two young constables grunted a kind of apology and even bought us a drink at the local shearers' pub. They advised us to stay indoors for the night and we were shown to a pair of filthy stretchers. We only got an hour's doze before dozens of bedbugs emerged to feast on our bodies—the bites took weeks to heal. No wonder shearers had to drink heavily before getting a night's sleep.

A local farmer took us on to Port Augusta, where we helped load crates of beer in return for a free ride on The Ghan, the antique narrow-gauge steam train which meandered slowly between Adelaide and Alice Springs. Every inch of the route was littered with mounds of empty bottles, and we added our quota, eating the occasional stale ham sandwich snatched from the dining car.

Arriving at The Alice near nightfall, we found our way to a long-distance truck depot. Here, we traded the promise of free beers along the track in return for a seat on top of bags of onions being transported up the narrow bitumen strip to Darwin; the remainder of the consignment consisted of magazines. We spent most of that long, boring, dusty trip trying to find a way to relax on those onions, while reading every comic book in the cartons, courtesy of Messrs Gordon & Gotch.

That evening, the truck's two drivers decided to stop at the Mataranka pub for a lengthy 'wet' at our expense. Plenty of beer was absorbed and sweated out that night, with our citified tales eventually giving way to the exploits of the blood-spattered buffalo shooters who stalked in and took over. This was our own genuine 'Wild West', but it bore little relation to anything I had seen on the silver screen—you don't quite get the stench of booze, blood and vomit in a cinema. There was some added excitement when, while walking naked from the truck to a makeshift shower enclosure, I stepped on a snake. It snapped away hissing in one direction while I disappeared at high speed in the other, cheered on by the few drinkers still left at the bar.

In Darwin, we were able to rest and scrub up at the house where senior *Herald* journos were accommodated by the paper when reporting on the town, a place then occupied by Hal Richardson and his wife. The Richardsons were extraordinarily kind to the two wayfarers who had suddenly appeared, feeding us great hunks of steak, making sure we had mosquito nets, and showing us what was to be seen around the postwar settlement. We found that Darwin was still pretty much a frontier outpost: dugout canoes lined the beach, Aboriginal people squatted in the bush not far out of town, and wharfies drank in a noisy bloodhouse, rioting and calling strikes if the beer ran out. Indeed, incoming beer had to be packed at the bottom of ships' cargoes, for once it was unloaded all work ceased. Meanwhile, the town's small 'establishment' yarned and drank at the

Darwin Club, similarly keeping reality at bay with enormous nightly intakes of alcohol.

Beyond the blanketing humidity and lethargic daily activity, an air of furtive shame seemed to hang over the town. No-one said much about it, but a number of bombed-out buildings and the vessels still half-sunk in the bay were constant reminders of the almost defenceless days of 1942–43, when the town was smashed up by waves of Japanese bombers. Largely unspoken, too, were the deeds of both courage and cowardice among civilians and soldiers when the first bombs hit. Now there was not quite as much certainty expressed about white man's superiority over the other races. Nevertheless, the territory's pubs and open-air picture theatres were still rigidly segregated: no-one thought twice about the relegation of local 'natives' to unhygienic living conditions on the town's outskirts.

To only a few unusual whites were Indigenous people worth a second glance. One whom we met in Darwin was the famed bushman Bill Harney, who lived on a deserted beach some distance away with his Aboriginal family. This quiet, friendly, gravel-voiced man was in town to guide a team of *National Geographic* photographers and anthropologists who had been sent to investigate the comparatively unspoiled life of Arnhem Land peoples. Before heading off, Harney organised his tribal brothers into staging a corroboree just outside Darwin.

Eventually, we were able to find an empty truck returning to Alice Springs. One of the drivers brought a rubbish tin full of water, in which he kept an 18-inch baby crocodile he had found in a river. He hoped to sell it down south, but it died a day after we left Darwin. We parted company at Tennant Creek, where we introduced ourselves to the local police and managed to get a lift in a departmental utility heading east to Townsville. There was no food on board, only the usual crate of beer, and few settlements on the way. On the first evening, a constable riding with us in the back spotted a dark speck in the distance heading towards the road, cocked his .303 rifle, and at a distance of 200 yards, brought the thing down with one shot from our lurching vehicle. Soon enough, we'd built a huge campfire and were feasting on the carcass of a roughly butchered, rather tough emu. Lying with full bellies under the brilliant stars brought a feeling of enormous contentment, and gratitude to a benevolent universe. Why should anyone want more than this?

Lifts were fairly easy to get down the east coast, as drivers had not yet learned to be suspicious of dangerous hitchhikers along the Bruce Highway. In Sydney, I called in at the old *Sun* office in Elizabeth Street, where George Johnston was now writing a daily column. Here was one of Australia's best potential novelists, forced to pick up scraps for evanescent paragraphs.

~

Back in Melbourne, my parents had finally split up. My father had moved to a room in a converted mansion at Jolimont where he lived a solitary life, isolated from the family love and respect he had once enjoyed. Smiles were infrequent on that once-cheerful face, but he bore his fate stoically, cooking his endless tins of M&V on a gas ring, listening to radio serials for companionship, and attending a sign-writing course at the Working Men's College in the hope of again 'improving himself'.

My mother had taken up with a prominent manufacturer of expensive fashion shoes. Malcolm Parker's parents had been brought to Australia as children on a sailing clipper of the gold-rush era, just as my mother's Grover antecedents had arrived. Parker senior had risen in the boot trade, and survived the dreadful 1890s era of strikes, depression and starvation. His only son enlisted during World War I and helped to chase the Germans out of Belgium. During the boom of the 1920s, Malcolm began manufacturing high-fashion women's and men's shoes at Clifton Hill. In World War II, he became an instructor of commandos on Wilson's Promontory. His first wife, Hilda, had met a tragic end: while walking along the pier at Flinders one stormy evening in October 1944, she was blown into the sea, whereupon her heavy coat filled with water and she drowned, leaving three daughters to be brought up largely at boarding school.

In 1947, Malcolm appointed my mother as Parker Shoe Co.'s public relations manager, so that she still had a separate income after leaving the *Argus*. She went to live at his Georgian mansion, called Sark, in Hopetoun Road, Toorak, which had been divided into two separate dwellings. I went to live there too, considering it the height of luxury to have a bedroom *and* a separate study of my own. It seemed rather a nuisance to have five young girls—sisters plus stepsisters-to-be—descending during school holidays, but at least we had a common interest in playing tennis on the lawn court and all got on pretty well. With the blindness of youth, it never occurred to me to ask about their mother, whom nobody ever mentioned. Not until years later, when by chance I walked by her tombstone at Flinders cemetery and noticed the inscription, did I begin to piece together what had happened.

Nor did the morality of my mother 'living in sin', which probably embarrassed the girls, trouble me for a moment. She and Malcolm were obviously in love and happy, and rich enough to travel the world, in addition willing to leave me to my own devices. Only my poor old Dad tried to discuss the situation with me. 'I want you to know that I've never loved anyone but your mother,' he once told me, on the verge of tears. With the careless brutality of youth, I muttered something to the effect that, 'These things happen—you'll find someone else.' He simply got up and walked away. A nasty moment, etched into the mind, and one for which I have never been able to forgive myself.

To make matters worse, my father took it into his head to move into a boarding house in Malvern Road, just around the corner from Hopetoun Road. I suppose he hoped to see his ex-wife and children a little more, as they moved grandly to and from their mansion. In the event, we rarely went to see him in his small room a few hundred metres away. What good did loyalty ever do to that simple, kind-hearted, unfortunate man?

Soon, Malcolm Parker was appointed managing director of California Productions, which had taken over a huge, disused munitions factory in prime minister Ben Chifley's electorate of Bathurst. The company's aim was to produce colourful swimsuits and other sportswear under licence from American manufacturers like Cole of California. Their modern styles caught on and their production gave comfortable employment to hundreds of people in Bathurst.

Partly out of the kindness of his heart, Malcolm decided to start a company journal, to be called the *Californian News-Sheet*, and employed me as part-time editor. Unlike my experience at Holeproof, this time there was no doubt about my access to factory areas. The employees willingly wrote personal pieces about their sections and local activities. I laid out the magazine, wrote some management notes, and arranged production at the *Western Times* office in Bathurst, much of which could be done by mail and phone from Melbourne.

The worst mistake I made was to feature Bernie Leser as 'The Man with the Stopwatch', whose job was to carry out time-and-motion studies on work practices. The communist newspaper *Tribune* attacked the 'remorseless speed-up system, the bitter divisions that spring up between workers', and the 'unemployment that follows a saturated market'. My observations of the factory floor were totally the opposite, but a strike was averted only when Bernie was transferred to other duties. He would later enjoy a meteoric rise as publisher and part-proprietor of *Vogue Australia* and other magazines.

By this time I had also begun to work for one of life's more interesting characters: Henry Drysdale, publisher of the Melbourne *Radio Times*. A Scot, Henry had enlisted in the Light Horse and fought in World War I, where a head wound had left him with the worst stammer I have ever heard. *Radio Times* became a sort of refuge for writers who were too radical to be accepted by the conservative mainstream media, but who were generally not quite radical enough to expound their ideas through the still-lively communist press of Melbourne. An exception was prominent party member Frank Hardy, who left the *Radio Times* just before I started there in order to concentrate on his remarkable work of 'faction', *Power without Glory*, a partially true novel based on the notorious John Wren.

By another of life's ironies, Hardy took the basis of his yarn from an article in the *Lone Hand* magazine entitled 'Wren and His Ruffians', which had been written anonymously by my grandfather from material gathered when he was working as a crime reporter. Due to stringent libel laws, little of the real story could be published in normal outlets. This left the field open for Hardy to adapt the known facts into a compelling tale of what might have happened in the Wren family.

Indeed, life in Melbourne would sometimes seem altogether too inbred. Years later I would marry Kerry Pearce, the daughter of TA ('Jim') Pearce, a solicitor who had inherited the senior partnership in Ridgeway Pearce & Co. from his uncle Percy Ridgeway, a famed criminal lawyer in his day. Among other things, documents had survived regarding John Wren's arrangements with his mistress, for whom he had bought a house near the Wren family mansion in Studley Park. For years I pleaded with Jim Pearce to let me copy the files. I think he was tempted, but legal discretion prevailed, and after discussions with John Wren, Jnr, the files were destroyed.

Henry Drysdale had picked up ideas from various sources. One was that the staff should call him 'Chief', as though he were another Hearst or Northcliffe. I thought this a humorous conceit but went along with it. From Bernard Shaw, Drysdale took the notion that all employees should be paid equal wages, regardless of their position. The printing industry union wouldn't let him get away with this in the composing room, but the journalists' union took no action. As the newest and youngest recruit on the staff, I was delighted to receive £10 a week, the same salary as the editor. For this, I had to review the week's new films, besides producing a full page of previews for the following week's radio programs, running to about 2500 words. The task was simplified by handouts from broadcasters as well as a comprehensive filing system describing practically everything ever recorded or broadcast. In doubtful cases, we consulted dear old Dr AE Floyd, the organist at St Paul's Cathedral, who tottered into the office each week with another erudite contribution on musical matters.

As well as their other duties, each *Radio Times* journalist was expected to contribute a decent news story every week. In an era just beginning to emerge from ultra-conservatism, there was plenty for a progressive journal to talk about. A taste of the times was the banning in New South Wales and South Australia of the film of Graham Greene's *Brighton Rock*, on the grounds that it was 'harmful to public morals, and tended to glorify crime, brutality and vice'. In Victoria, the film was cut by eight minutes and daringly shown at the Grosvenor Theatre in Little Collins Street, a cinema more usually remembered for serving cups of tea to its genteel audiences at interval. I enjoyed writing that story.

I continued a few freelance activities and began to save money again. The Mott family, which had established the Leader suburban newspapers, paid me £2 10s to spend a day each week walking around Coburg interviewing shopkeepers and association secretaries. For this modest sum, the flint-hearted Motts got a solid column called 'Around the Town', which ran to 1500 words in the *Coburg Courier*. The work gave me some insight into the lives of working people, but those items fit for publication were usually rather puerile. My favourite concerned a band of unwashed gypsies who used to camp on the Hume Highway out past Pentridge Prison, beg for petrol from passing motorists, and offer to read their palms and steal small items while their attention was diverted.

More interesting, to my mind, was a monthly journal called *Focus*, which was started by the scientist Oscar Mendelsohn in order to promote intellectual views and knowledge to a public assumed to be eagerly awaiting such pabulum. I rode my paratroop bike down to Oscar's attractive limestone farmhouse at Lara, to the north-east of Geelong, and gravely discussed how we could scientifically change the world's thinking—shades of HG Wells! My main contribution was a lengthy analysis of the fashionable Jean-Paul Sartre philosophy called existentialism, which denied the existence of a supreme mind in the universe. The gods must have been laughing quietly among themselves, for just as I was to take over editorship of the magazine, it closed down amid enormous public indifference.

I had read much about television experiments in Britain and America, and began writing in the *Radio Times* about the amazing new age to come, when instant visual communication would inform everyone and lead with little effort to a better world. It was practically a repeat of my folly in believing that Baden-Powell's ethics would transform the planet, if only everyone would take him seriously. But even I could see that it was necessary to study television at first hand, if I was to help the medium develop in socially beneficial ways. As the 1940s drew to a close, it was time to award myself a travelling scholarship and go to England.

CHAPTER 5

Adventures Overseas

A ONE-WAY PASSAGE TO England on the old Orient Line steamer *Ormonde* cost £90. I had managed to save about £140 from freelance work, so I felt I had plenty of spare cash for my trip. The *Ormonde* was making its final voyage to England where it was to be broken up for scrap, and it was sailing as a one-class ship. Yet, even though I was sharing a stuffy internal cabin with five other single men, there was little bickering: we all felt adventurous and carefree. In those days, emotional farewells were still common at Station Pier in Port Melbourne. My fellow passengers threw hundreds of coloured paper streamers to family and friends on the pier, before the frail bonds of alliance parted as we slowly edged into Port Phillip Bay. I could see people weeping onshore, but I didn't feel at all like crying. Rather, my spirits lifted as the big adventure began.

Friendships with other young men developed readily during those four weeks of isolation, especially among fortunate ones like me who didn't know what it was like to feel seasick. Endless drinking sessions at the bar, poker schools that lasted far into the night, even bingo and deck games, all seemed for a time to draw me closer to people than the intermittent encounters of suburban life. Young women, however, were scarce. Not many girls set out on their own travels in those early postwar days, and the few married women on board were regarded as untouchable, unless they took the initiative.

Only one of our group scored a heavy date. Before he left for her cabin, he opened his wallet and showed us the packets of condoms neatly tucked inside. While the couple were at dinner, however, two of us, having discovered the whereabouts of the willing woman's cabin, sneaked in, blew up a condom to balloon size, and tied it to the central light fitting. Romeo came back to our cabin quite early, in a fury of frustration. Some bastard, he said, had ruined his budding romance: when his intended partner had seen the inflated condom and realised that everyone knew what was afoot, she had furiously pushed him out the door. We sympathised with him: how could anyone play such a low trick on a mate?

A peculiar incident marred the succession of halcyon days and nights as we glided across the Indian Ocean. One night our poker school became particularly heated, and a player thumped his fist noisily on the steel partition separating our cabin from the next. An angry father burst through our door, demanding to know who was hitting the wall and keeping his family awake. For some reason he picked on me—perhaps I was smiling at him. He threatened to meet me on deck the following morning and teach me a lesson. In the accepted code, you didn't 'split' on the real culprit, nor did you back down if challenged. Better to be smashed up. So in the morning I dressed in singlet, shorts and sandshoes and walked around the deck, butterflies in my stomach, waiting for the promised fisticuffs to begin. However, the man's wife must have calmed him down, for he didn't appear on deck at all that day, nor even the next.

During the voyage I became friendly with the noted lawyer Julius Stone, who was travelling as cheaply as possible via London on his way to take up a professorship at the University of California's Hastings College of the Law in San Francisco. Julius tried to convince me that the rule of law would ultimately overcome the world's failings. I argued that this common delusion of lawyers could not succeed unless journalists were given access to all secret political decisions and actions. Relaxing in deckchairs overlooking the vast ocean, we finally agreed that legal ideals and public awareness must march hand in hand towards a bright and golden etc. etc.

A dozen or so years later, when Julius was appointed official observer to the trial of Nazi mass murderer Adolf Eichmann, I would wonder how his ideals were going to stand up to the reality of the ultimate human depravity. Do lawyers admit even now that the actions of Eichmann and his ilk were all performed under the rule of law, or that the law itself is not a sufficient protection for the rights of ordinary people?

When our ship briefly stopped at Colombo in what was then Ceylon (now Sri Lanka), my roommates and I paid a large fee to a taxi driver to take us out of the city to a typical 'native' village. We had no moral reaction to the squalid huts with their dirt floors, or the heavy odour of people living without sanitation. We thought that was simply the way local peoples existed until a beneficent civilisation like ours came along to 'uplift' them. However, in the Egyptian city of Port Said, at the Mediterranean end of the Suez Canal, the landing officials seemed not to agree with us that European control had improved their lot. Their manner was so surly and threatening that we were too alarmed to buy the pornographic postcards offered in the streets, in case that gave officials an excuse to detain us.

Eventually, the graceful old *Ormonde* steamed calmly into a pea-soup fog blanketing the English Channel. We had no radar and lay becalmed for four days until the fog dispersed and we were able to disembark at the River Thames port of Tilbury. London at last!

~

One result of the heavy drinking on board the *Ormonde* was that I arrived in England with only about £10 in my pocket. No matter—a sportswriter who'd also been on the boat had told me that the *Sydney Morning Herald* was about to start a new edition called the *Sunday Herald* and thought they might be taking on staff. And so it proved. London editor Irvine Douglas, a former private secretary to prime minister Joe Lyons, gave me a job as a general reporter, to start in a fortnight's time. Meanwhile, my interviews with disgruntled English migrants returning home on the *Ormonde* were featured in Australian newspapers, along with descriptions of what they were coming back to: a London still bearing most of the scars of the Blitz bombings.

When freelancing in Australia, one way I had found of earning a few extra pounds was to send news items about the developing field of 16-millimetre movies to film trade journals in Britain and America. The English journal was called the *Film User*, and at the urgent request of its editor I'd also sent regular food parcels for his family—the packages contained tinned food and other items still scarce in postwar Britain. So one of my first calls was at the editor's office where, after all my efforts, the least I expected was to be asked to lunch or dinner. Instead, I was treated to the frostiest of receptions. This balding, harassed-looking Englishman in a worn-out three-piece suit talked to me for two minutes and then sent me on my way, without even a cup of tea. Fortunately, he proved not to be typical of the English.

While waiting for the *SMH* job, I borrowed a pushbike from a friendlier acquaintance and set off southwards from London, working my way along a network of excellent youth hostels. These charged only a few shillings a night, and the price included a solid dinner and breakfast. It was late autumn, cold enough to make cycling a pleasure but not yet freezing. The countryside yielded a succession of picture-book scenes, with glowing fallen leaves littering the roadside and patches of forest hiding charming cottages. Farm labourers in the pubs seemed an unfriendly lot, uninterested in strangers, but the managers of most hostels were helpful, outgoing souls who belied English 'reserve'—one even offered me a labouring job on his extensive chicken farm. I rode down to Brighton, across to Devon, up to Bath and back to London with no misadventures. I even made a few pounds' profit, writing a long article for the Sydney *Sun* on my experiences.

Life in a London boarding house was the next eye-opener. I rented a small room with a gas ring and heater in a four-storey terrace in Harrington Gardens, South Kensington, for a pound a week—quite unaware that, close by, a serial killer named John Haigh had been murdering random victims and melting their bodies in acid baths. Already the area was filling up with Australians, several of whom lived in the same boarding house as I: we seemed to be the only ones who used the shilling-in-a-meter bath located on the top landing. The landlady dwelt in the basement, which had been converted from kitchens dating back to the days when it had been a grand townhouse. No lodger was ever permitted to descend below ground level or use the rear tradesmen's entrance. To summon the landlady to the ground floor, we had to ring an electric bell at the top of her stairs. Later, I discovered that this was because she ran an illegal but busy after-hours abortion facility in her quarters.

Meals were a problem for anyone used to extravagant Australian forms of nourishment. Four years after the war's end, extreme food rationing was still in force in London. The official weekly ration came down to a few sausages or two lamb chops, two eggs, a small lump of butter, a little fish and bacon, a few spoonfuls of sugar, and cheap filling in the form of bread and potatoes. I experimented with unrationed horsemeat but I hated the stringy, tasteless stuff. All this had to be fried in carefully saved dripping over the gas ring. I did find a medium-class restaurant in the Strand where, when funds allowed, I gorged myself on the rich, unrationed venison they could somehow procure.

Many young people far from home develop romantic liaisons. Mine was with an attractive Australian nurse who doubled with another nurse in a larger room on the same landing. We enjoyed the less-expensive sights and entertainments of London together, and it was not long before we were sharing, rather uncomfortably, my single bed. In the fashion of those days, this meant a good deal of kissing and cuddling, but not necessarily intercourse. That is, the woman would allow the man to go as far as fondling her breasts, but nothing lower down. If one persisted in desiring intercourse, the tradition among 'respectable' people was to get married. The male, often maddened by unfulfilled desire, felt impelled to propose. That is what happened to me. Also, I was twenty years old and in apparently steady employment, and my girlfriend seemed enthusiastic. But her widowed mother, upon flying over from Australia, forbade consummation. Her daughter was a few years older than me, and such a liaison seemed, in the moral system of the day, quite unnatural. The landlady then forbad any further 'visiting' between male and female boarders and asked me to find a room elsewhere, no doubt fearful of a pregnancy occurring right above her illegal basement activities. Robbed of propinquity and beset by parental disapproval, the romance faded.

I moved to an attic room in Notting Hill—unknowingly near the house where a former constable named John Christie was strangling women and concealing their bodies in various parts of his house. The English and their murders! They seemed to be happening all around me, but I paid them little attention. To kill seemed an aberration in life's grand plan: why would anyone want to waste time reading about such things? As a journalist supposedly attuned to public tastes, I was pretty much a failure.

Meanwhile, I had begun to work at the *SMH* office in Fleet Street. For what seemed a princely salary of £15 a week, I was instructed to cover events occurring at Australia House and various state offices in the Strand. There was plenty of straight news around: Arthur Calwell's massive immigration program was well underway, 'Stabber Jack' Beasley was still the outspoken high commissioner, and agents-general were working hard to attract new industries to their individual states. I became friendly with one young immigration officer who quietly fed me leads on several important stories.

My best series for the *SMH* concerned the P&O liner *Mooltan*, which had called at Bombay on a return voyage from Australia and picked up a passenger suffering from the early stages of smallpox. Before the danger was realised, the other passengers had dispersed to destinations all over Britain. At least twelve new cases of smallpox were admitted to one isolation hospital in Yorkshire, where five people died. My friend at Australia House gave the hospital's name and phone number only to me, so that for several days I was the sole reporter able to get the patients' names and Australian addresses. But after protests from other newspapers, the Health Ministry ordered a complete blackout on further information.

At this time I still liked going to the movies for relaxation. Another member of the *SMH* staff, who had been a courageous pilot in the Royal Air Force and won a Distinguished Flying Cross, asked late one afternoon if he could come with me. During the film, I was surprised and dismayed to feel his hand touching my knee and sliding up my leg. My instinctive reaction was to jump up and angrily walk out of the cinema. Thereafter, we scarcely spoke in the office.

Overt homosexuality seemed much more rife in London than in Australia. Not long after the cinema incident, I was walking home one night from a tube station when a well-dressed, middle-aged man followed me and then asked whether I would like to 'try the French method'. I spat out the words 'Piss off!' and squared up to smash in his face if he persevered, but he simply veered off in search of easier prey. I suppose that a horror of homosexuality had been imprinted on my mind after the expulsion of the two boys from my boarding school. It would take me many years to realise that no-one deserved to be persecuted like that.

One cold winter's day, I was tipped off by another contact at Australia House that professor Mark Oliphant, one of many scientists who had helped develop the first atomic bomb, was considering moving with his research team from Birmingham University to Australia. I informed Irvine Douglas and immediately left for Birmingham to interview the physicist. Oliphant, a stocky 47-year-old, seemed pleased by the opportunity to discuss his plans. He told me how he would create a department at the new Australian National University in Canberra to conduct fundamental research into nuclear physics. One practical spin-off, he said, would be the establishment of nuclear power stations throughout Australia. Another could be the decentralisation to Australia of British experiments in making the Commonwealth's own nuclear weapons, a sure deterrent to any aggression such as we had known during World War II.

Back at the *SMH* office, Douglas rang Jack Beasley and was able to strengthen the story on the basis of what he learned. The subject was splashed across the front page of the *Sunday Herald* on 26 February 1949. It caused consternation in Australia, particularly within the ruling Chifley Labor government, and was reprinted in many of the world's newspapers. Cables flew between Canberra bureaucrats, Birmingham and London. Finally, Oliphant wrote to the *Sunday Herald* to confirm that he would be carrying out nuclear research in Canberra, but that no secret work would be undertaken unless there was an 'imminent threat' of war involving Australia. 'The development of atomic energy must at this stage be carried out under conditions of secrecy which cannot be provided in a university,' Oliphant added. In other words, the *Sunday Herald* had exaggerated the prospects for nuclear energy and weapons for Australia.

Rupert Henderson, who controlled the day-to-day running of the Fairfax organisation, decided that a head had to roll. It could hardly be that of the London editor, but more fittingly that of the newest recruit—me. Irvine Douglas called me into his office and told me, apologetically, that I would have to go.

Ten years later, when I was an executive on the Sydney *Sunday Mirror* and Irvine was an elderly leader writer on the daily staff, he would still be apologetic about the incident. But it would not be until government documents were released under the thirty-year archives rule at the end of 1988 that the original news story would be borne out in almost every detail. The documents proved that Ben Chifley, when prime minister, had asked for Oliphant's recommendation on establishing a chain of nuclear power stations in Australia—in the best spy tradition, Chifley had even secretly met the physicist in a park to discuss the matter. Later, after the detonation of the first hydrogen bomb in 1952, Oliphant changed his views about the desirability of nuclear power.

~

In 1949, as far as I was concerned, there were plenty of other fish in the vast sea of journalistic opportunity besides the *SMH*. I walked across Fleet Street and introduced myself to Eric Baume, head of the Sydney *Daily Mirror* group in London, who had spent a fairly comfortable World War II sending colourful dispatches as a 'war correspondent' from his suite in the Savoy Hotel. He told me I could start work the next day, adding: 'I'm generally known as Baume the Bastard—and you'll find out why if you don't work hard enough.'

I had brought with me a half-prepared story on an immigration scam operating in London. Two Cockney spivs had advertised a £50 scheme for quick passage to Australia, claiming to save migrants the long wait in a queue for government-assisted passages normally costing £10. When I went to interview the two men, they accused me of being a detective from Scotland Yard who was posing as a reporter. I was flattered, but I quickly proved I was merely an Australian journalist. That said, after getting details of the pair's scheme and writing the story, I had no hesitation in telling Scotland Yard of the arrangement's suspicious nature. Their raid the following day gave me an exclusive story of the scandal type so loved by the *Mirror* in its heyday.

Most work for the *Mirror*, however, consisted of the unromantic business of checking and rewriting British press agency stories for Australian consumption. Because of the time difference, most of this had to be done at night. Being the newcomer, I ran the dreary 'dog watch' shift that finished about 2 a.m., when I caught a double-decker bus home. London could then be seen at its seediest, with prostitutes patrolling Piccadilly and London's clubland.

Many of my spare daylight hours were spent investigating BBC Television, then in its infancy. When they learned I was from Australia, the executives at Broadcasting House were extremely helpful, giving me an open pass to Alexandra Palace, where most TV programs were prepared and transmitted to a limited audience. The practitioners of this mysterious art were mostly enthusiastic young men who, amidst their busy lives, could still welcome another believer in the future of their medium. I was allowed to watch and photograph everything they did, beforehand and behind the scenes, until finally I was almost regarded as one of them. Exciting days were spent accompanying their primitive outside broadcast vans to sports events like tennis and ice hockey matches, where I noted how they set up their bulky equipment to fulfil what appeared to be the true purpose of television: the transmission of unedited live events in real time.

The result was a long series of articles, totalling more than 50 000 words, that would be published in the *Radio Times* between March and December 1949. No other newspaper seemed very interested in the coming media revolution, although behind the scenes the major press proprietors were planning to oust the Labor government and install the new Liberal Party under RG Menzies, who guaranteed them free licences for commercial TV operations. Ignorant of this at the time, I wrote on and on about the possibilities of this new form of information, convinced that Chifley would allow only a high-grade BBC form of television in Australia.

After a few months of continuous night work and a mediocre diet, I began suffering severe attacks of tonsillitis, and decided to return to Australia. I sailed back on the *Orcades*, a fairly modern passenger liner, but much less enjoyable than the *Ormonde*, mainly because of the rigid barriers separating first and tourist classes. I shared a tiny internal cabin with a silent elderly man. Still, a few days of rest and sea air began to cure my throat.

When I emerged in the bar, I was quickly picked up by a young, dark-haired Englishwoman fleeing an unhappy marriage. I was still technically a virgin, but whenever we could get my fellow passenger out of my cabin on some pretext (or even during dinner call), she expertly inducted me into everything she knew about sexual love. So intense did our activities become that if we couldn't use the cabin, we made love at night on the rear deck under the starry Mediterranean sky. It was enthralling, all-consuming, like a honeymoon without obligations. When we reached Melbourne, we parted with scarcely a backward look.

CHAPTER 6

Work, Love and Death

WITH MY MOTHER and stepfather often away on business trips, I was left in solitary occupation of the Toorak house for weeks at a time. Today, no doubt, this would be regarded by most young men as an ideal opportunity to develop relationships with the opposite sex. But I was so busy with grandiose projects that the thought barely occurred to me. Besides, most girls I knew seemed determined to preserve their virginity and were terrified of real sexual experimentation before marriage. My only foray ended in disaster.

A few doors down the hill, a live-in mothercraft nurse was caring for the children of a wealthy family. She was a tall, slender, blue-eyed blonde, about my age, and we often exchanged smiles as I walked past her residence to the tram stop. We began meeting occasionally to drink coffee and chat in Raffles cafe in Collins Street: usually she just listened patiently while I rambled on about the state of the world and my unique place in it. One night late in 1949, I asked her to come back to my empty house. After some desultory kissing, she acquiesced to get partially undressed in front of the log fire, but seemed ashamed of her slender limbs. I tried to massage some warmth of feeling into her body, but all in vain: even her lips remained unresponsive. She did not want to be seduced.

A few weeks later, I was dumbfounded to read that she had been in Sydney and had boarded the *Orcades* for the return voyage to Melbourne, but overnight had been reported missing. I possessed several good photographs of her. With my newspaper instincts aroused, I rushed into town and gave them to the *Herald*—today I cannot imagine doing such a thing, but at the time it seemed normal behaviour. *Truth* in turn bought one of the pictures from the *Herald* and featured part of the awful story in their next issue. I got the remaining details from FJ ('Bluey') Adam, the detective in charge of the investigation. According to his interviews with *Orcades* passengers, the woman had attended a party in one of the cabins, which developed into a drunken riot. Attempts were apparently made to rape her, although no man present would admit to succeeding. Later that night she must have jumped overboard, and by the time the alarm was raised, it was too late. Her body was never found, and no-one was ever charged over her disappearance.

I continued my weekly television articles for the *Radio Times*, concentrating on Australian moves to introduce the new medium. I adopted a lofty position, claiming that TV under a government-funded commission would quickly demolish lesser media. Television, I explained in November 1949, 'has a larger task than the press, or radio, or cinema', namely 'to bring an immediate, vivid, truthful picture of what is happening in the nation and the world—not what the press or radio commentator, or his boss, thinks we should read or hear'.

I even played a small part in the introduction to Australia of the closed-circuit TV transmission of surgical operations. Three months earlier, I had reported from London on the world's first such event. Bill Refshauge, medical superintendent of the Royal Women's Hospital, had read my article and asked electronics manufacturer AWA if the procedure could be tested in Melbourne, for the benefit of medical students. The company Pye and its partner Electronic Industries heard of the approach and attempted to arrange earlier transmissions from the Alfred Hospital. When I told AWA of the plot, its engineers worked all night to install the necessary equipment at the Women's Hospital, and it staged the first operation for the press and medical authorities one day ahead of its competitors.

That was all good fun, but I was more concerned at the prospect that major newspaper groups and the ABC, all conservatively run at the time, were likely to monopolise public television and dilute its cultural possibilities. This became an imminent prospect during the federal election campaign of late 1949, when Ben Chifley rejected all advice and remained steadfast in his objective of nationalising the private banks. He was slaughtered at the polls, and Bob Menzies became prime minister at the head of a Liberal–Country Party government.

A close relationship had long existed between Menzies and the Melbourne *Herald* group. In June 1940, Menzies had even appointed Sir Keith Murdoch as wartime director-general of information, with draconian powers of censorship. This appointment lasted less than six months, but during that time Murdoch antagonised every other pressman by demanding the right to insert official corrections of alleged errors in any newspaper. The tie between Murdoch, Menzies and the 'Establishment' continued for many years, culminating in the vitriolic campaign that defeated the Chifley government in 1949. Substantial paybacks were now due to be made by prime minister Menzies to the *Herald* and other newspaper groups.

In several *Radio Times* articles in early 1950, I warned that television was about to be 'diverted into the wrong channels under the wrong controls'. Sure enough, on 18 February, the new postmaster-general, Hal Anthony, announced that the government would licence both commercial and national TV stations, on the ground that Australians were 'well satisfied' with the dual system which already regulated radio stations. This, said Anthony, would ensure that TV would 'enrich our lives and broaden our vision'.

And the new government did not stop there. The Postmaster-General's Department used federal powers of compulsory land acquisition to acquire the multistorey *Radio Times* building at 300 King Street, allegedly for postal purposes, although plenty of other suitable buildings were available. Henry Drysdale, who had supported my troublesome articles at all times, was left in temporary occupation of the basement, where the presses were located, but with no way of getting the heavy rolls of newsprint in, or getting printed copies of the paper out onto the streets. At a stroke, the Menzies–Murdoch cabal had put itself in line to secure the main commercial TV licences, suppressed an awkward source of criticism in Murdoch's home base, and forced the closure of the sole rival to the *Herald*'s own weekly program guide, the *Listener-In*.

Drysdale tried to enlist the support of the *Argus* and the *Age*, pointing out that if the government could close down a weekly paper by compulsorily acquiring its freehold premises, it could put daily papers out of business at any time by the same method. Rebuffed by the floundering managements of both newspapers, Drysdale would turn to the courts for protection.

~

With my main source of freelance money now gone, it again became essential to find a regular income. My bulging book of cuttings impressed Harold Austin, a former war correspondent who had become a fairly relaxed newspaper executive. He gave me a job as a D-grade journalist on the *Age*. This well-established morning daily had begun life as a radical journal in the gold-rush days of the 1850s, and it generally remained on the moderately leftish side of politics, although its writing and presentation had become rather staid under a succession of cautious editors such as the incumbent, Harold ('Ham') Campbell. Above all, *Age* executives were scared of defamation writs. Several of my exposés—what are now described as 'investigative journalism'—were spiked before I realised that the

Age in those days would not take chances. I was forced to modify my approach in order to get one or two stories published on most working days.

At that time, the *Age* was still being produced in antique offices on the southern side of Collins Street, between Swanston and Elizabeth streets. It was printed on noisy old presses in the basement: rolls of newsprint had to be taken down a narrow alley off Flinders Lane, and printed copies were taken out the same way. The entrance to the editorial offices was up a narrow stairway off Collins Street. Battered desks, a couple of shared telephones, and a few old standard typewriters with faint ribbons were the sole equipment provided for reporters. The atmosphere was that of a newspaper which had seen its best days and now survived as a medium for classified advertisements mainly inserted by its loyal working-class readers. Seventy-two-year-old Oswald Syme, the last surviving son of the great proprietor-editor David Syme, was the main director and shareholder. His 54-year-old niece Katie Syme, another director, spent much of her time ensuring that reporters did not smoke while in the office—only the pungent men's toilet was safe from her regular tours of inspection.

Another young man had started work with the *Age* a few weeks earlier: Graham Perkin, a solid Methodist citizen from Sandringham. Perkin would eventually work in every journalistic and subediting position, and manage to avoid most of the usual heavy drinking sessions to produce large quantities of material suitable for publication. In 1966, a new chairman, lieutenant-colonel Edwin Neill (who had married Oswald Syme's daughter) would appoint Perkin as editor, with a charter to begin modernising the paper's writing and layout. Under Perkin's guidance, the *Age* appealed to a wider audience, especially university-educated readers. As the *Herald* and *Sun* began to go downmarket, circulation of the *Age* increased within a few years from less than 180 000 per day to about 250 000 a day. Unfortunately, Graham Perkin would literally work himself to death for the *Age*, dying in 1975 aged only forty-five.

In the early 1950s, I assisted on state political rounds, developing a knack for extracting amusing items from the generally flaccid debates in both houses of parliament. John Cain senior was Victoria's Labor premier: he seemed rock-solid and honest, rather like a local version of Ben Chifley. His attorney-general and best friend was Bill Slater, a self-educated solicitor who founded the radical law firm Slater & Gordon (many years later, I would write the history of that remarkable firm). Some of Cain's other ministers were notoriously dishonest, accepting bribes for assisting in pushing various schemes in which government might be involved, but the cautious *Age* executives never assigned anyone to pursue investigations in any depth. Such matters, as well as John Wren's continued influence over some Labor decisions, and his business dealings with Sir Keith Murdoch, were out of bounds. When Frank Hardy tried to portray the scene in fictional terms in *Power without Glory*, he was prosecuted by a later government for criminal libel, and undoubtedly escaped a long prison term only because a jury of ordinary people suspected that at least half of what he had written was true.

As a reward for learning not to rock the boat, I then became Trades Hall reporter, a position generally regarded as a pathway to higher things. Here, the old paper enjoyed lingering respect because of its radical past, but again, its great days seemed to be over. In a cosy arrangement, Trades Hall journalists shared all routine stories. The only scoops went to Jack O'Sullivan of the *Argus*, another eminent journal, temporarily rejuvenated after a takeover by the London *Daily Mirror* group. At least, they did up until the day O'Sullivan, for a bet, drank a full bottle of whisky and dropped dead on the spot. Alcohol abuse in fact stopped newspapers from having much influence on union affairs.

Late each afternoon, all three morning newspaper reporters would meet in one of the two main pubs in Lygon Street opposite Trades Hall, where we downed a few beers with any union official who happened to be around, and in this way kept reasonably up-to-date with union preoccupations. Their concerns were usually low-key, dealing with petty details of the meagre Arbitration Court awards which governed working relationships in those days. The big stories revolved around strikes in public utilities, and matters such as the jailing of tramways union leader Clarrie O'Shea, who was privately criticised not for his communist convictions but because he was placing union affairs too much in the limelight. In such cases, the pub meetings were useful for obtaining extra details or tip-offs on future moves. But the real action—and the libel-free headlines—usually came from parliament or the courts. Even Albert Monk, the likeable but pedantic head of the Australian Council of Trade Unions (ACTU) yielded comparatively little interesting news.

If there was nothing much doing from afternoon inquiries and the hotel round, Jim Davies of the *Sun* and I would usually amble down to another pub on the corner of Swanston and Bourke streets, which had a fine upstairs dining room. Here, we would eat a huge meal, usually steak, eggs and chips, and drink endless beers to see us through the evening. Ruled by the custom of shouting, I would try, and usually fail, to keep pace with Jim's consumption (he had an amazing capacity for drinking, and a physique to stand it, for he would survive until well over seventy years of age). I was almost incoherent by the end of dinner, not knowing that I was a potential alcoholic and that my true capacity was one or two glasses. Beyond that, I found it almost impossible to stop drinking. The walk back to Trades Hall through now-deserted streets saved me from complete disaster. We divided up the evening union meetings to be attended, usually with members and officials who had also had too much to drink. When meetings were held in camera, we waited in draughty corridors until the secretary could tell us of any newsworthy results. Jim and I shared all such news items, being now sober enough to make sense of them and phone the results through to our papers before 11 p.m. This became easier after a little experience, for most 'news' is merely a slightly altered version of what happened the last time around. Then it was home to sleep it off in preparation for the next day of similarly turgid work.

Thankfully, I was put back on general reporting. With my bag packed in advance, I was ready to go anywhere at any time: to a mine collapse at Yallourn, bushfires in remote areas, on a delightful trip following Charles Sturt's route down the Murray River. This was a better life for a young man, full of stimulus and intensive learning. My final reward came when I was selected to accompany HMAS *Australia* to the Antarctic region. Dr Serge Udovikoff, the only surgeon at the small Australian base on Heard Island, had been stricken with severe appendicitis. Obviously, he could not operate on himself, so he had to be picked up and given medical attention. The aircraft of those times could not reach the island, so the only solution was to send a naval vessel, at enormous expense.

For such events, the Australian media divided itself into two competitive camps: the Murdoch press versus the remainder. The *Herald* sent one of its best reporters and even a photographer; I went along to ensure that the *Age, Sydney Morning Herald* and smaller independent papers did not miss out on the story. Within an hour of being given the assignment, I had my suitcase down at Princes Pier and was preparing to board a huge old cruiser, on which junior officers were grumpily vacating their cabins to make way for the gentlemen of the press.

The voyage southwards began serenely enough. Our time was mainly spent drinking and playing poker in the officers' mess. We also wrote 'specials' about shipboard life, which had to be submitted for censorship by the captain, GC Oldham, before being radioed to Melbourne: 'A thin white line of hope for a man in danger was cut through the Southern Ocean today …' As we steamed through mid-winter seas, the waves increased to massive proportions, the temperature dropped to well below freezing, and blizzard after blizzard struck the ship. Our camera shutters jammed, and atmospherics prevented many radio messages from being sent. But on 8 August 1950, when we arrived at Heard Island, a morning of silent frozen calm greeted us. The ship hove to about a mile offshore and a cutter was quickly lowered to beat the next violent storm.

I was now faced with a peculiar dilemma. Radio communications were open again but might last only a few minutes. We were not permitted to send messages unseen by the captain, but he was directing operations on the bridge and refused to be disturbed. Well, what was life but a constant risk? As soon as I saw the cutter returning at high speed, I scribbled the words 'Udovikoff off' on a message pad and ran to the radio room. 'Captain seen this?' grunted the operator. 'Yes,' I lied, as he turned to his transmitter. The message reached Melbourne just as our western sky began to darken again—no radio communications would be possible for the next two days.

The *Age* subeditors now rose to the occasion. With only my two words to guide them, they described a wonderful drama: 'Luck was with us today … As if by a miracle the seas were dead calm … only slight snow and a few showers fell.' They told of how the grateful patient was being examined by ship's doctors to see if an immediate operation was necessary. The tale was copied all over the world, leaving the Murdoch press far behind for once. Even the Navy had to learn from the *Age* that the mission had been successful.

When communications resumed and complaints were radioed to captain Oldham, he didn't say much, apart from sternly reminding me that censorship was obligatory. Circumstances brought him a mixed revenge. On our triumphant return voyage, we struck a submerged iceberg at moderate speed, loosening some of the *Australia*'s plates. The captain absolutely refused to let me radio the story back to Melbourne, which meant nothing could be published until we landed. The *Australia* limped on to Sydney, where it was put into dry dock for repairs.

I disembarked to find journalists still talking about how the *Age* had scooped the mighty *Herald* group with my message. One result was an approach from Sydney *Daily Telegraph* manager Duncan Thompson, who offered me a promotion from C grade at the *Age* to B grade in Sydney. I told Harold Austin, who immediately arranged the same deal. I then wrote what must have seemed an egotistical note to Thompson, who passed it on to his boss, the as-yet-unknighted Frank Packer. I received this memento:

> Dear Mr Cannon,
>
> Mr Thompson has passed on your note. My reasons for wanting to see you were that Mr Thompson assessed you as a very bright, clever young journalist with a future. He also said he thought you were interested in coming to the *Telegraph*.
>
> The most disturbing thing about it is not that you are happy where you are and not coming to the *Telegraph*; no doubt we will manage to struggle along without you. But I am shocked at the decline in Mr Thompson's usually keen, shrewd judgment of character. This is evidently on the wane. I cannot see how any young man with such conceit can have a really great future.
>
> Yours faithfully, Frank Packer, Managing Director.

As if Packer had glimpsed my future, my career with the *Age* began to go downhill. The local news and features I wrote began to seem trivial and pointless, scarcely worth staying up most of the night to complete in order to meet the paper's deadline. I felt there must be exciting people and movement somewhere outside the grey columns of a still-conservative *Age* and the grey skies hanging over an ultraconservative city. Perhaps I shouldn't have been so cheeky to Packer's messenger.

I resumed contact with Henry Drysdale in his bunker at 300 King Street. While a large damages claim for illegal closure of the *Radio Times* was being prepared, justice Wilfred Fullagar granted Henry a Supreme Court order instructing the Commonwealth to allow reels of newsprint to be taken down to the presses. In his inimitable way, Drysdale decided to increase the stakes by starting an afternoon daily newspaper in opposition to the *Herald*, then nearing the height of its circulation and power. Drysdale asked the new *Age* editor, Keith Sinclair, if I could be seconded for a few months to edit his new paper. Sinclair refused, so another young man, Kenneth Hince—who would later become a noted antiquarian bookseller and *Age* music critic—was appointed to try to get the *Melbourne Times* off the ground. It was a hopeless battle from the start. Drysdale had no overseas or interstate news services, relying instead on rewrites of BBC broadcasts and airmailed journals, and his local reporting and photographic staff was almost non-existent.

I helped as much as I could with anonymous items and tip-offs, particularly those which the *Age* would not use. Probably my best story, published in December 1950, told of how a winner of the Miss Australia beauty contest had been signed up by a Hollywood producer of sex films. But even this sensation didn't do much for the *Melbourne Times*'s circulation, because Drysdale could distribute only several thousand copies to city newsagents, forsaking the huge home-delivery market. Within a few weeks he was forced to close down the paper and concentrate on his complex lawsuits against the federal government.

To help fight his court cases, Drysdale engaged a young, brilliant but almost blind barrister named Gillespie-Jones. I think they must have disagreed, probably over payments, for Drysdale ended up representing himself in court. On a slack day I attended one hearing, where justice Fullagar tried to assist the layman but was eventually driven to exasperation by Drysdale's crippling stammer and his persistent jumps into the 'lessons' of ancient history. A few months later, Henry Drysdale's complicated legal affairs reached the stage of a High Court application to appeal to the Privy Council. I helped typeset his application, for such documents had to be in printed form, but leave to appeal was refused. The Commonwealth had won.

Later, I heard that Drysdale had settled all his outstanding claims against the government for £75 000—not a bad sum when you consider that £5000 bought you an excellent house in those days. However, *Radio Times* employees, working on verbal mateship agreements and weekly rental payments, received no compensation at all, although they were able to find other jobs easily. And the plant on which we had lavished so much time and effort became so much scrap metal. Today, I suppose the presses that printed the first *Ginger Meggs* colour comics would be regarded as part of Australia's national heritage. But in the 1950s, by order of the federal government, they were deemed fit only for the wrecker's hammer.

~

With the high salary I was earning from the *Age*, and additional income from freelancing, I felt it was time to launch into my own form of publishing, and try to build it up to the point where I would not have to work for other people. My duties at the *Age* did not usually start until 2 p.m., so I had every morning free, as well as two days off each week.

Television seemed the most likely field for publishing opportunities. Tenders for construction of the first government TV transmitter at Gore Hill, Sydney closed late in 1950. By the following month I was the proud (part-time) publisher of *Teleview*, trumpeted on the front page as 'Australia's first television magazine'. Tam Mappin, former manager of *Radio Times*, handled business affairs for me at an office he had opened at 473 Bourke Street, while Alan Spalding, then a subeditor at the *Age*, helped me to gather and rewrite material in our own version of *Time* style ('Backwards ran the sentences until reeled the mind').

Since there were no TV broadcasts at the time, it seemed sufficient to publish *Teleview* quarterly, at 2 shillings a copy. For the first issue, postmaster-general Anthony agreed to write an article explaining the government's caution in selecting the correct technical standards, far in advance of the BBC's standards of the time. Larry Fanning, chairman of the Broadcasting Control Board, who privately believed in a government monopoly akin to the BBC, wrote that the medium would 'exercise a tremendous influence'. Ben Chifley, meanwhile, sent me an article 'regretting very much the delay' in introducing national television. These high-powered contributions were supplemented by technical and program articles.

For the second issue of *Teleview* in April 1951, Labor member of the House of Representatives Arthur Calwell wrote an article attacking moves to introduce commercial TV, arguing that the 'profit motive must not be allowed to debauch this valuable addition to the enjoyment of living'. If licences were granted to 'those concerned merely with the idea of getting rich quickly', he continued, the medium could become 'a national menace'. I asked prime minister Menzies's office in Canberra for a response, to be published in the same issue, but nothing was forthcoming. Soon after publication of Calwell's article, the manager of Ramsay Ware, which printed *Teleview* at its King Street works, called me to say he could not obtain enough glossy paper to print the next issue. I went to Edwards Dunlop, the wholesale merchants, and managed to scrounge enough reams of the paper to complete another edition, then returned to Ramsay Ware with the good news. The manager was taken aback, but he recovered his wits enough to say, 'Sorry, the production schedule has already been filled up.' He would not admit that instructions had come from his conservative directors to cease printing 'socialist propaganda'.

Meanwhile, the *Age* and I had reached the end of one road. In an attempt to tie me down, I was given the boring job of waiting all afternoon and evening in the pictorial department for photographers to return from their assignments and process their films. My task then was to write captions from their often sparse information. After a few weeks of this, I pleaded with Harold Austin to put me back on more interesting work. He appeared to relent, promising to assign me to general rounds from the following Monday. That day, glancing in the duty book, I saw I was down for caption-writing yet again. I walked straight out of the office, almost in tears, and never returned to the full-time staff.

Even with money in the bank, I had to find some income to continue publication of *Teleview*, which so far had attracted only about 500 subscriptions and the same in bookstall sales. The *Radio Times* plant was now lying derelict in its King Street basement, so

I approached Henry Drysdale and arranged to rent the composing room and its equipment for a few pounds a week. The ancient single-magazine linotypes had not been properly serviced for years. I engaged RMIT technicians and *Argus* operatives to strip down the machines in their spare time and get them working again.

The priority was to get out another issue of *Teleview*. This was typeset on the first linotype put back into service. I hand-set the main headings in battered fonts from *Radio Times* days, made up the pages, and lugged the heavy trays of lead to the communist printery in Corrs Lane, where they ran off 2000 copies on the glossy paper I had bought from Edwards Dunlop. Later, I was able to print the magazine myself on a rickety old Wharfedale poster-printing machine in the *Radio Times* works. That meant learning the art of cutting underlays to enable halftone blocks and worn type to print properly, not to mention hand-feeding large sheets of flat paper into the machine—I still have nightmares of being caught between revolving cogs and drawn into giant machinery.

I battled on with *Teleview* until the end of 1952, but with the federal government still unable to make up its mind about a starting date for television services, I was forced to abandon it. Not until 1956 did TV become a reality for the public in Australia, with the accompanying TV guides selling in the hundreds of thousands each week.

My takeover of the *Radio Times* plant was the beginning of four extremely arduous years. The part-time linotypers taught me how to dismantle the thousands of working parts in Ottmar Mergenthaler's Heath Robinson invention. All these parts had to be cleaned, examined for excessive wear, replaced if necessary, and reassembled in the correct order. We had eight linotypes, but three of these had not yet been converted from gas-fired pots which supplied the molten lead necessary to cast the slugs or 'lines-o'-type'. We wrote off those machines and concentrated on the others, cannibalising for parts where possible, and replacing such expensive items as the mold-wheels, which had become warped after decades of use. After much

Jessie Grover nee McGuire, my great-grandmother and journalist, 1880. *Johnstone O'Shannessy & Company, Melbourne.*

Montague 'Monty' Grover, my grandfather and journalist, 1908.

Ada Sarah Grover, nee Goldberg, my grandmother, c. 1890.

The first known picture of me as a baby, 1930.

Arthur Cannon, my father, as a radio operator on SS *Niagara*, c. 1927.

My mother Dorothy ('Dolly') as a reporter, interviewing police in Camperdown for a story, c. 1938.

In Melbourne, c. 1937.

Dad's frozen solid underpants, Cobden c. 1937.

With my sisters Jill and Dina, 1938.

House of Guilds committee, 1945: John Bechervaise centre front, me and Fred Elliott back row on right, Jack Duigan front right.

At Dad's bush block in Seville, 1947.

Hitchiking in South Australia, on our way to Darwin, c. 1948.

In Collins Street, Melbourne 'walking the block' with 'Gwenda', 1948.

As a young journalist at the *Age*, 1951.

Dolly and Malcolm Parker on their wedding day at Sark, Hopetoun Road, Toorak, 1953.

John Monks, my sister Dina and I working on *Newsday*, c. 1958. *Courtesy John Monks.*

With the twins Sarah and James, 1966.

The extended family at Paul's 21st birthday at Goosehill, Main Ridge, 1977.

Launch of *Life in the Cities*, with Premier Ruper Hamer, 1975.

The publication of *Melbourne After the Gold Rush*, 1993.

In the State Library of Victoria archives researching *The Historical Records of Victoria*, c. 1998.

At Fernhyll, Gippsland, 1999.

With James, Sarah, Paul and Patrick at the Royal Historical Society of Victoria for the *Land Boomers* function, 2016. *Courtesy David Eckstein.*

Sitting on John Stanley James's ('The Vagabond's) grave in Carlton Cemetery, 2016.

time and expenditure, we had five workable machines on which good operators could churn out slugs about half as fast as today's computerised typesetters.

As fate would have it, an expert lino operator in London's Fleet Street, who was an acquaintance of mine, decided to emigrate to Australia, and we went into business as commercial typesetters. With few overheads and cheap rent, we could cut costs considerably, as long as customers were content with the restricted range of typefaces on offer. In those days, all letters of the alphabet were represented on small but expensive brass matrices, kept in channels in heavy brass magazines, and machine-assembled into lines against which molten lead was squirted to form the solid slugs suitable for printing or stereotyping. Each new font and magazine cost about £200, and separate fonts were needed for each size and style. Instead of investing too heavily in new fonts, we decided to offer quick service at low prices, and this drew in enough customers to keep us going. Soon, we were setting much of the *Footscray Advertiser* and doing semi-legal work every Wednesday to typeset starting-price lists for SP bookmakers. Whenever we ran short of linotype metal, we melted down some of the old *Radio Times* stereo plates and exchanged them for fresh ingots suitable for typesetting.

Since my partner was working in the *Herald* composing room before putting in a few hours at King Street, I was forced to become sufficiently expert as a linotype operator to fill urgent orders during the day. I would arrive at dawn, climb into a boiler suit, proof and correct the previous night's typesetting, phone through any necessary orders for supplies, clean up the place, answer inquiries at the front desk, perform all the office work, and grab a sandwich when I could. Only when our part-timers began to arrive each evening could I parcel out the work and sit back to think about the next issue of *Teleview*. I even had time then to stroll into the stillness of the pressroom and gaze at the great grease-covered Goss presses, wondering how on earth I could get them back into service with only a few hundred pounds of capital to my name.

At midnight it was home to the clean luxury of Toorak, four or five hours' sleep, and up again at dawn—I usually did this six or seven days a week.

Conditions at King Street remained appalling, no matter how much we tried to partition sections and clean them up. Like every old Melbourne building, ours was infested with rats. Our entertainment was to hurl pieces of type metal at rodents that appeared between the cases of hand-set type; once I managed to hit one between the eyes. We tried traps and poison, but the stench of droppings remained, especially around the tea-making corner, where crumbs dropped from sandwiches and cakes provided a nightly feast for our unwelcome visitors.

My unscarred hands became ingrained with fragments of lead, graphite and grease, which no amount of scrubbing with sandsoap would remove. Little was known about lead poisoning in those days: most of us suffered from mouth ulcers, later recognised as one of the early symptoms of excessive lead in the body. A couple of the wiser operatives would wash their hands before eating a sandwich, but most would simply handle lead slugs while picking up a cigarette for another puff, transferring minute fragments of lead to their lips, as well as smoke to their lungs. Similarly, while melting used slugs into fresh ingots, masks were never worn to filter the fumes we all breathed.

~

Teleview had attracted the attention of the Radio & Electrical Retailers' Association in Sydney. The president, a Crows Nest retailer named Ernest Tree, was anxious to break Ossie Mingay's trade publishing monopoly. I agreed to negotiate.

One of Mingay's most profitable ventures was a listing of the retail prices of all electrical products, which also acted as a trade catalogue of goods available in that market. In those times, when selling prices were fixed and rigidly enforced by manufacturers and importers, it was vital for retailers to be advised of all authorised changes. Ernie Tree's idea was for us to start a new journal called *Price News* that would fulfil the same function but more cheaply, and with his retail clout and buoyant personality, Ernie would be able to attract a fair amount of advertising from manufacturers. We would overcome the main technical problem by setting the prices on separate slugs alongside product descriptions, so that new prices could be typeset quickly, dropped in, and circulated promptly to retailers. It all seems rather pointless in today's more competitive market, but at the time the idea had commercial validity. Eventually, however, my partner and I found printing and finishing this large journal problematic. We heard of a printer at Highett who wanted to retire, so my partner agreed to leave the *Herald* and run that printery, taking *Price News* with him, while I maintained the typesetting operation at King Street.

By this time, Jack Bellew, the former publisher of *Tomorrow*, had also 'gone commercial'. Under the name Atlas Publications, he built up a large pulp publishing venture in Clifton Hill, producing a string of colour comics as well as Western and crime novelettes. He also published a somewhat more upmarket men's magazine called *Squire*, an obvious pinch from the American *Esquire*. Jack's oddball monthly concentrated on male interests but included such things as out-of-copyright short stories by Guy de Maupassant, and sophisticated cartoons clipped by Peter Bellew from contemporary French journals. Jack heard what I was doing at King Street and sent down his manager, Peter Ryan, to investigate, mainly because a large amount of typesetting was needed for the various Atlas productions. We were soon able to make arrangements that proved profitable to both sides. The reconditioned linotypes showed their worth, pouring out vast quantities of slugs from which I and a part-time compositor made up the pages.

My rapidly ageing father was now working as a clerk for the State Electricity Commission. A couple of evenings a week, he came to King Street to have dinner and refresh his keyboard skills on the machines, helping to cut through the great amount of typesetting. With the extra money he earned, he was able to buy a larger bush block to the east of Melbourne, this one with a small house on it. Whenever I could manage it, I rode up there on my motorbike for a day or a weekend. One hot summer day, we foolishly set fire to a pile of rubbish. Sparks leaped into the air and flames began to race up the hill towards a group of houses near the main road. I revved up the bike and, feeling pretty heroic, roared at high speed into Seville to summon the local fire brigade. It took them all day to extinguish the blaze.

A few weeks later, I was riding back to Melbourne at dusk in a line of traffic when a car approached from behind to pass me on a blind corner. The driver cut in suddenly to avoid an oncoming vehicle and swerved into my front wheel. We were doing about 45 miles per hour. I was knocked clean off my bike, turned a somersault in mid-air, and skidded on my backside along the bitumen highway. Few riders wore crash helmets in those days: another half-spin in the air and I would have been killed. A truck driver stopped to help, while another driver pursued the one who'd hit me but had failed to stop. (The driver was fined £15 in a court in Lilydale a few weeks later.) The truck driver took me and my bike home, where, feeling almost paralysed, I fell into bed. The next day an X-ray revealed that the coccyx bone at the end of my spine had been shattered. I could not sit down for several weeks and was forced to eat my meals off the mantelpiece. That was the end of my motorcycling: I sold the remains of the bike for £50.

Henry Drysdale was now making enough money from renting various parts of his basement to buy a smaller car than the Bentley he usually drove. He selected a revolutionary Czech sports machine called a Tatraplan, based partly on the much larger eight-cylinder Tatra but reduced to a four-cylinder design more akin to the Volkswagen. I suppose Drysdale thought he was being generous in offering to sell the £1350 car to me on low-interest terms. Indeed, for a few months I had fun at weekends taking the thing at high speed over various bush and alpine routes. But ultimately the purchase proved a disaster. At 15 000 miles, the gears started to fall to pieces, and replacement parts could not be obtained from Czechoslovakia. I sold the almost useless car at a dealer's auction for £550 and began motoring life anew as the owner of second-hand four- and six-cylinder Citroens.

~

One day in 1954, Peter Ryan came to King Street to tell me he had had a row with Jack Bellew and was quitting. Jack, meanwhile, had appointed a man named 'Robby' Robinson as manager of Atlas Publications and was casting around for someone to do the editorial work. Would I be interested? Since I still couldn't figure out how to get the rotary presses at King Street into profitable operation, I agreed. In this way, at twenty-five, I became managing editor of a pulp publishing firm. Atlas took over the typesetting operation at King Street, with the best linotype operator promoted to foreman and myself remaining in general superintendence.

Jack had done so well out of pulp publishing that he was able to buy a two-storey mansion in Queen's Parade, Clifton Hill and convert it into offices for his expanding staff. Jack himself selected comics which he thought would do well in Australia, choosing them from the vast range of overseas material offered by Yaffa Syndicate. He also commissioned a local effort called *Captain Atom*, which was well drawn and sold in reasonable numbers—about 20 000 copies of each monthly issue.

My immediate task was to increase the output of text magazines. Through Yaffa we obtained the most popular American titles, such as *Ellery Queen's Mystery Magazine*, and adapted them for the Australian public. We invited local manuscript submissions, but most were of poor quality. After being edited, the American stories were produced in stapled editions of 96–128 pages on newsprint, plus a colour cover on glossy paper, retailing at 2 shillings a copy.

They usually sold between 10 000 and 20 000 copies per title, leaving a fair margin for returns from newsagents and bookstalls.

As an experiment, I started Australia's first regular science fiction magazine, *Science Fiction Monthly*. Yaffa obtained for us the rights to reprint stories and illustrations from early issues of *Amazing Stories* and similar sources, and we included news from the growing number of science fiction clubs and fans in Australia. Unfortunately, we could not reach the 10 000 minimum sales needed to justify a print run, and the magazine ceased after about eighteen issues. I also converted an American satirical magazine called *Ballyhoo* for the Australian market, including about one-third local material, but it lasted only a year. Richard Walsh and his friends did the job much better a decade later with *Oz* magazine, successfully defying censorship laws.

Our men's magazine, *Squire*, was going through a curious period. Originally it included 'artistic' nude photographs, many of them shot locally by leading fashion photographers, and these undoubtedly led to buoyant sales. At first, the permissible definition of 'nude' was that the models' breasts could be shown but nothing below the navel. However, even this led to protests, mainly from the Roman Catholic Church. So Gordon & Gotch instituted an unofficial censorship procedure, and since they enjoyed a near-complete distribution monopoly outside the major newspaper groups, we were forced to follow their wavering dictates. Each month, I had to parcel up the pictures intended for the upcoming issue of *Squire* and take them to the city office of Fred Crystal, Gordon & Gotch's national circulation manager. Fred, steeped in Victorian rectitude, was simultaneously attracted and repelled by our images of beautiful women. In a confusion of embarrassment, he would okay photographs of the Hollywood film star type and reject those of the army pin-up type, without ever being able to clearly explain what was acceptable and what was not.

The morality campaign of the 1950s finally reached the stage where no hint of nipples were allowed—even *Truth* had to have these symbols of sexuality airbrushed from its photographs, sometimes with ludicrous results. We didn't want *Squire*, of which we were quite proud, to go down that path. I tried commissioning an excellent Melbourne artist, Wes Walters, to do a series of paintings of attractive models, more or less along the lines of the famous Varga girls who had done so much for *Esquire*'s readership. The Walters girls, printed in colour on art paper as centrespreads, began to do the same for *Squire*'s flagging sales. But they, too, worried Fred Crystal. In the end, he guiltily insisted on reducing their curves and increasing their clothing, so much so that, as our circulation again dropped, there seemed little point in continuing.

Jack Bellew had a permanent lunch table reserved in the upper dining room of Florentino at the top of Bourke Street. Almost every day we sat there gazing through a large window at the premises opposite, where couples learning the art of ballroom dancing gyrated in Arthur Murray's School of Dancing. Most of our equally circular discussions revolved around ideas for breaking into 'big time' magazine publishing. The problem was that, in any field, we would be competing with the large newspaper groups, which controlled practically all mass-printing and distribution facilities. Finally, we evolved a scheme to buy local rights to the American *Family Circle* magazine, 'Australianise' it, print it in colour on cheap paper, and distribute it at sixpence a copy through pharmacies instead of newsagents.

The president of the Pharmaceutical Guild was Eric Scott, my stepfather's cousin. He agreed to the distribution scheme, believing that magazine sales would bring extra customer traffic into the shops of his several thousand members. Also on side was the old-time *Argus* journalist Keith Attiwill, who was in charge of public relations for the guild. And on hearing of the deal, Frank Packer became interested too, to the extent of agreeing to print the magazine each month at his rotogravure plant in Alexandria, which in those days produced the *Women's Weekly*. On the editorial side, we were advised by 'George' Warnecke, a sixty-year-old journalist who had achieved stunning success with the *Women's Weekly* after he and Frank Packer had started the journal in 1933. I assumed the grand title of editor-in-chief, while as editor we employed the experienced Melbourne journalist Elizabeth Auld, followed by Marjorie McNeece. The art director, an important position in a new type of magazine, was Frank Eidlitz, whose modern design work had won him many accolades in the advertising world. George Stokes drummed up enough colour advertising for us to be able to launch the first issue in November 1955.

Family Circle purveyed a romanticised version of domestic life. The ideal family was seen to consist of a dominant male breadwinner and a subservient wife who stayed at home to care for—frugally but lovingly—the couple's two or three children. Our short stories, usually by English or American writers, were based on the heroine who had to decide between two outstanding men of different types, both of whom were anxious to marry her: our very first story was entitled 'The Heart Must Decide'. Factual articles warned that 'emotional maturity' was necessary for a successful marriage. One of our most popular picture-strips showed how 'normal' babies should look and behave during each stage of development. Also included were the usual features on new films, astrology, teenage problems, beauty tips, cooking, patterns, medical advice and the like. George Warnecke's only complaint was that the magazine was not 'personalised' enough. I attempted to remedy that with an 'Inner Circle' page of snippets by Ida Elizabeth Jenkins, a well-known radio commentator.

The magazine sold reasonably well, considering that we had almost no spare funds or facilities for widespread promotion. However, we were really competing for readers' sixpences against the gigantic success of the *Women's Weekly*, a fat colour tabloid which even then sold more than 800 000 copies every week. Our best circulation was about 160 000: anything we did editorially, the *Weekly* could do far better. From all points of view, it was easy to sell advertising space in the *Weekly*, but difficult to win it for *Family Circle*. Even *Woman's Day*, at that time edited by Cyril Pearl and published by the Melbourne *Herald* group, outstripped our puny efforts. The losses on *Family Circle* soon began to drag down the previously profitable pulp business. After a year of constant effort and disappointment, I felt I should resign and give someone else a chance to put it right. Unfortunately, Jack Bellew then fell seriously ill and died. His widow and Marjorie McNeece tried to carry on the business but it was too far gone, and after a few months it went into liquidation. *Family Circle* had killed the golden goose.

~

During the hectic early 1950s, I was so busy working twelve to sixteen hours practically every day that I had few relationships, of any kind, with women. Business was run almost exclusively by men, and drinking and mateship were male activities. Ambition seemed to sublimate most sexual longing: occasional night-time fantasies occurred, but usually I slept soundly in deep exhaustion. I had one brief affair with a woman in her thirties whose main concern seemed to be that, when making love, we should at all costs avoid handling each other's genital areas. Her ex-husband had insisted on this, and she felt impelled to pass on the puritanical tradition. Love, even lust, seemed to have passed me by.

And then it happened, blasting out of a clear blue sky. Here was I, a hardworking young man in his mid-twenties, and still unmarried. Girls of similar age, friends of sisters or family, old school acquaintances, they could not stand it. I was invited to various dances and parties, which were obviously part of the mating game but of little interest to me. Still, very occasionally I accepted an invitation. In one of those rare episodes, I went to a party in Melbourne's eastern suburbs, and there she was.

Don't ever believe there is no such thing as love at first sight. Immediately I began talking to a tall blonde named Susan, I knew that we would be married, and I am sure she felt the same way. All that I can recall of that moment are the waves of electricity that seemed to flow back and forth between us, accompanied on my part by an overwhelming desire to take her in my arms there and then. We left the party early, scarcely even making farewells, and spent most of the night hugging and kissing and murmuring to each other in my car as it sat parked on a quiet stretch of Yarra Boulevard.

At twenty-one, Susan Neville Ussher was in her final year of training as a nurse at the Alfred Hospital: soon after we met, she topped the state in her nursing exams. But work suddenly diminished in importance. We were in the grip of nature's biological imperatives and spent every possible moment together. I had never felt so close to anyone.

A common interest, which reinforced our own longings, was found in romantic light classical music. The 1950s saw the introduction of long-playing (LP) vinyl records which went around at 33 revolutions per minute instead of 78 rpm. This enabled most compositions to be contained on one or two sides of each LP. The World Record Club exploited the new technology to the full: every month we eagerly awaited their new catalogue and bought one or two records. Practically every family invested in the new type of record player that was fitted with a diamond stylus, which overcame the problem of constantly changing the steel or bamboo needles required to play the old 78s. The musical result, although possibly inferior to today's technology, was a major advance which seemed to bring the world's best orchestras and singers into the living room, on demand. This, before television, was our main form of escapism, and the method by which dreams of eternal love were stimulated.

I was living alone in a flat in the bayside suburb of Elwood. Susan and I walked endlessly along the magic moonlit beach, which had previously seemed so ordinary, before returning to my place for food and cuddles. We even went to bed together, but not in the way it is understood today. Susan whispered the confession that she had had difficulty preserving her virginity against the onslaughts of medical students and doctors, in fact had nearly been raped in a car after one outing. In the accepted way of the times, she was determined to obey parental precepts and go to the altar a virgin.

One time, after Susan had finished her nursing course and was living back at the family home, we went on a winter car trip to Woods Point, a small town on the Goulburn River to the east of Melbourne. We were delayed in the snow and did not return until 3 a.m. Her parents' house was ablaze with lights: they were anxiously pacing the floor, having already phoned the police and hospitals. Perhaps they secretly believed that we had gone and 'done it', as relations remained strained for some days. A midnight curfew was set for future outings.

Although Susan's aged grandmother muttered darkly that no good could come from any relationship with the son of divorced parents, Susan and I were married in March 1955, in Holy Trinity Church in Kew. I had carefully prepared for this important occasion by changing our Citroen's engine oil, fitting a shooter's spotlight, and buying a .303 rifle with a few hundred bullets, so that, if we felt like it, we could spend our honeymoon blasting crocodiles somewhere in northern Queensland. I leave it to psychologists to explain this weird ambition. Immediately after the ceremony, we got into our car and headed north at high speed towards our first stopping point, the chalet at Mount Buffalo.

The consummation of our long-suppressed desires began with a near-fiasco. On my previous visit to Mount Buffalo Chalet when at boarding school, the building had seemed a haven of luxury. Now, despite the fact that I had booked one of its best double rooms, it seemed grubby, with a general atmosphere of decayed gentility, on top of which our dinner was almost inedible. That night, Susan was in her nightgown and in bed before I could even see her body. A feeling of mutual embarrassment, almost of fear, seemed to envelop us. We kissed fiercely and tried to drive away these negative feelings. Yet her body, which had once seemed to melt into an accommodating shape, was now tense and stiff. As for mine, it was unresponsive. After half an hour of bewildering effort, and increasing feelings of humiliation and inferiority, I began to shed tears of dismay. What ghastly mistake had we made? But when she saw that

I, too, was in anguish, Susan's attitude changed at once. She became protective and maternal. Her body softened, and she held my face to her breast, saying over and over, 'It doesn't matter, it doesn't matter.' Then, amazingly, we were passionately as one. We spent all night wrapped in each other's arms. In the morning, as we looked shyly but lovingly into each other's eyes, the bedroom and the rest of the chalet seemed to have been transformed into a wonderland. Trite, I suppose, but unforgettable.

We then drove over frightful back roads via Yackandandah and Albury, to finally arrive at a hotel facing Bondi Beach. Just as we arrived, the front-wheel-drive mechanism of the Citroen collapsed and the car had to be towed to the nearest garage. All of our belongings—including the suspicious-looking rifle wrapped in a large towel—had to be taken by taxi to the hotel. That was as far north as we got, the planned slaughter of crocodiles averted. It mattered not. We were in a quiet part of that old-fashioned hotel, and a million miles from the world's daily concerns, revelling in the discovery of each other's sexuality and the intimate confessions that come from the merging of two bodies and souls. After days in the surf, and evenings devoted to food, music and wine, we were ready again most nights to see how far the limits of sensuality could be pushed. What had begun as a disastrous honeymoon turned into a private triumph.

We began househunting on our return to Melbourne. Housing supply had not caught up with the cessation of building during the war, and we were anxious to find something more spacious than the minimum-sized standardised boxes being built in suburban streets. In a further rush of romantic longing, we answered an advertisement to rent a bush cottage near Eltham. This turned out to be located on the Yarra River farm of Dr Donald Thomson, a noted anthropologist whom I had once interviewed for the *Age*. The property was guarded by a couple of half-starved loping Irish wolfhounds, and maintained largely by Thomson's youthful second wife, who on one occasion had thought nothing of swimming in the Yarra while pregnant in order to rescue a boat swept away in a flood. The main house was decorated with Aboriginal artefacts. The cottage itself, a few hundred metres away, was pretty rough but liveable. When Thomson agreed to have electricity connected to the abode, we promptly moved in our belongings. When nothing had happened after several weeks, we moved everything out again.

My father died at about this time. He had earlier lost all hope of reconciliation with my mother and married his landlady, moving with her to the outer reaches of Toorak Road, Burwood, where she ran a lending library while my father drove to work each day to the State Electricity Commission at Lilydale. He had suffered from a duodenal ulcer ever since his air force days, with ignorance of dietary factors making it progressively worse, until finally he was diagnosed with cancer of the stomach. An operation seemed to save his life, but he continued to go downhill. We last saw him at the Epworth Hospital in Richmond, his once bulky body diminished to about 70 pounds. Frightened and repelled by my first sight of imminent death, I could do no more than take his hand and stroke his forehead. 'It's goodbye, son,' he whispered. Susan was much more used to death than I. She cradled his head and kissed him lovingly, making up for my strained attitude.

Susan and I continued searching for a house in the Eltham area, finally discovering a cottage on a large block near the top of a hill in Montmorency. The house was a simple self-built construction of weatherboard and asbestos–cement sheets, but it was the best we could do on a £500 deposit. At least it was ours: we were young and vigorous, appreciated the clean country air, and could stand the often-freezing climate.

Inside, the house seemed rather dank. I discovered after we moved in that the 'drains' were merely earthen channels dug under the house that had become blocked with green scum. So I carted in glazed pipes and cement and built drains that emptied kitchen waste into an open gutter in our unmade street—in the outer suburbs in those days, few people bothered to apply for council permission or employ a qualified plumber. The next problem was the smelly outside dunny, which was festooned with dusty spider webs. My stepfather sent out a couple of men from his shoe factory, who dug a large hole for a septic tank and connected a flushing toilet situated on our enclosed back porch. Again, we didn't trouble the council with plans or permits. My enjoyable contribution was to smash down the old asbestos–cement dunny with an axe, squash the tarantulas and red-backs, and set fire to the lot.

Meanwhile, Susan had become pregnant. She enjoyed an easy and peaceful pregnancy. In April 1956, when the contractions began, we drove hurriedly into St Andrews Hospital in Melbourne, where our son Paul was born. From the start he was a happy, healthy, extroverted child, rather like me around the eyes, but with his mother's blonde colouring and the pronounced grandpaternal family jawline.

~

After quitting *Family Circle*, I had to look around again for an income. Robby Robinson, the one-time manager of Atlas Publications, was now working for the publisher of a rag-trade journal called *Clothing News*. By coincidence, he too lived at Montmorency. A likeable and honest fellow, he suggested that we go into partnership to start a superior type of fashion trade journal, one that would adopt an independent editorial policy rather than kowtow to advertisers, and generally win us fame, fortune etc.

Robby had a reasonable asset in the form of his house, which he had built himself on a large block of land. I had almost no money left, but my stepfather agreed to guarantee a £1500 overdraft. On that frail capital base, we registered a business under the name Australian Fashion News. Robby was to do all the legwork, selling advertising space and gathering material. I was to be the editor, which meant selecting the best press releases and photographs, which poured in from manufacturers, and trying to write objective stories about textile tariffs and other general matters. Who was to typeset, make up and print the journal? After getting some fearfully expensive prices for printing it on glossy paper, I decided to do it myself out of the double garage attached to my house. We lined this to keep out dust and damp, while a friendly electrician illegally installed a large single-phase meter board.

While all this was happening, the *Argus* had been swallowed up by the *Herald*—in January 1957—and ceased publication. From the vast range of *Argus* equipment on offer, I selected a Model 48 linotype with three magazines full of useful fonts. This was one of their most modern machines, called a mixer because you could set roman, italic and bold typefaces on the same slug, after which the machine would automatically distribute the matrixes through a complex mechanism back into their correct magazines. This beautiful machine I bought for £500, about a tenth of its true value. Meanwhile, a printer friend at *Truth* told us they were replacing a Model 6 Miehle flatbed letter-press printing machine in their jobbing section. This we got for £600: the heavy machine would print solid blacks on glossy paper. It was designed to work on three-phase power, of which there was none in our residential area, so we were forced to buy a gigantic 5-horsepower single-phase motor to turn the press over. Every time we switched it on, the lights in the surrounding streets went dim, and the few black-and-white TV sets in the district went crazy.

Apart from such annoyances, everything proceeded smoothly enough. It was almost like being back in the basement of the *Radio Times* building, except that I was only a few metres' walk away from the house where my wife was nursing our small son. Occasionally she would bring him in her arms to the shed full of clacking machinery, no doubt wondering what strange sort of person she had married.

I had no way of making new metal ingots for the linotype, so I simply cleaned the used slugs with kerosene and put them straight back in the machine's own small melting pot, with no harmful effects. The linotype, being almost new, tinkled out fresh slugs at high speed. I used a few fonts of new handset type for headings and made up the large pages and advertisements with ease. We bought glossy printing paper by the ream from various wholesalers, saving the cost of transport by loading it into Robby's 1926 Essex sedan or my Citroen with the rear seats folded down, the neighbours nodding sadly as they saw each fresh load arrive. At press time, the *Truth* printer came out (at 10 shillings an hour) and helped me to master the quirks of the gallant old Miehle, where great care had to be taken with the quality of photographic reproduction. After printing, we loaded the large sheets back into our cars and took them to a city bindery for folding, stapling and trimming.

The rag trade, then based mainly in Flinders Lane, took some persuading that it needed to spend £50 a page on advertising in our publication. Robby turned out not to be the hot-shot salesman required to open the purse strings of these shrewd, miserly, often emotional manufacturers and agents. Consequently, after several issues, most of our capital was gone, and outstanding accounts that meant the difference between profit and loss began to look rather dodgy. I wanted to press on to the limit, but Robby was more nervous, so we agreed to finalise the partnership. I spent the last of my savings and overdraft buying his share at cost price, and I then employed a professional advertising salesman on commission and began to print the next issue. Fresh misfortune lay in store for my little bush printery, however. My neighbours became so incensed at the interruptions to their TV programs that they complained to the local council, which served me with a notice ordering immediate closure.

One door closes, another door opens. Alan Maller, a compositor who had built up the large Excelsior Printing Works in Hawthorn, heard of my difficulties and wanted to know if he could purchase *Fashion News*. This seemed a good way out, especially since, on top of everything else, I had little interest in the fashion and textile industries. Alan paid enough to discharge all the debts and the overdraft, plus £800 for the linotype. I sold the press and ancillary equipment to another suburban printery.

My next employment was as an account executive in the peculiar field of professional advertising. Peter Ryan got me the job after being appointed assistant director of United Service Publicity, an advertising agency formed by several ex-servicemen which had developed into one of Australia's biggest agencies. My first task was to help promote a new line of refrigerators being produced by the Australian offshoot of a large American company. Up to this time, refrigerators had been manufactured with a bulbous exterior and rounded top, but some clever American had had the idea of cutting these down to a 'sheerline' design with a rectangular side and flat top, and offering consumers a choice of colours. For our photographs, attractive models would open the fridge door, pretending to be typical housewives. Mechanically, the fridges remained practically the same: badly designed and jerry-built, so they would break down after a few years of use. This, I was told, was 'selling the sizzle, not the steak'.

After some rather shameful success in this endeavour, I was put onto drafting ideas and writing copy for Shell, the multinational petroleum company, in an attempt to prove that Shell petrol was the best and that the service at Shell-owned stations was incomparable. Car engines were typically inefficient, polluting the atmosphere and depositing quantities of unburned minerals on top of the pistons, which required expensive decoking every so often. So we claimed that Shell burned 'cleaner' than any other brand, even though we had no technical research I was aware of to support the claim. No consumers' association existed to carry out independent tests, and government seemed totally uninterested. Many manufacturers got away with wild, unsupportable exaggerations in their advertising.

Work became more interesting when I was given the job of promoting the products of Electronic Industries, which produced a large range of Astor TV and radio sets under an agreement with Pye. The best thing I ever did for that company was to rewrite my old *Radio Times* articles into a booklet called *How Television Works*, which was given free to every buyer of its TV sets. But again I became disillusioned with the way in which we were told to produce press advertisements, selecting some minor technical feature of the sets, inventing some grandiloquent name for it, and claiming it as an 'exclusive' breakthrough giving superior reception. In fact, all TV sets were pretty much the same, with reception depending more on location and a good aerial than any brand's alleged technical advantages.

~

One night early in October 1957, our little family stood by the front fence in Montmorency gazing into the clear starlit sky. I had one arm around Susan's waist, and in the other I held our sturdy eighteen-month-old son. We were waiting for one of the most amazing events of the century. Suddenly, low on the horizon, we saw the first Soviet Sputnik satellite carving a majestic path across the heavens. Not just us but everyone we spoke to later felt presentiments of a new age dawning. Surely, this time, humanity would know how to forge a better era for itself, the earth, the universe! Once again I swore to do everything I could to help cure the world's ills.

As part of the upwardly mobile process in which we all tried to participate, Susan and I contracted to buy a superior new house being built down in Beaumaris, on the eastern shoreline of Port Phillip Bay. As it faced golf courses on two sides and was reasonably near the beach, it seemed to offer something better than cramped suburban living. With improvements to the cottage at Montmorency, we were able to sell it for a good price, pay a substantial deposit on the new house, and still have some money left over. Was the capitalist system as bad as I had assumed?

By the beginning of 1959, I was ready to make a new bid for freedom, free speech, truth and a better life for all. Naturally, this would take the form of a publication in which no holds would be barred, and the Cannon version of reality would be seen as the correct medication for the ills of humanity. At a cost of £2, I registered the name Newsday Publications. Office-sharing arrangements were made with a friendly photographer, Michael Jackson. In his small studio and darkroom, a converted brick stable behind number 7 Collins Street in Melbourne's CBD, he took messages for me and I did the same for him when he was absent. We cooperated on photographic jobs, the result of which was a standard of magazine photography that still looks good today. To help us cut production costs on our new publication *Newsday*, Alan Maller allowed me to use the *Argus* linotype I had sold him, as well as a Ludlow machine on which bigger headings could be cast on lead slugs. He would print the first two issues of *Newsday* on his biggest letterpress machine, while Gordon & Gotch agreed to handle wholesale distribution to newsagents.

By March, the first issue was ready. It was small, a sixteen-page stapled tabloid on glossy paper, but it contained plenty of reading matter because I did not bother trying to sell any advertising space. Aiming high, we printed 20 000 copies, to sell at a retail price of 2 shillings. The editorial content was considered quite radical in those conservative days. *Newsday* attacked the Taxation Department for levying several hundred pounds' tax on repatriations paid to former inmates of Nazi concentration camps who were now living in Australia. The first piece in a series called 'Architectural Monstrosities' criticised the aluminium Sidney Myer Music Bowl, which was being built on a previously tree-covered slice of the Kings Domain parklands. An Aboriginal schoolteacher complained about the half-guinea fee she had to pay to register as a citizen of Australia. The Police Department gave us horrifying pictures of bodies lying scattered after a road smash, which the daily papers refused to publish—we lashed their motoring writers for not telling the truth about the badly designed machines being produced by Ford and General Motors. In an echo of Sputnik, a professor at the Jodrell Bank Observatory in England had written an article entitled 'The Incredible Universe'. An Australian professor of a more naive type, Manning Clark, was taken to task for letting himself be hoodwinked on his visit to the Russia of Stalin and Khrushchev, after which he'd written a nonsensical series of articles for the *Age* about the 'cultural renascence' inspired by the Bolshevik revolution.

Newsday's lead story was even more provocative. By extraordinary good luck, the American Baptist evangelist Billy Graham was about to begin an emotion-ridden Australian crusade designed for the showy public repentance of guilt-stricken souls. Across its front page, *Newsday* plastered the slogan 'BILLY GRAHAM GO HOME', followed by a strong article advising him to 'pack his carpet-bag'. Australians, we said, did not need to be sold religion by the same methods by which soap was marketed. The Billy Graham article attracted widespread attention and was reprinted throughout the world. Newspapers as far away as Boston and South Carolina printed cables about *Newsday*'s stand and gave American reactions. Our inaugural issue was a sellout, and we even showed a small profit.

Encouraged, I foolishly decided to double the size of the second issue, keeping the price at 2 shillings but increasing the print run by a few thousand copies. This meant endless hours occupied by gathering information and contributions, then spending every weekend setting it in type. My long-suffering wife and small son were left almost alone in our Beaumaris house while I lived on sandwiches and adrenalin.

The new issue led with the story of how RG Menzies had outmanoeuvred Stanley Bruce, Billy Hughes and Earle Page to become the conservative pre-war prime minister, but had then left Australia almost defenceless to face Japanese attacks during World War II. Other journalists around Australia had seemed to like the first issue of *Newsday*, and the editorial burden was now lightened as they sent in contributions not considered suitable by their own papers. One who had followed the adventures of the actress Ava Gardner contributed an amusing assessment of her flamboyant activities on and off the set of the film *On the Beach*. We warned against the dangers of subliminal advertising, and congratulated Western Australia on its introduction of Australia's first anti-monopolies law.

From the office of *Fashion News*, editor Don Joinson wrote a long, anonymous attack on flaws in the promotional policies of the Australian Wool Bureau, then being run by William Gunn.

Joinson's comments on the bureau's ineptitude and waste of woolgrowers' funds seemed fair enough, and soundly based on inside knowledge. But in the rush to produce the enlarged second issue, I failed to notice one sentence that in effect alleged that a secret commission had been paid by one advertising agent to another during a change of agencies. *Newsday* number 2 had been on the streets for only a couple of days, and was selling very well, when a writ for libel arrived at the old stables off Collins Street—one of the agents had decided to sue for damages, although the other individuals named kept very quiet indeed.

A few hours later, a phone call came from Gordon & Gotch to say that they, too, had received a writ, and that, under the circumstances—but without giving me a chance to try and show that the allegations were substantially true and in the public interest—they had decided to withdraw the current issue from sale. Gordon & Gotch duly sent a circular to every newsagent in Australia worded as follows: 'Agents are requested to withdraw from sale IMMEDIATELY the April issue of NEWSDAY and return to this office without delay.' The result was that the writ against Gordon & Gotch was withdrawn and about 17 000 copies were returned. This was almost ruinous, for I still had to pay the printer, and it was impossible to redistribute the dated copies in order to get some income. After much bitter argument, Gordon & Gotch paid me for copies sold, and I was left to consider what to do next.

I searched around for a tough solicitor to fight the libel case, hoping that the publicity would boost future issues of *Newsday*. I was referred to Ray Dunn, who told me that an unsuccessful court case could cost me the family home and even lead to bankruptcy. Nonetheless, I decided to proceed. Thankfully, he was a brutal negotiator and bullied the opposing side into settling privately for £50. His bill totalled another £50, which I paid with gratitude.

I also found a way to continue the magazine. Many years earlier, the Fitchett brothers had established a small printing and publishing outfit in West Melbourne called Southdown Press. It possessed an almost-worn-out web-fed letterpress machine, worse even than the *Radio Times* plant, on which it printed *New Idea*, *TV Week* and a racing form guide. The boss, an old journalist named Bill Bednall, was happy to take on *Newsday* to help fill up his press and distribution facilities. Alan Maller continued to allow me the use of his typesetting plant, so it was back to the old days, transporting heavy, made-up pages of lead to Southdown Press for stereotyping and printing. Bill's plant was also capable of making the zinc halftone plates necessary for photographic reproduction, and his charges were quite low. In this way I was able to carry on for a few months.

In issue number 3, I headlined the claim that this was 'The Paper They Can't Suppress!', and I reprinted the Gordon & Gotch circular to newsagents which had nearly put *Newsday* out of business. I admitted that the journal had 'not achieved much so far', but asserted it might one day 'be the kind of newspaper that Australians will be able to point to with pride as being among the great newspapers of the world'. Some hope!

The author David Martin began writing for us, pleading for such books as Brendan Behan's *Borstal Boy* to be unbanned by the repressive Menzies regime; he also wrote the first-ever exposé of the Scientology racket. We had another large-selling issue with number 5 (I had learned the hard way not to put a date on issues), in which we published the first extensive biography of BA Santamaria and 'the Movement' that had shattered Labor's chances of regaining power. We simply couldn't get enough copies to supply bookstalls near St Francis and other Roman Catholic churches. Yet the following issue, with Reginald Ansett on the cover, did very poorly, selling only 8000 copies out of the 20 000 printed. We could not maintain this boom–bust cycle—*Newsday*'s run would soon end.

~

During these crises, Susan helped support the family fortunes by working part-time at night as a nurse at Wahroonga Private Hospital in Sandringham. She had also fallen pregnant in the summer of 1959, and we were both looking forward to the birth of our second child in October. But midway through the pregnancy, she suffered a sudden haemorrhage and had to stop working. Her usual doctor was overseas, so she was examined instead by another doctor who put her into St Andrew's Hospital, where she seemed to recover. After ten days I went in to take her home, but just as we were about to leave she collapsed on the floor in a pool of blood. An emergency operation was performed and the pregnancy terminated. Doctors in those days didn't attempt to explain underlying causes, even when the patient was a senior nurse. We were simply assured that Susan would be all right after a further spell in hospital, and that future pregnancies should be trouble-free.

I think it now best that I quote from a deposition which I had to make later that year:

> After leaving hospital my wife had been prescribed sleeping sedatives and she had tried to reduce the dosage over a period, with varying degrees of success ... Sometimes she was all right, but other times quite depressed. Periodically she attended [a doctor] after leaving the hospital for tests and examination. She suffered insomnia ... on occasions only sleeping one night in three.
>
> Late in July 1959 my wife was reading one of her nursing textbooks and read a description of a 'mole', which was described as a cancerous growth on the foetus, and considered it to be the complaint that had caused her to lose the baby in June. She showed me the textbook and stated that she was now fully aware of the trouble. Shortly after ... she stated that the doctor had given her a clearance from any cancer complaint, but she was worried that it may recur in future children.
>
> During August and early September the condition of my wife in respect to the insomnia had improved, but she still seemed under tension ... About the end of August my wife and I went

to Surfers' Paradise, and during that time she seemed very much improved, and on our return she seemed to sleep one night in two.

After we returned from the holiday we sold our house at Beaumaris as it was on a busy road and the traffic affected her sleep. We arranged to move into my parents' home in Hopetoun Road, Toorak, during their absence overseas ... My wife was quite happy at the idea of selling our home and staying at Toorak, and was in good spirits on the 20th September.

On the morning of Monday 21 September, I woke up at about 7.30 a.m. and turned towards Susan. She was lying on her back, staring at the ceiling but with a distant, glazed look in her eyes. I asked her how she felt and she said she had not slept at all. Still drowsy, it didn't occur to me that she might have been worse than usual. I got up, had a shower and shave, and dressed. On my way back to our bedroom, our little boy called out, 'Someone's taken the car.' When I went downstairs, I found a piece of paper torn from a spiral notebook, with a seven-line pencilled note:

> Goodbye my darling
> & God bless
> forgive me for what
> I'm doing to you
> The car will be
> at the Auburn railway
> gates

Forgive? She did not need my forgiveness. I needed hers, for not realising the truly desperate nature of her depression. Gasping and trembling, I rang the police radio centre, which had a car close to Auburn. But by the time they got there, it was too late—Susan, still in her dressing gown, had thrown herself under a train.

I had just enough strength left to phone her father. He, poor man, would have driven past the scene to get to Toorak, but I never dared ask him what he had seen. When he arrived, I simply threw myself into his arms and wept on his shoulder.

The succeeding days were an agonised blur. My mother immediately flew back home from overseas to help look after our son. Susan's father arranged for her clothes to be taken away and burned, so that we would not be stricken by these reminders of her. The funeral seemed to be attended by hundreds of relatives and friends—I spent the whole time bathed in tears and sunk in dark depression.

Later, my mother did her best to jerk me out of it, saying, 'You've got to carry on, for the boy's sake.' That helped a bit. Yet all of my easy optimism had vanished. If an innocent woman and beloved wife could be struck down like this at the age of twenty-five, what was the point of anything? As for myself, now aged thirty, my life seemed to be finished too, my heart slashed and interred with her remains in the family grave at Box Hill Cemetery. During the service, the grave had seemed a vast, black, echoing cavern into which I wanted to fling myself, to be buried on top of her coffin, forever clawing at the lid and seeking a final embrace.

There she lies still, eternally beautiful and uniquely courageous, like all who die young. We who are left behind must watch as, year by year, our skin slowly crumbles, our strength seeps away, our eyes become dim, our memories assume gigantic shapes. When I finally let go this clutch on life, there will not be many left who remember my Susan. Those who read this, please recall that love once walked free in this world, and it fought against every monstrous thing that ever was. Now my soul is purged of youthful guilts, and goes soaring with hers once more towards the stars. Forced to return for the time being to earthly concerns, I rely on the firm promise of the Book of Revelation:

> And God shall wipe away all tears from their eyes;
> and there shall be no more death, neither sorrow,
> nor crying, neither shall there be any more pain:
> for the former things are passed away.

PART III

LIFE REVISITED

CHAPTER 7

Reckless Rupert and Other High-Flyers

Ambition is the only power that combats love.

Colley Cibber, *Caesar in Egypt*, Act I

EVERYTHING HENCEFORTH HAD an edge of darkness, but life, and the ability to struggle against its crises, always begins again. For me, after a hellish couple of weeks, that meant a painful climb out of the grave and a slow return to 'normal' life. This was greatly assisted by my mother, who helped look after my son, then three and a half. Many years later, he would tell me that he could remember nothing at all of this period: not even me sitting on his bed and hugging him and telling him that God had called to his mother and that she was now living with the angels. He was surrounded by love, material assets and a series of doting foster-mothers. It could have been much worse.

In the wake of the *Newsday* debacle, Alan Maller offered me a job back on *Fashion News*. This was still being edited by Don Joinson, who had made a great success of the journal, transforming it into a glossy production of 100 tabloid pages each month, with square binding that enabled colour sections to be incorporated into mailings to retail buyers. Now Don was planning an even more ambitious project: a down-to-earth journal to be called *Australian Fashion & Beauty*, intended to compete with *Vogue Australia*. So I became editor of *Fashion News* again while Don concentrated on the new magazine.

The huge workload proved helpful. As 'beauty editor' of his new journal, Don chose a model I had occasionally seen at functions, whom I will call Joan. She was rather tall, blonde, athletic, and with high cheekbones which made her one of Athol Shmith's favourite photographic models. Joan made little secret of the fact that she was attracted to me. God knows why—it was one of fate's ironies that I should edit a leading fashion journal. We progressed from cups of coffee to dinners at Maxim's in Toorak, which I could barely afford, to long conversations in her nearby flat. She had a shrewd brain as well as a glamorous exterior.

One day Joan announced that she was going to take a bath. 'Why don't you have one too?' she suggested. A bath in the middle of the day! What kind of strange behaviour was this? I said no thanks, but she left the bathroom door open and I could hear her splashing about. As she dried herself, I saw an occasional flash of naked limbs. Then she walked out, with her blonde hair piled high on top of her head, wearing only a bath towel, and with a questioning smile on her face. I took her in my arms and kissed her. The towel slipped away and she led me into the bedroom.

For me it was a return to sensuality, to a level of desire I thought had vanished forever, accompanied by a healing force which felt as though my heart and mind and soul were being bathed in exotic balm. It helped greatly to keep me from the abyss into which I might easily have fallen. And this only a few months after the death of my beloved first wife! No doubt some relatives were shocked, but I was simply fortunate, and deeply grateful to a woman who had appeared out of nowhere to save me from endless, damaging grief.

In the interests of social history, I must record that it was Joan who introduced me to the idea of male deodorants. The average urban male who changed his clothes every day and showered each morning—especially if he used Lifebuoy soap to help prevent BO—considered that he was reasonably inoffensive. The advent of non-iron, synthetic-fibre shirts changed all that. After a hot day in such a shirt, people stank so badly they could even recognise it themselves. Just to save the labour of ironing cotton shirts, men were forced into the woman's world of underarm spray or roll-on deodorants. I must say the world has had a better aroma ever since.

~

Cyril Pearl, a legend among radical journalists, had watched the struggles of *Newsday* with wry sympathy. He was one of the outstanding writers on the Melbourne *Star*, which the *Argus* published from 1933–36 in a vain attempt to break the *Herald* monopoly of the evening newspaper field. When the *Star* collapsed, Frank Packer gave Cyril a job on the Sydney *Daily Telegraph*, then appointed him founding editor of the *Sunday Telegraph* late in 1939. Under Cyril, the Sunday edition was the best newspaper published in Australia. Every page packed a punch, jammed full of genuine news, humour and iconoclastic comment. Cyril was at his best in April 1944, when federal information minister Arthur Calwell used his wartime powers to censor items critical of his administration. Cyril attempted to publish his paper with blank spaces, but even this was considered illegal, and most copies were confiscated at gunpoint by federal police, caught on camera by *Telegraph* photographers.

After ten years of success with the *Sunday Telegraph*, Cyril was backed by Frank Packer in publishing a fascinating magazine called *A.M.* (*Australian Monthly*), intended to encourage the best in Australian creative talent. Unfortunately, Cyril aimed well above the potential market, and after five years of losses, *A.M.* faded away. He then helmed *Woman's Day*, a rotogravure Herald & Weekly Times magazine meant to compete with Packer's enormously successful *Women's Weekly*—his trainee journalists included my sister

Dina Cannon, and a woman who would come to play a big role in my life, Kerry Pearce.

Sir Keith Murdoch's only son Rupert now enters our narrative. By the end of the 1950s, Rupert had mastered the newspaper trade through his inheritance of the Adelaide *News* and Southdown Press, bequeathed to him as part of his father's estate. At the time I first met him, in May 1960, the empire consisted of the *Mirror* papers in Sydney; the Sunday *Truth* in Brisbane; *Truth*, *TV Week* and *New Idea* in Melbourne; the *News* and half the *Sunday Mail* in Adelaide; the *Sunday Times* in Perth; and a number of minor publications and radio stations. He had the makings of a national daily newspaper chain, a Sunday newspaper chain, and a national magazine chain, an astonishing achievement for a man so young—barely thirty years of age. He became admired and hated almost in the same breath, and struck me as a curious mixture of quixotic idealism and ruthless entrepreneurial genius.

When Rupert Murdoch first moved to Sydney, he left the old cadre of crime and sex specialists in charge of the sensationalistic *Daily Mirror*. With the *Sunday Mirror*, however, he decided to experiment with an upmarket formula, partly because the opposition's more respectable *Sun-Herald* and *Sunday Telegraph* controlled most of the retail advertising directed to middle-class households, especially North Shore customers. To achieve this transformation, Rupert appointed Cyril Pearl as editor of the *Sunday Mirror*, leaving it to him to select his own staff—which was when Cyril first rang me.

Curiously, although our paths often crossed, I had never spoken to Cyril. Now, I found myself having an extended, wine-drenched feast at the old Society Restaurant in Bourke Street, which continued long after the waiters had turned off most of the lights. Cyril must have been satisfied: he offered me the job of associate editor, which I accepted instantly. A few days later I was interviewed in a dingy office at Southdown Press by Murdoch himself, who ground his teeth in quiet despair when told that Cyril had offered me the princely salary of £60 a week—at that time the basic wage was about £15, a figure more to Rupert's liking.

A strange interregnum followed. Ever since he'd taken over the *Mirror* interests, Rupert had been considering closing down the wild Melbourne tabloid *Truth*, largely at the behest of his highly respected mother, Dame Elisabeth. Cyril suggested that it would be preferable to convert *Truth* into a more generally acceptable type of weekly paper, probably a weekend review published on Friday or Saturday, since Sunday newspapers were forbidden by law in Melbourne at that time. At a meeting in early July 1960, Rupert accepted the idea that I should oversee this enterprise as acting managing editor, with assistance from Cyril before he went to Sydney. This would enable the *Sunday Mirror* to work in tandem with the new Melbourne weekly and enjoy a considerable interchange of suitable news and features.

Jeff Utting, the editor of Melbourne *Truth*, was understandably alarmed to learn that his favourite blend of crime, sex, racing tips and rumour was to be supplanted by a family-oriented newspaper. It was with considerable reluctance that he provided an office and a pile of layout sheets so that Cyril and I could work out a formula for the new paper. Meanwhile, Utting complained privately to Murdoch that the newcomers were about to ruin a valuable property, losing untold thousands of readers by dropping the midweek racing tips. So in mid-July, Murdoch summoned Utting and myself to Sydney, where he declared that Utting had given valuable service to the company and 'had to have his chance too'. At a further conference in Melbourne a few days later, Murdoch announced without consultation that an ex-*Herald* journalist, Lyle Cousland, would become editorial director of a revamped *Truth*, Jeff Utting would remain as editor, and I would revert to the original plan of accompanying Cyril to Sydney.

Cyril somehow persuaded me, as well as his long-suffering wife, that Rupert had good motives for these decisions. Certainly the trumpets had sounded for Cyril: at fifty-four, he was eager to re-enter the arena where his greatest journalistic years had been spent. We were farewelled with a riotous whisky breakfast in front of a blazing log fire at the Ryan household in Armadale, where Peter enjoyed himself by making gloomy prognostications about my future. I then drove to Sydney in a non-stop twelve-hour endurance test and pursued an old dream by buying an elevated house in Dress Circle Road, Avalon, far out on the city's northern beaches. This was not as impractical as it would be today, for it was possible then to make a fast run through Frenchs Forest and over the Harbour Bridge to the News Ltd building in Surry Hills. Soon, my curious new family group was established in this beautiful location: myself; Joan; my small son, now just old enough to start at the local primary school; and a housekeeper in the person of an elderly relative.

~

On the floor above the *Daily Mirror* bearpit, Cyril and I occupied the former offices of departed *Truth* editors Lindsay Clinch and Ray 'Gander' Beckett. Our first act was to get rid of the loaded revolvers which lay in the editors' top drawers. Our next move was to disconnect the red alarm buttons set underneath the desktops, which had once brought armed guards from all parts of the building to evict angry readers swept up by the muckraking of *Truth* proprietor John Norton.

Murdoch expected a transformation of the *Sunday Mirror* such as Cyril had achieved with his magnificent wartime *Sunday Telegraph*. But he would not provide, and probably could not afford, the same editorial resources that Frank Packer had been smart enough to permit. Nor could he afford large-scale promotion in a city where the major newspapers controlled the leading commercial TV and radio stations. So our full-time creative staff numbered a mere half-dozen, apart from the sporting department. The best of them included Frank O'Neill, who could turn his hand to anything; Elizabeth Riddell, who supplied much-needed cultural input; and Keith Newman, a dogged investigator from the tough but intelligent old school. The subeditors, Jack Plummer and Guy Morrison, turned out a presentable paper from the scrappy material supplied. Soon after we started, news editor Alan Green walked out, on the grounds that he would not be told what to do by a brash young Melburnian (me). I had to take on his job, as well as look after the feature pages and write a weekly opinion column.

There were some compensations. My old London boss, Irvine Douglas, who had left the *SMH* and been reduced to writing 'pop' leaders for the *Daily Mirror*, now treated me with wary respect, almost fear. Eric Baume, bounced from the *Mirror*, came up to me at a function and pleaded for casual work as a film reviewer. Frank Browne, publisher of an often-defamatory news-sheet entitled *Things I Hear*, tried to get in the door too. Cyril peremptorily rejected Baume and Browne, as he did our scandalmongering but rather likeable social editor.

My best contribution to the new paper was to institute a regular page of debate on public issues, with 'Yes' and 'No' sides contributed by leading personalities. This enabled me to meet such diverse personalities as Bill Walkley, founder of Ampol Petroleum, who financed the annual Walkley Awards for journalism; and GJ Dusseldorp, a property mogul who supported government action to remove tenants standing in the way of large land developments. Through the friendly bookseller Alex Sheppard, I managed to obtain an uncensored copy of CH Rolph's *The Trial of Lady Chatterley*, the circulation of which was being held up by Customs officials, and by publishing a favourable full-page review I helped to shame them into releasing it to the public.

To give the paper a solid base of features, Rupert persuaded his great-uncle, professor Walter Murdoch, to resume the excellent weekly essays that had once been a hallmark of the Melbourne *Herald* under Rupert's father. We also asked the noted foreign affairs commentator Peter Russo to write a weekly analysis. Wise in the ways of newspapers, Russo extracted a written guarantee that his column would be printed in full exactly as he wrote it, and that it would continue for a minimum of twelve months. (Nine months later, when Rupert sacked Cyril Pearl, he would also break the agreement with Russo, ceasing publication of his column.) Cyril also arranged for Keith Newman to accompany the artist Russell 'Tas' Drysdale on a tour of outback Australia, concentrating especially on Aboriginal camps and pub scenes. The drawings and text were published in the *Sunday Mirror* as a series of four-page lift-outs, no doubt puzzling those readers more accustomed to lift-out racing guides—I made time to watch Drysdale completing the work in his Kings Cross studio.

I also had time to spare for the great journal *Nation*. If I could not get out to the Anglican Press printery at Chippendale on *Nation*'s press night, the following morning I went to the journal's upstairs office on George Street to get an early copy. The tiny office was a shambles, stacked high with unreviewed books and mislaid manuscripts, and decorated with a collapsed armchair in which visitors sat at their peril. In the midst of this mess sat publisher Tom Fitzgerald and his equally brilliant assistant George Munster, whose quacking voice over the phone sent shivers up the spines of crooked company directors and politicians.

My week's activities occupied six long working days, including a sixteen-hour Saturday. There were interludes, such as when Murdoch took his first wife Patricia, Cyril, Joan and me out on his new motor yacht to tour Sydney Harbour. We docked at Balmain quay, where Tom Fitzgerald and his wife Margaret joined us for drinks. This entry into high-powered circles was more to Joan's taste than the social isolation at Avalon, but it led nowhere. In the end, she became bored by the fact that most of my waking hours were spent working, and she returned to Melbourne at about the same time Patricia left Rupert, no doubt for similar reasons.

Given his limited time and constant crises, Rupert tried to be friendly in other ways. He took me to lunch at the Sportsmen's Club, but immediately I started discussing newspaper policies he wandered over to the poker machines and played them glumly until it was time to return to the office. On our long Saturdays, he was horrified to discover that after the first nine hours, Cyril and I would stroll to the nearby Journalists' Club to have a decent dinner and a bottle of wine, often with the taciturn poet Ken Slessor. One evening, unannounced, Rupert joined us, with the question, 'What happens if a big story breaks right now?' He was barely satisfied on being told that the interstate edition had gone to press and six hours were still in hand before the main edition. As well, Jack Plummer was on tap if a major event occurred, sitting at his littered desk and most likely savagely munching a cold egg-and-bacon sandwich from the *Mirror* canteen.

For interstate news, we were forced to use the unreliable *Truth* and the more reliable Adelaide *News* facilities. The Melbourne office of *Truth*, still under Utting, usually didn't bother to answer our inquiries. The *Mirror* office in Canberra was supposed to provide us with a weekly political news story. One day when I rang and asked the *Mirror* man to track down a hot political rumour, he simply transferred himself to a copy-taker and dictated a piece off the top of his head, using my unsubstantiated rumour as the basis of his story.

Considerable consternation at the changes we were making occurred among *Daily Mirror* editors who were fearful that our new ideas might actually work. These bitter old hands were forced to respect Cyril's reputation, but they spread the story that I had been made his heir apparent because I was supposed to be an illegitimate son of Keith Murdoch. I don't know who was the more libelled by that tale. Another shade of dismay occurred when Ian Smith, a cleverly sensationalist editor of the daily paper, made what he must have thought was a friendly approach, offering to 'fix' the police who'd caught me in a radar speed trap on the totally deserted Frenchs Forest road at about two o'clock one Sunday morning. I indignantly rejected the idea that a journalist should be involved in such a deal, and he never spoke to me again.

About this time, Rupert visited Cuba as part of a world trip, and, true to his earlier socialist convictions, he sent us a long cable extolling the virtues of Fidel Castro's revolution. This made an excellent double-page feature, being contrary to the extreme pro-American policies being promoted by every other important media outlet in Australia. Late one Saturday after his return from overseas, Rupert brought together Cyril, myself and Arthur Calwell, then leader of the federal Labor Party, in his private dining room. But for whatever tactical reason, Calwell spurned Murdoch and the *Mirror*, turning instead to Warwick Fairfax and the *SMH* for newspaper support against Menzies in the run-up to the 1961 election—which Menzies managed to win despite a severe recession.

The rapid transformation of the *Sunday Mirror* from a rough-and-tough tabloid appealing mainly to Sydney's working class, into a paper of moderate intellectual interest, predictably led to a substantial decrease in circulation among old readers. But regrettably, we could not replace them quickly enough with North Shore readers, and within a few months we were down from 380 000 sales a week to 330 000, and still falling. Murdoch became alarmed, and he listened even more closely to the *Daily Mirror* doomsayers. And so it was that, in May 1961, Murdoch arranged secret conferences with Cyril in pubs and clubs well away from the *Mirror* building, the details of which Cyril never revealed, even to me—I presume that confidentiality was the essence of the final settlement.

Douglas Brass, a competent journalist of the old school whom Murdoch had appointed editorial director, soon called a meeting of the *Sunday Mirror* staff and told the assembled journalists that Cyril Pearl had 'resigned' and that Bill Lean—one of Ian Smith's henchmen from the *Daily Mirror*—had been appointed editor. After each staff member had expressed their dismay, I asked Brass about my position as associate editor, and he said I would remain in that post. But when I came into work the following week, I found that another *Daily Mirror* executive, Brian Hogben, had taken over my desk. I was relegated to a small back office and instructed to write a two-page news review called 'The Week'.

In October, Alan Maller offered me my old job back as editor of *Fashion News*. I accepted, on the proviso that I be paid the same salary I was receiving at the *Mirror*. That having been confirmed, I was delighted to at last be able to send a stinging letter upstairs to Rupert Murdoch, protesting against what had been done and requesting recompense for my return to Melbourne:

> Dear Mr Murdoch,
>
> As you know, I came to Sydney with Cyril Pearl with the task of changing the *Sunday Mirror* into a 'quality newspaper'. I do not wish to rake over the coals of the past at great length. Suffice it to say that, for reasons which have never been explained to me, we were prevented from carrying out our assignment, and the money was spent instead on the *Sunday Mirror News-Pictorial* ...
>
> I regret to say that ... my position as Associate Editor has become a farce. Mr Lean has never consulted me on the conduct, contents, or policy of the paper; apart from the obligatory consultation of the Tuesday morning and Saturday night conferences, and the writing of the editorial. On the contrary, Mr Lean has attempted to put me on the subeditors' table; and more recently has apparently instructed the News Editor to give me news stories to handle.
>
> On Saturday nights my main function appears to be considered that of copy boy, passing messages from Mr Lean to the subeditors, the sporting staff, and the composing room. I had previously imagined that my time as a copy boy had been served on the *Argus* 16 years ago. I should like to make it quite clear that in any crisis I am willing to perform almost any function on the paper, but a crisis does not last for several months.
>
> I must therefore record the strongest possible protest against what appears to be a deliberate and sustained campaign to undermine my position, when my only desire has been to assist the newspaper and the Company to the best of my ability.

> In view of the total picture presented by the events of the last 11 months, I feel the best course is for me to return to Melbourne. I would be willing to continue writing 'The Week' on a contributory basis if desired for the sake of continuity and content. I should also point out that shifting back to Melbourne involves considerable financial loss on agents' fees and solicitors' charges for buying and selling my house, transport costs, etc. However, there does not appear to be any satisfactory alternative …

When I heard nothing in reply, I took Cyril's advice and consulted a prominent Sydney solicitor, Ralph Larkins, widely feared after the many rugged negotiations conducted on Frank Packer's behalf. Larkins wrote to Murdoch claiming wrongful dismissal from my post as associate editor. The following day, Murdoch summoned me to his office and, after a heated conversation, told me to clean out my desk and leave the building immediately.

Several weeks later, Larkins held a conference with the *Mirror* solicitor, who agreed that no-one at the *Mirror* office could be found to complain about my work, and that I had shown 'no resentment or personal ill-feeling' towards Bill Lean, the new editor. He agreed to pay three months' salary plus six weeks' holiday pay in lieu of notice, and this was accepted so that the matter 'could be settled amicably'. Meanwhile, I had arranged to lease my house at Avalon and headed south with my son to live with my mother and stepfather again in Hopetoun Road.

CHAPTER 8

Back to Old Melbourne Town

My return to Melbourne was made easy by the fact that Don Joinson had hatched a scheme with suburban newspaper publisher Peter Isaacson to start an opposition rag-trade paper called *Fashionweek*. They figured that a weekly paper would rob *Fashion News* of much of its timeliness and would soon run it out of business. They miscalculated badly. *Fashionweek*, printed cheaply on newsprint, was not at all what the rag trade wanted. At its middle and upper ends, fashion depended on the illusions and glamorous mystique best conveyed at that time in the pages of *Vogue*, the Australian edition of which was in the process of being taken over by Bernie Leser. Understanding this, Alan Maller installed a colour offset press in his Hawthorn printing works, enabling us to offer superb colour pages to our trade advertisers. With an expert advertising staff that included Cathie Stokes and Norah Riches, *Fashion News* simply went from strength to strength, while *Fashionweek* soon faded away. All I had to do was sit in a comfortable Flinders Lane office, dream up interesting editorial page layouts, and write up occasional interviews, which left me with time and energy to undertake other work.

Peter Ryan, at the instigation of his friend professor Macmahon Ball, chairman of the board of Melbourne University Press (MUP), had by now been appointed director of the press, with the immediate task of cleaning up the mess left by his predecessor, the learned, likeable but unbusinesslike Birmingham-educated Gwynydd Francis James. Ryan had also taken over from Cyril Pearl the task of writing the jocular, almost defamatory 'Melbourne Spy' column each fortnight for *Nation*, but he was now too busy with his new occupation. So from December 1961, I took over, continuing the column through most issues until January 1969. It was a very satisfying way to research and write. Highlights included the revelation that many rare and expensive books were disappearing from the holdings of the State Library Victoria; the dangers of Malathion chemical sprays, which could cause insanity among farm workers; and the forced eviction of Aboriginal residents from Comalco's mining leases around the Cape York town of Weipa. None of these subjects were being tackled by the wimpish Melbourne newspapers of the day.

I made sure that my own name appeared on a four-page feature in 1963 that analysed confidential memoranda sent by Keith Murdoch to his senior executives on the Melbourne *Herald* in the late 1920s. These came to me through his former editor Syd Deamer, who had become a close friend and drinking companion at the Journalists' Club in Sydney. After the *Nation* analysis appeared, Rupert Murdoch asked Tom Fitzgerald if he could have a look at the originals. I sent them up from Melbourne, and that was the last I ever saw of them.

By September 1963, things were going so well at *Fashion News* that I was able to change to part-time employment: three days a week. I used the extra time for consistent research into Australia's late-nineteenth-century land boom and bust, in the hope of being able to produce a book. Cyril lent me his rare copy of the suppressed edition of Meudell's *Pleasant Career of a Spendthrift*, which gave first-hand recollections of the period. Cyril also advised me to consult Harry Nunn, the chief archivist at the State Library, who had received several crates of contemporary official documents from the bowels of the Crown Law Department. These documents, consisting mainly of details of 'secret insolvencies' of the 1890s, had been dumped unopened in the Verdon Basement beneath the library. As I unpacked them in dim light, up to my elbows in long-undisturbed dust, excitement began to take hold of me. Here were details of the dirty doings of most participants in the land boom—all the chief financiers like WL Baillieu, the sly solicitor Theodore Fink, and crooked politicians like James Munro and Thomas Bent. The archives had no photocopying facilities at that time, so week after week I painfully transcribed every relevant detail of all the ambitious individuals and their fraudulent company flotations.

On the domestic front, meanwhile, my stepfather Malcolm had become concerned about the amount of time my mother was devoting to my seven-year-old son. I would deliver him to Trinity Grammar each morning, and my mother would pick him up most afternoons and lavish attention on him. One day in the garden at Hopetoun Road, Malcolm suddenly burst out, 'You'll have to take the boy away.' I was able to use Rupert Murdoch's payout to put a deposit on a 2-acre block and cottage in Hogan Avenue, Warrandyte, where we soon moved to begin enjoying country life. A childminding service picked up my son from school each day, after which we drove to Warrandyte, then back again early the next morning.

I began to understand my stepfather's anguished state of mind within a few months. Just before the severe recession of 1960–61, he had ambitiously expanded from the Parker Shoe factory at Clifton Hill by taking over the old, established and much larger Harkness Shoe Company in Collingwood. Instead of employing about 200 folk, he now had to find the wages each week for more than 600 skilled tradesmen and women. Simultaneously, the bottom had dropped out of the local shoe market and cheap imported shoes had flooded in. Malcolm continued to employ his workers for much longer than financial prudence dictated, as unsold shoes piled up in the stockrooms of both factories. Finally, he was forced by the

ANZ Bank, with whom he had dealt all his business life, to close down the facilities and dismiss all his staff. But even when the freeholds were sold at knockdown prices, there was still a considerable shortage of funds to pay off his debts.

The bank allowed him to keep temporary possession of his two large houses at Toorak and Flinders until the market improved and one house could be sold, but there was now no income at all. The shock to Malcolm's mind was enormous, and he began to lapse into a state of vegetative bitterness. Just to get money for food and pay other domestic bills, my mother took a reporting job with the Leader newspaper group, distinguishing herself with a fine series of articles about conditions inside Pentridge Gaol—later, she would be awarded an MBE for her 'Services to Journalism'. Transferring to Flinders, where Malcolm became even more withdrawn, my mother became the main publicist for the pioneering 'Angel of Mercy' helicopter ambulance service.

Then, Lady Viola Tait, who lived next door to my mother and stepfather's mansion in Toorak, asked Dorothy if she would write the history of J.C. Williamson Theatres, a subject on which her late husband, Sir Frank Tait, had left reams of material. My mother agreed to do this for £30 a week plus royalties, on the understanding that both their names would appear as joint authors. But when Lady Tait saw the completed manuscript, she refused to allow publication, saying in a letter to my mother that it disclosed 'too many intimate business matters which were never intended for public reading'. My mother rewrote the book three times in consultation with Lady Tait and the other directors of JCW. After several quarrels, Lady Tait took over the material, censored it, and arranged to publish through Heinemann under her own name. Threatened with legal action, she reluctantly paid my mother a further £500, the settlement including a proviso that my mother should not reveal who had actually written most of the book.

~

One day, the woman who would become my second wife, Kerry Ann Pearce, walked into my life. The daughter of a leading Melbourne solicitor, she had worked on *Woman's Day* and the *Herald* some years previously with my younger sister Dina, and now, after a long stay in Greece, was looking for part-time work. At my suggestion, she interviewed many of the small shopkeepers who had rented space in the large new Southern Cross Hotel complex in Exhibition Street, and found that they were doing badly, especially the fashion shops. This made a good front-page story for *Fashion News*, demonstrating that even trade journals could have teeth. After that, she got a secretarial job in the Department of History and Philosophy of Science at Melbourne University, under the formidable Diana Dyason.

We fell in love and married in April 1963 at St Stephen's Church, Gardenvale. Kerry was twenty-seven years old; I was thirty-three. By the end of that decade, we had produced three delightful children: our twins, James and Sarah, were born in March 1964, and another son, Patrick, was born in October 1969—just as my latest venture, the *Sunday Observer*, was also struggling to be born.

Even before the twins appeared on the scene, the far-flung location of Warrandyte was becoming a problem. We were able to sell the 2-acre allotment back to the original owners, for the same price. By this time I had also sold the house in Avalon, enabling us to buy a small cottage in Orchard Street, Brighton. This was near my wife's parents, who proved a tower of strength during her difficult pregnancy with the twins.

Our marriage would last eighteen years, with what I thought at the time were normal ups and downs. I do not propose to write much more about it, or the anguish caused on both sides, for there are people still living who would be hurt again by what would necessarily be a one-sided view of events. But a mea culpa is necessary: I remained the overambitious idiot I always was, concentrating too hard on my work, not devoting enough time to my family, and excusing myself with the notion that to support them financially was enough. It never is, but I learned that lesson too late.

I have not written much about my children in these pages, for they each have their own perspective and their own stories to tell. But briefly, Paul has been successfully self-employed as a builder for a long time and has two children—his support for me over the years has been extraordinary.

Of the twins, James showed a remarkable early aptitude for music, and when quite young became a guitarist of uncommon quality. He has gone on to become a lecturer and researcher of French at La Trobe University, has spent much of his life travelling between France and Australia, and wrote a notable historical work on the poorer sections of Paris known as 'The Zone'.

Sarah prefers to be called 'Za' by family and friends. This originated in early childhood when James could not say 'Sarah' and called her 'Zaza' instead. Za has spent many years in bookselling and academic publishing, and at the time of writing is the senior marketing coordinator at Monash University Publishing. Za has had more challenges than most, yet—like her son—she wakes most mornings with a smile.

My youngest son Patrick works for himself as a designer and typesetter in the publishing industry and has two girls and two boys.

Suffice to say that I remain extremely proud of all four healthy, hardworking offspring and the next generation they are producing.

~

While my wife Kerry was suffering in silence, I was working like a demon on my part-time project. Peter Ryan introduced me to Hugh Brain, the chairman of T&G Assurance, who had been closely associated with the WL Baillieu interests and for some reason was anxious to tell me what he knew. He also allowed me to photograph an extraordinary list that the National Bank had produced in 1895 for confidential circulation to its branch managers, showing many secret insolvencies which did not appear in the Crown Law Department's records. All this began to give me a more personal insight into the characters who had manipulated the land boom and its aftermath—I was not aware at the time that my own great-grandmother's diary of the awful 1890s depression was hidden under an apartment block in South Yarra. On the front verandah of the Orchard Street cottage, I hammered out about 200 000 words for a book which I named *The Land Boomers*. Kerry and I discussed many details of the publication while pushing our babies in a twin pram around the historic streets of Brighton, trying to visualise life in its boom-time mansions.

As well as Cyril Pearl's wise advice, other assistance came from the artist Horace Brodzky, son of Maurice Brodzky, editor of the old *Table Talk* weekly magazine, and the Melbourne trade union solicitor Spencer Brodney. For the chapter on GD Meudell, the retired floor manager of Robertson & Mullens booksellers, Frank Campbell, was willing to reveal all. This wonderful old bookseller could extract from his prodigious memory of tens of thousands of book titles every detail connected with the way in which the Baillieu and Fink families organised the suppression and bowdlerisation of Meudell's tale of land-boom scandals of the 1890s. (In fact, this was the same floor manager who had apprehended me when I'd attempted to filch a HG Wells title from his store twenty years earlier—his powers of recall being what they were, I wondered if he remembered me.) The scars of the great boom and bust had lasted for seventy years, and it was time the full story was told.

I did not think I had any hope of getting the manuscript published in the rigidly stratified conservative Melbourne of the time, and got ready to buy a small printing machine to produce a version for private publication. However, Peter Ryan asked to see the bulky manuscript and then passed it on to Geoffrey Blainey for an opinion. Geoff thought that it might safely be published, provided its length was cut by about half. I spent some months typing out a shorter version, which was then worked on by an experienced MUP editor, Beryl Hill. After she tactfully explained to me the meaning of editorial style, footnotes and a bibliography, I revised the manuscript yet again. This became the shortened clothbound edition of which 4000 copies were published in 1966, selling at $7.50 each. (One copy would eventually make its way into the State Library's Rare Books Collection.)

Before publication, Peter Ryan sold serial rights to *The Land Boomers* to the *Financial Review* in Sydney. A few days later he received an apologetic letter from the editor, Vic Carroll, saying that the Fairfax solicitors had banned publication in their newspapers, because of the provisions of the *NSW Defamation Act* covering possible damage to descendants. Such laws, if universally enforced, would put an end to the honest writing of history—even true crime stories could not be published because descendants of the criminals might suffer. MUP's Sydney representative, Alex Sheppard, found similar problems among NSW booksellers who were wary of displaying the book. Eventually, Sir Frank Packer's *Bulletin* accepted whatever risk was involved and serialised parts of the book over three weeks in November 1966.

Melbourne booksellers, not inhibited by the draconian NSW libel laws, went wild over the book. It sold out in seven days, and after generally delighted reviews appeared in most papers (with the notable exception of the *Herald*), copies were changing hands at up to $50 each. The comments which pleased me most were those of Walter Murdoch in two successive articles in his nephew Rupert's *Australian*. Murdoch had wished as a young man to train as a doctor, but was prevented from doing so when his widowed mother lost her ample savings in the crash of the Commercial Bank in 1893. He found my book 'admirable and horrifying'. However, the families of some of the people who had made fortunes out of land speculation were not so impressed.

Many editions and variants of the book followed, with annual royalties that assisted my financial position. I would later wonder if it is good for a writer to have such an instantaneous first-book success. The heady success of a bestseller leads people to expect that you can do the same again and again, and expands your ego to the point where you begin to agree with them. However, a note of caution came from the knowledgeable professor Weston Bate, who claimed in *Historical Studies* that my general account of the late Victorian period was 'oversimplified and often grossly inaccurate'. Uneasily aware of my lack of deep historical knowledge, I did not reply, but simply tucked the judgement away and thought, 'One day I'll show you buggers.'

~

At *Fashion News*, I made myself thoroughly unpopular throughout the rag trade by exposing financial shenanigans connected with the Gown of the Year contest. This was conducted each year, allegedly for charity, by garment manufacturers and the Models & Mannequins Guild. In fact, it was simply an annual booze-up, a tax-deductible dinner, and an excuse to promote the new season's fashion ranges. Models gave their services for free and got nothing out of the show except publicity. When the most recent balance sheet arrived to show that the entire profits had been eaten up by manufacturers, leaving nothing for charity, the guild secretary was so disgusted that she gave me the audited results, and I published the document in full, causing a sensation in Flinders Lane. The president of the association that represented garment manufacturers was so overcome by shame and guilt that he persuaded several firms to withdraw their advertising from *Fashion News*. Alan Maller later accused me of deliberately sabotaging the magazine, but that was not so: I felt I was simply doing my job.

Alan also made a mistake in building an office floor above his printing factory in Hawthorn and relocating the magazine there, closing down the *Fashion News* office in Flinders Lane. It is always foolish to remove editorial and business offices from the main scene. Advertising manager Walter Woods and I resigned and started our own paper, called *Fashion Pictorial*. This soon faded, due to a lack of capital, but it took enough advertising away from *Fashion News* to make Alan sell up to—of all people—Rupert Murdoch.

Murdoch shifted the paper back to Flinders Lane and appointed as its editor a bright 27-year-old *Age* journalist named John Ross.

John Burgess, head of the Textile Council of Australia, then gave me a job writing the council's newsletter and assisting its attempts to preserve tariffs that protected local textile manufacturers. It was interesting for a while to see inside the operations of industry leaders like the Foletta family and Bruck Mills in Victoria, and Bradmill in Sydney, and to lobby Canberra bureaucrats in the Department of Trade. But I was not cut out for that kind of work, sometimes embarrassing people by questioning whether the protectionist argument could be justified—free trade sounded like a much better idea.

Then, a new opportunity. Peter Ryan, the fairly new director of MUP, was worried by the state of the Melbourne University bookshop, which was owned by the publisher and was supposed to provide all the textbooks required by staff and students. The bookshop was suffering the effects of years of gentlemanly mismanagement, being crammed full of unsaleable superseded books, and showing trading losses of about $50 000 a year, which ultimately would have to be met from university funds. Ryan asked me if I could try to sort out the mess, with the encouraging advice that things couldn't get any worse, and therefore any changes must be for the better. In this way, without any book trade experience whatsoever, I found myself both a bestselling author and in charge of a million-dollar-a-year business with about twenty-five staff, all of whom knew far more than me about the details of the operation. I didn't even have a Master of Business Administration.

Fortunately, an experienced bookseller, Roy Farrell, had taken over as temporary manager, and he introduced me to the mysteries of ordering textbooks for the following year's student intake. Another stroke of luck was that Terry Unwin, a middle-aged English bookseller who had survived a spell as a navigator in RAF bombers over Germany during World War II, agreed to move from Ell's of Newcastle to become my assistant manager. I planted him in charge of each department in turn—shop floor, back office, despatch—so that he could make first-hand observations of their operating problems. His first success was to enable us to get rid of the drunken despatch foreman.

The next step was to get academic book ordering under control. The practice was for each lecturer or professor to supply us with lists of the books required as well as an estimate of enrolments, so that we could order books to arrive at the beginning of first term. However, the lists had become outdated over the years, comprising large numbers of titles that were no longer available. Even regarding the books still in print, the citations were often faulty and so the wrong books would arrive. Academics' estimates of the number of students willing to buy new books were wildly astray too—many youngsters bought second-hand books, or waited for them at the Baillieu Library, or just didn't bother procuring them. It was necessary for me to visit each faculty and explain the economic reality of bookselling life which I had just learned. This did not increase my popularity among university staff.

One result of previous practices was that the damp stone basement underneath the bookshop was overflowing with books from earlier years that had been bought and never sold, some of them half a century old. We pioneered the system of 'sale or return', sending back to publishers as many books as we dared. I suppose they simply pulped them. Fortunately, we were in a strong position, as our retail turnover of expensive textbooks was probably Melbourne's biggest. We got rid of thousands more old books at a monster sale at 50 cents each. The remaining old stock we simply sent to the local paper mill, to be converted into rather more useful cardboard and wrapping paper. One Saturday we undertook the delightful task of taking axes to the cubbyholes which had concealed the stock in the basement, and converted the area into an open ventilated space where all titles could be seen at a glance.

Ominous rumblings came from some of the older bookshop staff. A former manager, who had been found a sinecure in the back office, hinted that the staff were so upset by the changes that I might be faced with a strike, and that I should back off. I called in the remainder of the staff one by one, starting with known troublemakers. I asked them whether they were willing to express their loyalty to MUP and stay, or whether they wanted to hand in their resignation on the spot. Half a dozen accepted severance pay and were out of the building the same day; the remainder heaved a collective sigh of relief and set to work continuing the changes which logic dictated. Within a year we had made up the bookshop's trading losses, introduced new departments such as LP records and art prints, and were able to report large and continuing profits.

I was now promoted to assistant director of MUP and asked to solve the problems of its book printery, situated some distance away in Cardigan Street. The printery and its twenty-odd employees had slipped into a state of lassitude over the years, using as their excuse the great amount of hand labour necessary to produce fine books. This was partly valid, but wage rates and other costs had gradually risen so high that MUP's own printery could not compete with outside book printers who operated on a larger scale with more advanced technology.

The solution I found was simple enough. We converted the small plant into a two-shift operation, changing its entire economics. If employees did not want to work overtime because of family commitments or other reasons, we simply employed outsiders at night, in the manner I had perfected at the old *Radio Times* plant. The elderly manager of the printery was aghast at the thought of having to work after 4.30 p.m., so I let him handle the morning work, then I came in about lunchtime and supervised the evening shift myself. Soon, work was flowing in and out of the printery at nearly double the previous rate. We were able to typeset, print and bind every new MUP book, half of which had earlier gone to outside printers at higher rates than we were now charging. The wider university heard about our speedy turnaround of job printing, and soon we had more work from there than we could handle, all at good profit margins.

Once these changes had been made, there was not a great deal for me to do. So I used my free mornings and lunch hours to begin another intensive research program at the State Library, skimming through almost every nineteenth-century Australian book, newspaper and journal it could offer. A wealth of neglected material lay before me. The first fruit of this activity was the rediscovery of an eccentric journalist named John Stanley James, who had disguised his identity to get jobs in various institutions during the 1870s and 1880s, thereby obtaining first-hand information for scarifying 'inside' articles for the *Age* and *Argus*. (Under the codes of ethics that would later be enforced, requiring journalists to disclose their identity, such intimate reportage became almost impossible.) I condensed his collected *Vagabond Papers* into one volume, discovered his true identity, and wrote a long biographical introduction for the MUP 1969 edition.

By now, our family could afford to move into a bigger Victorian-style weatherboard house in Landcox Street, East Brighton; we'd sold the little Orchard Street house for about $7000, which paid for half of the new house. We now had four large bedrooms, one of which I used as my study. Later, we built an extra bedroom on the back, overlooking a large garden in which the children could play happily and safely.

~

In July 1969 I received an offer I simply could not refuse.

The Liberal government of Sir Henry Bolte, realising that there was no way of stopping the sale of tens of thousands of Sydney Sunday newspapers in Melbourne, acted to legalise the publication of Sunday newspapers in Victoria. Ambitious new publishers thought they saw an opening, and one small paper, the *Sunday Post*, quickly started up. But the newsagents' monopoly refused to allow home deliveries on Sundays. The *Post* was on its last legs when another new entrant came from Sydney, looked into its pathetic sales figures, and declined to take it over.

The new arrival was John Crew, an ABC journalist who was acting as the front man for self-made millionaire Gordon Page Barton. Gordon had been forced to flee from Indonesia at the age of twelve with his Dutch mother when the Japanese invaded in 1942, leaving all their possessions behind. In Sydney, Gordon worked as a newsboy after school, swearing that one day he would control his own newspapers that featured his favourite colour comics. He bought a truck and started an interstate parcel-delivery service, which developed into a company, IPEC Australia, that operated hundreds of trucks. Barton then branched into various finance and property companies, becoming a takeover specialist in partnership with a financial genius named Greg Farrell.

Ironically, in view of his background, Barton was always opposed to Western colonialism in Asia, regarding it as a basic cause of international conflict. When prime minister Menzies began to send Australian 'advisers' to support US forces in the Vietnam War, Barton formed the Australia Party, whose objective was to achieve a balance of power in federal parliament and help end the Vietnam conflict. One of his candidates was the idealistic, enthusiastic but rather bumbling young man 'Smiling John' Crew.

On his arrival in Melbourne in mid-1969, Crew set himself up in a suite at the old Savoy Plaza Hotel in Spencer Street. Perhaps he and Barton had read my vigorous attacks on Australia's Vietnam involvement, published in the *Sunday Mirror* as early as October 1961. Perhaps they had consulted Tom Fitzgerald and George Munster about the most suitable person to edit their Sunday paper—I meant to ask them but never did. Prompted in whatever way, John Crew rang me at MUP and, during an interview at the Savoy Plaza, offered to give me a free hand editorially as well as double my salary to $12,500 a year.

I was delighted at what I thought was an unprecedented opportunity, one that was unlikely to occur again. Before accepting, though,

I thought I had better meet the proprietor. With keen anticipation, I went to the office of Tjuringa Securities in Sydney, where I met the tall, gangly, almost cadaverous Barton. He was friendly but preoccupied. It was only when we went to his home for lunch and were served by a nurse that I learned his wife Yvonne was dying of cancer in an adjoining room.

Barton wanted to talk about anything except newspaper and business affairs, preferring to proudly show me how he had beaten the paint companies' 'propaganda' by allowing the bare outside timber of his house to weather until it became rock-hard. I was puzzled, but decided, perhaps foolishly, to go along with the rambling discussion. Then he gave me a copy of his impressive 1966 pamphlet *Australia in Asia*, which expressed his party's foreign policy and defence views much more clearly than he could in person. I was completely won over. Barton wanted to proceed with my appointment on a mere verbal understanding, but after my experiences with Rupert Murdoch, I was determined to get a watertight contract. As signed by Barton, Crew and me on 1 August 1969, this gave me complete control (at least in theory) over the hiring and firing of editorial staff as well as the total contents and layout of the paper.

In long sessions at the Savoy Plaza over the following nights, I was made privy to more details of my masters' plans, and became steadily more perturbed. Their basic idea was to produce some sort of paper in order to catch the end of the football season in mid-September. This would only have been sensible had we owned a large-capacity plant in good working order and some kind of distribution system. In fact, John Crew had discovered from Gollin & Co. that a \$700 000 eight-unit Goss Urbanite web offset press had been ordered by Rupert Murdoch for Melbourne but was no longer required. It was capable of producing up to 40 000 copies per hour of a 96-page tabloid newspaper and seemed ideal for a large Sunday publication, particularly since it also had four-colour capacity for comics and news photographs. Barton ordered the press, and he also leased a large galvanised-iron warehouse, previously used for storing new Datsun cars, on the southern bank of the Yarra in Fishermans Bend. My historical knowledge told me that this was a landfill area, previously subject to flooding, and I expressed my doubts, saying we needed a city location. Barton disagreed, and Gollin's engineers began sinking massive concrete foundations through the mud to support the 12 000-kilogram weight of press and folders.

These delays meant we would have to use small suburban printeries if we wanted to produce our first issue in September. Even then, however, we had no staff of any kind, apart from me. The task seemed almost impossible, no matter how much money was available. The following morning, after a sleepless night, I gave notice, probably setting a new record for brevity of editorial tenure. In my letter of resignation, I urged that the order for the press be cancelled if possible, or the goal of September publication be abandoned, or a much smaller paper be started by buying out a suburban plant such as that of Progress Press, at that time still outside the Murdoch net. I also protested against the proposed selling price of 15 cents a copy, as most daily papers were selling at 5 cents.

It quickly became obvious that Barton didn't want to know about any of the real problems involved in starting a good newspaper. He assured me that Peter Isaacson's printery in Prahran could handle the first issues, printing the colour comics separately and inserting them by hand. He also agreed that the selling price should be reduced, to 12 cents, and with these sweeteners I foolishly agreed to give the project a try.

We now had four weeks left to gather a staff and produce a dummy run. Most newspapers were still using 'hot metal' typesetting—linotypes etc.—but we planned to be among the first to utilise new technology: IBM typesetters controlled by small computers which adjusted type styles, the justification of lines, and sizes up to 14 point. While John Crew scurried around getting these installed in our warehouse, I placed a half-page advertisement in the *Sun News-Pictorial* calling for 'courageous journalists' who wanted to write for a different kind of newspaper. Not one of the big names in daily journalism applied, but from the *Age* we managed to recruit the enthusiastic 29-year-old Bill Green, whom I immediately appointed to the key post of news editor. Kerry Walsh, another good writer, took on the women's pages, with Freda Irving providing columns of social events. A well-known model, Helen Homewood, wrote interestingly about matters which were becoming important to young women of the day.

The most obvious gap was in sport, one of the crucial departments for Sunday papers. Not a single sportswriter had applied for a job. In a flash of inspiration, I rang Harry Beitzel, who was running his own sports news service in St Kilda Road. In return for lots of money, Beitzel agreed to take on the entire twelve-page sports section, including providing photographs of all the main Saturday sporting events. He did it superbly, creating one of the paper's best features and relieving me of all the worry. He even persuaded then Collingwood Football Club captain Des Tuddenham to write an analysis of the leading football match of the day.

For other editorial features, I tried hard to get Clive Turnbull to revive his old 'Free Speech' column that had once delighted me in the *Herald*. On my third visit to his Collingwood office, I began to realise one of the problems of ageing: at sixty-three, Clive no longer believed in anything much, and hence had nothing to write about. All illusions gone, I left in sadness, turning to a left-wing academic named John McLaren whose commentary 'This Week' proved an acceptable substitute, although lacking Turnbull's unique way with words.

Once again, Cyril Pearl was a tower of strength with constant advice and suggestions, as well as writing a witty weekly feature. David Martin, who had helped me so much on *Newsday*, and the historian Niall Brennan both agreed to contribute weekly columns: their political and religious views were diametrically opposed, but together they stirred a refreshing breeze through the corridors of Melbourne conservatism. For Canberra news and views, I engaged Don Whitington, who had once been the *Sunday Telegraph*'s expert political correspondent and now had his own media firm. On the lighter side, Alan Fitzgerald contributed a satirical column which prevented our readers from taking any politician too seriously. With Melbourne's large Italian population in mind, we bought many articles from leading Italian magazines; these were translated by the bilingual Michael Costigan, a former priest and *Advocate* editor who had joined our news staff.

Barton agreed that we should buy the rights to material from the *New Statesman*, providing us with a solid base of world features. He seemed to spend the rest of his time on the phone to Paris, attempting to negotiate Australian rights to the sexy science-fiction comic strip *Barbarella*. He failed, but we managed to get *Dick Tracy*, *Mickey Mouse*, *Prince Valiant*, *Alley Oop*, *Brenda Starr*, *Tarzan*, *Bugs Bunny* and other favourites. These arrived as black-and-white artwork that had to be expensively converted to colour by local artists.

I arranged with an old *Radio Times* stalwart, Denbeigh Salter, to review films. Bernard Boles, a rather oddball but knowledgeable art critic who was out of favour with the art establishment of the day, appeared from nowhere to give his controversial views, which had the almost unique virtue of being understandable to the general public. I wrote most of the book reviews late at night or very early in the morning, supplemented by a column of authoritative book trade news from Ted Sayers. Perhaps my best coup was to discover the identity of the mysterious 'Veritas' who had once written the popular TV pages for *Truth*. He was the horseracing world's John Pacini, who agreed to contribute his outspoken views on TV programs to the extent of two full pages each week, as long as his new pseudonym of 'Paul Jacks' was strictly observed.

All in all, despite the shortness of time, the features seemed to be shaping up well. Bill Green had been busy searching for and appointing a skeleton news staff. Covering police rounds is a major problem for a small Sunday paper. However, the ABC roundsman Harry Lovett ('Harry the Horse') agreed to give us the nod whenever anything big was brewing. A nervous young man named John Steed proved himself capable of extracting humour from almost any interview: we promoted him as 'Our Man Steed', after Emma Peel's partner in the popular TV show *The Avengers*. Even better was Alan Young, who was willing to imitate 'The Vagabond' or 'The Melbourne Spy' and take jobs anywhere under false names in order to get at the underbelly of public affairs. His reminiscences of an attempt to join the army were side-splitting, while his temporary work as an encyclopaedia salesman exposed rackets in that field. Other notable newshounds who joined the staff included Noel Turnbull, who contributed many front-page stories before becoming a leading figure in public relations, and John Goode, an old friend from Atlas Publications who was particularly adept at writing news features.

More rapidly than I had expected, we were coping with most of the editorial difficulties. But the home-delivery problem that had been a key factor in the downfall of the *Sunday Observer* still needed to be resolved. At that time, the Victorian Authorised Newsagents Association (VANA) was totally under the thumb of the daily newspaper proprietors, while no newsagent wanted to work on Sunday morning if it could be avoided. VANA escaped a restraint-of-trade action by ordering 60000 copies of the *Observer* to be sold over the counter through their subagents, mainly milk bars, which opened on Sundays.

This was not nearly good enough for the ambitious Barton. He approached Bob Hawke, then president of the ACTU, and offered that organisation a share in running the paper if it could convince the Transport Workers Union to instruct milk vendors to deliver the *Observer* with the morning bottles. Hawke refused the offer—just as well, for home deliveries of milk were soon to be phased out. Barton was forced to organise his own distribution system, using fleets of IPEC trucks to deliver bulk supplies of the paper to milk bars early each Sunday morning. At the same time, he advertised for 2000 newsboys to home-deliver the paper and sell it by the roadside; a prize of a new bicycle was offered to those who sold the most copies.

The time of our first and only dummy run approached too quickly. It was on 7 September 1969, exactly ten years after my own *Newsday* had ceased publication. A large telephone switchboard had been installed at Fishermans Bend, although few people knew our number. United Press teleprinters chattered away in one corner, spewing out vast amounts of paper but with no-one to clear them. I'd had no time to appoint subeditors and was forced to work on the old *Radio Times* theory that the editor could roughly lay out most pages, leaving the finer details to typesetting staff. But during that awful first Saturday, we discovered that the imported machine for setting large headings couldn't work fast enough. We were forced to paste up the text and leave space for many headings to be set by our friends at Peter Isaacson, who had contracted to print the first issues. Even so, the dummy issue contained many blank spaces. It looked truly amateurish.

By the time the first real issue was due to be produced on 14 September, I had managed to find a couple of moonlighting subeditors to help straighten out the layout, and extra photosetting machines had been installed. But the production generally remained a shambles, not helped by the fact that Gordon Barton lurked near the make-up benches, reading the pages in progress and complaining to all in earshot that rebel forces in Vietnam were being described in United Press cables as 'Reds'. I stared at him angrily and shook my head. He took the hint and disappeared from the editorial and composing room areas. His main contribution after that was to send me a handwritten note, which I have preserved, complaining that there weren't enough crossheads and the columns were 'sometimes very cramped'. This at a time when we were balanced on the edge of not appearing at all!

At 2 a.m. on the Sunday morning of publication, the last pages still had not gone to the printer, where platemakers and machine hands were enjoying large overtime payments while sitting around with sandwiches and keeping awake with much coffee. John Crew went to the Isaacson printery in Prahran to make sure that all possible plates were on the machine. At about 3 a.m. I wearily took the last sports-page paste-ups from the benches, put them in my car, and drove as fast as I dared to Prahran. Within a few minutes the presses were rolling, but even at maximum speed they could only turn out about 100 000 papers before breakfast.

I staggered home, asking my heavily pregnant wife to wake me after a couple of hours' rest. At about 9 a.m. we drove down Bay and Church streets in Brighton, searching for our newsboys and posters—not a sign of one. About an hour later, the papers were delivered to a couple of local milk bars, and a solitary newsboy appeared, tying an *Observer* poster around a tree near the corner of New Street. The Sunday paper revolution had begun, even if it was about five hours late.

~

Although our production, advertising and distribution departments were hopelessly inefficient—Barton and Crew's fault, not theirs—we were lucky with many of our news stories. The great dread of Sunday newspaper editors is that nothing will actually happen on Saturdays apart from sport, and in their worst nightmares a giant headline appears that reads 'NO NEWS TODAY'. But the rapidly growing radical movement in the eastern states knew about our efforts and provided many leads for exclusive stories that were in tune with our editorial policies.

In our second issue, we were able to disclose shocking bastardisation by permanent army officers against national service trainees being prepared for the bottomless pit of an Asian land war. The minister for the army was forced, much against his will, to take action. Then, a new journalist, Michael Crewdson, joined our staff, bringing with him several sensational stories from his friend Dr Bertram Wainer, the pro-abortion crusader. In late September 1969, three days before the birth of my youngest son, we disclosed that a number of senior police officers were extorting bribes from the operators of illegal abortion clinics. Chief secretary Arthur Rylah tried to bury the issue, but the officers were eventually jailed and abortion laws greatly liberalised.

These stories were published at the risk of huge damages being paid for defamation claims. Later, justice William Kaye, appointed by the government to inquire into Bert Wainer's allegations, and himself protected against libel suits by absolute privilege, had the audacity to criticise the *Observer*'s presentation of whatever facts we could establish.

The *Sunday Observer*'s proudest moment occurred on 14 December 1969, when we published Ron Haeberle's incredible colour photographs of the massacre of the entire population—men, women and children—of My Lai village in Vietnam. In the United States, *Life* magazine was not ashamed to publish the visual evidence of what some American troops were doing in Vietnam, but no Australian newspaper would touch it: local editors were too squeamish and cowardly. In our office, John Crew's finest moments were spent buying the transparencies from *Life* and then arguing for hours with Customs officials who wanted to ban them on the grounds of extreme horror. John's threats of High Court action won the day.

The pictures were rushed to Wilke's, a printing firm paid large amounts to prepare an eight-page colour supplement at short notice. The pages were dramatically laid out by our new chief subeditor, David Robie, while I took the decision not to include the most sickening close-ups of babies with bullet holes through the middle of their foreheads. That Sunday we sold out our entire print run of 150 000 copies. Dr Jim Cairns attributed the huge success of the Vietnam moratorium rallies of 1970 at least in part to the utter disgust of most people in Melbourne about what we had shown to be happening in Vietnam. At a time when all other newspapers were decrying protest marches, and frequently forecasting they would lead to street violence, the *Observer* alone consistently supported the anti-Vietnam rallies.

Other incidents bolstered the view that the battle for free speech was being won. We printed an anti-war cartoon showing a naked soldier with a small cannon between his legs, an obvious reference to male aggression as a cause of war. A Prahran magistrate fined Peter Isaacson $50 for printing the cartoon, but the verdict was reversed on appeal, with judge Trevor Rapke chastising the police for wasting everyone's time. Then John Crew was fined $100 in the Port Melbourne Court House for publishing material which incited young men not to register for compulsory national service. Judge Thomas Shillito of the County Court reversed that magistrate's decision.

These were stirring times, and I remain grateful to Barton and Crew for allowing me to share in some of them. But as the weeks went by, I began to realise that my rather pedantic, perfectionist nature could not cope with their freewheeling attitude to daily problems. I began to show signs of extreme stress: sleeplessness, depression, migraines, and other reactions by which human physiology tells you it has had enough. I resigned as editor, agreeing to stay until January 1970 and to continue writing editorials each week.

While winding down on the *Observer*, I began to plan other ways of earning a living. The boom in Australian books seemed to be continuing, much to the surprise of most book-trade experts. With the assistance of Patricia Reynolds of the State Library, I decided to publish a facsimile edition of the *Australasian Sketcher*, a monthly illustrated journal produced by the Melbourne *Argus* in the 1870s and 1880s. I selected 1880, mainly because Ned Kelly was hanged that year, and the woodcuts of his final battles and extinction were superb. Pat lent me one of the library's precious rare volumes, which I took to Graham Enticott, who ran a nearby lithographic film company. He agreed to carefully photograph the pages onto process film, as long as I held the volume open and flat under the arc lights. That was the probable cause of the skin cancers that would later appear on the backs of my hands.

Dai Nippon printed the huge volume beautifully on heavy art paper in Hong Kong for about $3 a copy, and I resold them mainly by mail order for six times as much. For as long as the Aussie dollar held up, and Asian printing remained reasonably cheap, it seemed like money for jam. I followed the *Sketcher* with about a dozen other facsimile reprints of scarce and valuable books, most of which sold equally well while the boom in Australiana lasted. Then everybody got into the act and the game was up.

Meanwhile, the Barton press empire was going from bad to simply pathetic, despite the investment of millions of dollars. By late 1970, David Robie had resigned as editor and Barton and Crew asked me to return. Ignoring my wife's dismay, forgetting the hell on earth which was Fishermans Bend, and deluding myself that I could out-manipulate the top dogs, I agreed to talk. At our first meeting, I discovered that a number of crazy schemes were being floated to use up surplus press capacity on weekdays. There was to be a weekly women's paper placed free in every Melbourne letterbox, and supported totally by advertising revenue, although we had no top-flight advertising sales staff. The next day, the idea had changed to a daily tabloid newspaper which would unquestionably knock the stuffing out of the *Sun News-Pictorial.* Heaven knows where otherwise rational people get such illusions.

Yet I agreed to return as editor-in-chief, provided that all such schemes were abandoned and that we produce something within our limitations. This would be a second Sunday newspaper, quite upmarket, to be called the *Sunday Review* and aimed at the field occupied in London by the *Sunday Times* and similar papers. The new weekly would take the best features from the *Observer*, which would go slightly downmarket to occupy the same niche as Sydney's Sunday papers. The *Review* would be printed at about 9 p.m. on Saturday, just before the *Observer* went to press with its much bigger circulation and late sports news. Both papers could be distributed to milk bars on the same run and might eventually achieve home delivery. They would also help publicise each other.

Kevin Childs was appointed editor of the *Observer* and given his head on producing a mass-market tabloid, which he did very well. Bill Green came over to the *Review* as my assistant editor, which meant effective control of the new paper. I would, thought I, control both papers from a leisurely distance, devoting most of my energies to combating the well-meaning amateurism that constantly tried to invade the operations from above.

With a tiny staff consisting mainly of Michael Costigan, Richard Beckett and John Hepworth, we managed to get the first issue of the *Review* out on time, on 11 October 1970. We relied heavily on freelance contributors, taking Cyril Pearl, Barry Oakley, Bernard Boles, Niall Brennan and Alan Fitzgerald from the *Observer*. Perhaps my best idea was to get George Munster of *Nation* to fill page two with items of mainly Sydney origin: his first contribution forecast that an unknown writer named Germaine Greer would soon become famous. We transferred most of the *New Statesman* material from the *Observer* and also bought the rights to *Spectator* material, giving us spectacular overseas contributions. Other fine writers in the early issues included professors Geoffrey Sawer and Sol Encel, Barry Humphries, Vincent Serventy, Beatrice Faust, Mungo MacCallum, Bruce McGuinness and Barry Jones. Best of all, Mike Leunig came to work for us, drawing brilliant page-one cartoons on current events. I wrote a satirical summary entitled 'Another Week', and David Wilson contributed book news.

In our third issue, Bill Green wrote the only full report of the obscenity trial in Melbourne of the Philip Roth novel *Portnoy's Complaint* that any paper dared to publish. Leunig's cartoon showed a courtroom full of possible phallic symbols: Gordon Barton insisted that we remove the glowing red tip from the magistrate's nose.

I was extremely proud of these early issues of the *Review*, which served up a feast of worthwhile material to anyone who wanted to read and think about current affairs. Encouragingly, given the organisation could provide little promotion beyond a half-page advertisement in the previous day's *Australian*, the first issue sold all 40 000 copies at 15 cents. It is a common mistake to think that curiosity sales of a first issue will be repeated, but we managed to maintain respectable sales of between 20 000 and 30 000 copies each week, almost solely in Melbourne.

~

Shortly before the *Sunday Review* started, Gordon Barton bought a controlling interest in the historic publishing and bookselling company Angus & Robertson (A&R). A fundamental part of my agreement to return was that A&R would take over my little publishing firm and any remaining copies of the books I had produced. A&R's managing director, George Ferguson, persisted in regarding the books as remainders and would not offer more than a dollar for each for them. I was tempted to walk out and claim breach of contract, but by this time we were committed to the *Review* and I did not feel I could abandon our small staff.

After we had published our first few issues of the new paper, Barton walked into my office, which was being shared by other *Review* staff, told me that Ferguson had left A&R, and asked me whether I would fly to Sydney each week to run the company. I was stunned: what lay behind this kind of madness? I was not willing to leave my family during the week, not willing to move back to Sydney, and not willing to continue working for such a rackety organisation. In mid-November, in a renewal of my earlier rages, I resigned and went home to continue producing and selling my own books. I expected that Barton and Crew would have no alternative but to appoint Bill Green in my place, and indeed he did carry on successfully for some weeks. But he had a fatal habit of telling the truth, even shouting home truths at his wayward proprietor. So early in 1971 they employed a young Sydney man, Richard Walsh, to come to Melbourne and show the locals how to do it. Walsh was famous, some would say infamous, as one of the original publishers of *Oz*, an irregular periodical that had broken many taboos in the 1960s.

In Sydney, meanwhile, Tom Fitzgerald was despondently battling the falling circulation of *Nation*. Barton bought it and amalgamated two papers into *Nation Review*. Under Walsh's editorship, this became much cheekier and achieved a higher circulation for a time. However, huge losses on attempts to expand the *Sunday Observer* forced Barton to close it down in March 1971 and auction the Fishermans Bend plant. The press was eventually sold in situ to self-made Greek publisher Theo Skalkor for the derisory figure of $362 000. The years during which Peter Isaacson continued the *Sunday Observer*, from 1977 to its extinction, would be dealt with in the final issue published 11 June 1989; after that, the established daily papers would be able to monopolise the Sunday newspaper field.

Richard Walsh tried to carry on *Nation Review* by taking it to other offices and printers. But he also accepted the vacant post of publisher at A&R, a move which led only to the decline of both enterprises. Walsh would give one version of these events in his 1993 compilation *Ferretabilia*. He was criticised by some former staff members for not giving due credit in certain areas, but such harsh feelings were probably inevitable. There is no question of Walsh's brilliance in using the ideas and efforts of others, which is one of the hallmarks of a successful editorial administrator. No doubt it was this attribute which prompted Kerry Packer to appoint him managing director of Consolidated Press. Once upon a time, Walsh would have led the way in satirising such pap, but we all grow older and sometimes wiser.

CHAPTER 9

Books *Are* Different

IT WAS WITH not a little pleasure that, as 1970 came to a close, I was able to abandon the frenetic and frustrating world of newspapers for the more satisfying work of writing and publishing books. As part of deeper research into historical sources, I had extracted many passages from *Age* editorials of the 1850s gold-rush era. I selected them not so much for their long-term significance, but for the power and passion of the writing. The best were collected into a little book called *The Australian Thunderer* and published through my firm, Heritage Publications. Its 1000 copies were sold out at $3.60 each, leaving me with a modest profit.

I had also been working up some other research into a general survey of the nineteenth century, which I rather grandiloquently called 'Australia in the Victorian Age'. My method of working was quick and wide-ranging. Photocopying was coming into general use, and as with microfilm was relatively cheap. So as I rapidly traversed the holdings of major libraries in Melbourne, Sydney and Canberra, I ran their copying departments almost ragged by ordering copies of thousands of passages. The criterion for selection was anything that threw light on the development of Australia through its dramatic or human content. All of it helped to build up a general picture of the nation's pioneering years, albeit slightly distorted perhaps by my fondness for the revealing anecdote. But most lives are fairly boring in their daily routine: it is only the highlights, the humour and the tragedies that are remembered.

I studied this material more carefully at home, where firm outlines of chapters began to take shape. In the end, I discarded more than 90 per cent of what I had garnered. Then, having heard of the Menzies government's Commonwealth Literary Fund, I wrote to ask if they would be willing to finance the extensive research and writing required for my project, and was gratified to receive a grant sufficient to keep myself and my family for twelve months. The result was the first volume of a general history of Australia in the Victorian era entitled *Who's Master, Who's Man?* This was published by Thomas Nelson at the end of 1971, in a clothbound edition designed by the painstaking, brilliant layout artist Alison Forbes. Its 5000 copies sold out almost immediately and it had to be reprinted several times in hardback and paperback editions.

A few academic critics refused to be impressed. Some were puzzled by the title, not appreciating that a major theme of our history is the weakening of old-world class systems through the end of convictism, the era of free immigration and the gold rush, and similar features of frontier society. Other academics thought I had relied too much on my sources. But if you don't believe first-hand observations, what are you going to accept? Professor Manning Clark, however, could see what I was trying to do and lauded my work in the *Australian*. The book received the inaugural Barbara Ramsden Award for the best collaboration between author and editor (Sue Beaven, later Lady Ebury). That seemed to silence most of the critics, at least for the time being.

The royalties from the book were gratifying, but I could see that they would not continue to support my family in reasonable comfort. What to do next? I had often thought that the full version of *The Land Boomers* as originally written would make a good historical source book. I approached Peter Ryan at MUP, who kindly allowed me to take back the hardback rights for incorporation into a new edition. The original MUP publication had consisted of twenty-two chapters: I added twenty-eight chapters of further research, making a book of more than 400 large pages. I then found more illustrations and had the whole thing reset and expertly printed by Dai Nippon. To avoid confusion with the MUP edition, which was still in print, I changed the title to *Land Boom and Bust* and issued 1000 numbered and signed copies at $15 each. All sold within a few days, leaving me several thousand dollars in front.

About this time, Stuart Sayers asked me to begin reviewing Australian non-fiction for the *Age* Literary Supplement, which I did for about five years. Max Suich asked me to do similar work for his new Fairfax weekly, the *National Times*, which set out to be a more professional Sydney version of the *Sunday Review*. In a front-page *National Times* story in October 1975, I was able to point out the similarities between Gough Whitlam's then constitutional crisis and events in Victoria a century earlier, when most public servants had to be sacked because the Legislative Council refused to pass a radical government's budget.

In 1972, Rupert Murdoch had succeeded in another of his dazzling coups by taking over the Sydney *Daily Telegraph* and *Sunday Telegraph* from Consolidated Press. Early the following year, Murdoch dispatched his chief editor, James 'King' Watson, to arrange a Melbourne edition of the Sunday paper, with the result that the little-used former *Sunday Observer* plant at Fishermans Bend was leased to print the paper on Saturday nights. Watson asked me to resume my old Sunday column 'This Week', giving me the whole of page two to spread my views. This was profitable fun for a few weeks, but it was an activity I found difficult to keep up without support from a regular newsroom and the inside gossip on which columnists mainly subsist. It was back to books for me.

In the State Library, I read a rare copy of EBF D'Auvergne's biography of the Irish-born adventuress Lola Montez, published many years earlier, in which he described her medical problems in considerable detail. At the same time, I studied one of the library's few works on venereal disease, for the prevalence of syphilis in past centuries seemed to shed light on many otherwise inexplicable historical events. Many of Montez's symptoms and actions fitted precisely with medical analyses of the time. I asked a leading Melbourne venereologist for his opinion, and when he agreed with my perspective, I wrote a rather different version of the one-time dancer's outrageous life entitled *Lola Montes: The Tragic Story of a 'Liberated Woman'*. This I also published under the Heritage imprint and sold the 1000 copies within a few weeks.

I published two more books in 1973. Patricia Reynolds gave me free access to hard-copy newspaper files in the State Library, enabling me to plan and publish a large-format book entitled *Famous News Pages in Modern Australian History, 1923–1973*. Starting with the front page of Monty Grover's *Sun News-Pictorial* of 5 November 1923, with its remarkable photographs of the Melbourne police strike, I selected the main news event of each year. Then I had to load each heavy volume of bound newspapers into the back of my station wagon and take them to Enticott's, where they were filmed as same-size negatives, whereupon I could return the files and get another load. This book, too, sold its 1000 copies without difficulty. By this time, Hong Kong printers had nearly doubled their charges, so I moved on to cheap but competent printers in Taiwan, enabling me to stay afloat financially while making the books available at reasonable prices.

Pat Reynolds also recommended me to the well-known English publishers David & Charles, who were producing an international series of photographic histories. For my contribution, entitled *An Australian Camera 1851–1914*, I was allowed to go through the La Trobe Library's entire collection of more than 100 000 original photographs and take selections to be copied on Enticott's litho camera, which enabled superb reproduction. This venture also introduced me to numerous other sources of pictures that were little used at that time, such as the Australian War Memorial and the NSW Government Printer, many of which were just beginning to realise the value of their neglected files. Cyril and Irma Pearl had pioneered the interpretation of history through photographs with *Our Yesterdays* in 1954, and I was happy to follow in their footsteps.

Also in 1973, the Whitlam government abolished the Commonwealth Literary Fund and set up the Australia Council under Geoff Blainey, with specialised units that included a new Literature Board. One of its first awards, granting me a three-year fellowship at $9000 a year to continue historical writing, revolutionised my life. To be paid a living wage to do what I liked best for such a long period—this was a fantastic windfall.

The grant also enabled my family to enjoy for a few years the dream of moving to the country, away from the worsening noise and pollution of Melbourne's suburbs. After some searching and false starts, we found Goose Hill, an established property on Old Main Creek Road, Main Ridge, near the southern end of the Mornington Peninsula. On the allotment were the original timber homestead and a huge barn, while the surrounding land had been whittled down to a manageable 6 acres of gently sloping paddocks. We quickly sold our house in East Brighton and moved to Main Ridge in time for Christmas. We were among the first urbanites to invade that isolated apple-growing and grazing district, and were no doubt resented by some of the hardworking pioneer families who maintained almost a backwoods approach to life and its necessities. Few services were available: if something needed doing, you did it yourself, and no-one worried much about council regulations.

We soon discovered the kinds of stresses endured by country families, but despite some (ultimately amusing) misadventures, there were many compensations. No other house could be seen from ours: we existed adrift from the world like a Swiss family Robinson. Climate became all-important. One could almost soar aloft on the winds which swept through the ancient pine and cypress trees fringing our paddocks. One calm, warm evening yielded sheer magic:

when we walked to a nearby hilltop to catch the last of a vivid sunset, flight after flight of swifts came swooping out of the southern sky, skimming close to the ground and passing with a rush of wings like miniature angels.

In this isolated setting, I managed to complete the second volume of the 'Victorian Age' trilogy, ironically enough titled *Life in the Country*. By 1975, the final volume, *Life in the Cities*, had been successfully published, and launched by premier Rupert 'Dick' Hamer at the Mitre Tavern in Melbourne. All three volumes went through several editions, selling about 80 000 copies in all. I also published several more facsimile volumes in short runs of 500–1000 copies, notably the three-volume versions of Garryowen's *Chronicles of Early Melbourne*, and another classic, *Victoria and Its Metropolis*.

Since our farm income was only a few hundred dollars from the sale of hay, it was just as well we had these ventures to fall back on. In addition, Kerry was offered a job as secretary to the principal of the new Woodleigh Anglican school at Baxter, which helped greatly with reduced fees for the twins as they began secondary education. But while our finances remained stable, the same could not be said for our relationship—by 1978, our marriage had come to an end. Goose Hill was sold for the low figure of $75 000. My wife moved with the children to a house in Mount Eliza, while I moved to a house in South Frankston, then managed to buy a small cottage on an acre of land in another part of Main Ridge. Before departing Goose Hill, however, I had to undertake the worrying task of disposing of our six old 'boilers'—hens which had long stopped laying. I caught the first one with some difficulty, held it with one hand over an old well, and brought down a razor-sharp axe on its neck. The other hens immediately went quiet, almost paralysed, as though they sensed that the end was near. The incident so impressed my youngest son that years later he did a frightening painting of the scene with me as axe murderer.

~

Another cogwheel of destiny now began to slot into place.

Throughout his years as chief archivist at the State Library, Harry Nunn had been quietly working away behind the scenes to have the government records hived off into a separate institution, along the lines of Britain's famed Public Record Office. In 1973, Harry had succeeded in persuading the new Hamer government to introduce his draft of the first Victorian Public Records Bill, largely copied from the British act. The Nunn–Hamer action was long overdue. For 140 years, documents of all kinds had been piling up in government and municipal offices throughout Victoria, or had been randomly destroyed to make space. The State Library basement could hold only a fraction of the most historically important records, and the sorting and research facilities there were appalling—some documents had even been stolen by private collectors. After Harry's bill had slipped through the state parliament, he discovered a spacious, air-conditioned warehouse at Laverton in Melbourne's south-west. The government bought the building for the bargain price of $1.6 million and turned it into the main repository for official records.

Harry Nunn had written into his legislation a seemingly innocuous clause stating that the keeper of public records (himself) was responsible for publishing suitable extracts from the records. As the inaugural publications officer, he appointed the same Gwyn James who had been director of MUP until Peter Ryan took over. Gwyn produced for Victoria's Public Record Office (PRO) a few reprints of early Blue Books and the like, and a collection of documents on the Eureka rebellion. When in 1978 Gwyn reached the compulsory retiring age, Harry asked me if I would be interested in applying for his job.

I had another look at the holdings, which at that time consisted mainly of nineteenth-century records. It seemed that the best way to make them accessible to the public was to reprint the most important records bit by bit in a series of volumes, along the lines of *Historical Records of Australia*, which had proven such a boon to researchers.

By August 1978 I was established at the Laverton repository and had worked out a plan for publishing a series to be called *Historical Records of Victoria* (*HRV*).

In order to break down the huge mass of material into manageable units, I proposed to begin with a 'Foundation Series' of several volumes, to cover the first period of permanent government from 1836 to 1839, when William Lonsdale was in charge of the new settlement. Each book in the series would be devoted to a particular topic, such as Aboriginal people, Crown lands and so on. Within each volume, every official document that could be found would be printed in full, in chronological order. When that series was completed, we would undertake a second series, perhaps more selective, dealing with the 1840s, when CL La Trobe was in charge of the district.

As these matters were being considered, I was busily photocopying everything I could find from the late 1830s. In a portable safe that had been dumped outside the keeper's office, I discovered dozens of files of original documents, most of them written by Lonsdale himself, and unknown to historians. The safe had obviously been tipped on its side while being transported to Laverton: the files were a mess, clearly out of order and never re-sorted or properly accessioned. By photocopying the lot, I was able to arrange the copies in sequence and leave the originals for someone else to sort out.

In addition, in a dark corner of the repository, simply thrown on a shelf, with no name and no location number, I discovered a crumbling ledger book that I named 'Geelong Court Register', for it contained a magistrate's quill-written records of Geelong's first legal cases. Other documents were simply falling apart through dampness or old age, while the ink on many was fast fading into illegibility. These are only a couple of examples of the appalling state into which Victoria's most historic documents had sunk over many years of neglect.

For photocopying, I used one of the earliest Rank Xerox machines, the only plain paper copier available at the time. Its drum had a tendency to stick—within a few seconds, the paper wrapped around it began to char as the heat-setting element remained on. One had to quickly open the machine and extract the paper before it burst into flames. After two small fires, I kept a fire extinguisher handy while copying.

Fairly soon, by delving into every corner of the archives, I had enough copies to begin sorting them into logical order. This process made it apparent that thousands more documents from the early settlement period were missing. Generally, these were loose letters from colonial headquarters in Sydney, easy to misfile, destroy, lose, or allow to be acquired by collectors of Victoriana. I also discovered that, during World War I, officials had permitted philatelists to rummage through the files and cut the old stamps and postal marks off letters, which they would then sell in aid of Red Cross funds. To this day, many of those irreplaceable documents have neat little rectangles cut in them, obliterating the wording on the reverse side.

I wondered if other file copies of the missing or mutilated documents might have been preserved in government quarters in Sydney. The director of the New South Wales Archives Authority was Ian McLean, who had been Harry Nunn's chief assistant when the Victorian archives were held by the State Library. Ian was enormously helpful, allowing me to roam through the stacks in Sydney, where he placed a desk and a modern photocopier at my disposal. The results were overwhelming: practically everything missing from the Victorian archives was there in pristine form as originally written or dictated by Sydney officials, before their clerks made fair copies for despatch to William Lonsdale. Even better, many documents bore the governor and colonial secretary's confidential minutes, which were never meant for Melbourne eyes. I went home after a week's concentrated work bearing about 2000 photocopies, and later made more trips to pick up specialised items overlooked the first time.

Excited by the possibilities, Harry began diverting some of his authorised staff to work on the material I was gathering. One typist, Judith Gillard, completed the difficult task of transcribing the first Melbourne police court records, dating from 1836 to 1838, from a thick volume kept mainly by William Lonsdale in his capacity as magistrate. The second volume, for the years 1839–40, was never found. Former magistrate WJ Cuthill told me that he had located the first volume in an empty cell at the City Court when he started work there in 1925, but that the second volume was missing even then.

Judith Gillard was soon joined by her friend Jocelyn Macmillan. Together, they pounded out vast piles of typing from the photocopies, doing their best to lay it out in a form suitable for future typesetting. Computers and word processors were almost unknown for office work, and Harry, or perhaps his superiors, resolutely set their faces against purchasing the new IBM golf-ball electric typewriters. I often felt sorry for our two typists, but even so, their productivity was about ten times the normal public-service standard.

Up to this point, we had disguised the magnitude of our publishing plans. But so much time and money had been invested in our (unannounced) project that we had to come clean. At Harry Nunn's request, in May 1979 I redrafted my original proposals for the *HRV* series into a form suitable for ministers and other departments to consider. Harry coolly took this lengthy report, removed my name from it, substituted his own, and added an introductory paragraph. In the event, Harry, supported by history professors Alan Shaw and Geoff Blainey, managed to obtain the funding.

Seething because of Harry's actions, I resigned from the permanent staff in mid-1979. After being pressed to stay, I agreed to continue editing *HRV* material on a part-time basis, as long as I was able to resume my own work, in my own time. This agreement took effect at the beginning of 1980, when I was appointed editor-in-chief of the whole project—still part-time.

~

The first project I tackled was a re-examination of the life of that demonic character John Norton, proprietor of the *Truth* newspaper chain for most of its early years. Norton was such an extravagant and extroverted character that his own writings provided copious information and detail. By comparing these with verbatim court reports of the day, and the versions of colourful events written by Norton's plentiful enemies, it was possible to get somewhere near the likely truth of his actions and motivations. As I had suspected, there was much to admire as well as despise about Norton, for how else could one explain the enormous loyalty of the working class towards the old *Truth*, in those innocent days before pictorial sex became its mainstay?

The results of my work were published in 1981 as *That Damned Democrat*, along with extracts from Norton's writings on baby farming scandals, trade monopolies, women's rights and many other questions of social justice. Peter Ryan leapt on the manuscript for publication by MUP and soon sold 4000 hardbacks at under $13 each. Even better, the *Sydney Morning Herald* bought the serial rights and published my complete text in daily episodes.

Then a former Royal Australian Navy officer named Al Knight, who had been my publisher at Nelson's for the final two 'Victorian Age' volumes, started his own publishing company: Hyland House. He asked if I had anything suitable for him. I was able to rescue more of the Vagabond's work, consisting of his descriptions of rural Victoria in the 1880s and 1890s. These forgotten articles were collected into a book called *Vagabond Country*, beautifully designed by Alison Forbes and published in a lavish edition. Knight managed to get a subsidy of $6000 from the Victorian Ministry for the Arts, of which I received $2000. Despite good reviews, however, the book didn't sell too well. I suppose its natural audience, living in towns scattered throughout the state, were not large purchasers of books.

I also acted as historical adviser for a Film Australia series called *The Migrant Experience* that was shown on SBS television. The director was a lawyer and filmmaker named Ben Lewin. To obtain visual material cheaply enough, he used re-enactments shot during the silent movie period.

One day, towards the end of 1981, I received a call from John Ross, who had long ago left the editorial chair at *Fashion News* to become a successful book publisher, first at Macmillan, then with Lloyd O'Neil in South Yarra. John had worked out a deal with the State Library Victoria to publish one of their most valuable holdings, a large album of original watercolours by the colonial artist ST Gill, entitled *The Victorian Gold Fields 1852–3*. I provided a lengthy biographical introduction, and descriptive captions for each of the paintings.

As interest in Australiana was booming at that time, the following year, John suggested that we plan a pictorial essay to be called *Australia: A History in Photographs*. After I prepared a framework of major historical events since 1788, my niece Jane Fenton visited every Australian capital city to search for relevant, good-quality photographs. From several thousand excellent pictures, most of them unpublished, we selected a few hundred. I again wrote the chapter introductions and captions, and the book was published in 1983 in what seemed to me a huge edition of 36 000 hardbacks. Wonderfully, a Sydney book club had ordered 16 000 copies to sell to its members as the recommended book of the month. Most newspapers gave the book extensive reviews, so the remaining copies soon vanished, too.

The success of this photographic history made John Ross keen to see if a similar approach could work using historical 'genre' paintings. People were beginning to plan for Australia's bicentennial celebrations in 1988, and we could foresee a flood of competition unless we got in first. The planning for this book, on the positive side of Australia's development from 1788 to 1983, and called *Australia: Spirit of a Nation*, made me think deeply for the first time about what aspects of Australia I really admired. This was a jolting experience: I began to realise that it was easy to criticise the movers and shakers of society for their occasional mistakes, and not give them enough credit for their constructive activities.

What was it that made me proud and glad to be an Australian? The continent, I realised, could have been snatched from the

Aboriginal people by anyone—Dutch, Indonesian, Japanese, Chinese. It was a mere historical accident, and a fortunate one, that lieutenant James Cook 'discovered' the fertile east coast on behalf of an expanding British Empire that possessed tens of thousands of surplus convicts to export as a cheap labour force. I worked my way right through the remarkable story of how free Australians had shaken off this convict heritage, explored the huge continent, made the land bear fruit, fought in Britain's wars, established a federated democracy, achieved high living standards, and produced some of the world's best sportsmen and women. It was not difficult for picture researcher Debby Cramer to find excellent paintings and other illustrations to illustrate my 120 000 words, mainly in the nation's public galleries and libraries. These works had mostly been completed at times of great national passion and were a true reflection of the ambitions that have made Australia what it is.

Reviewers like Dinny O'Hearn and Russel Ward were generally enthusiastic about this cheerful approach to the past, but David Grearson in the *National Times* thought it was 'a queer sort of history indeed', suitable mainly for 'third-form history classes'. Thank goodness general readers disagreed, purchasing most of the first edition of 15 000 copies. The heads of Australia Post then saw the book, liked it, and ordered a second edition of 10 000 copies, to be sold for almost $100. This became part of their bicentennial effort, issued in conjunction with replicas of historic stamps. All copies of this edition sold immediately.

A book that did not do so well was *The Long Last Summer*, a study of Australia's embryonic upper class before World War I took so many of its sons. The work and its title were suggested to me by editor Valerie Haye, who also did the picture research. After contacting as many established families as I could list, who seemed willing to cooperate, Valerie came up with a good collection of photographs copied from their old albums. I planned the chapters, tried to impose unifying themes, and wrote the introductions and captions. The book was published by Nelson's in 1985 and launched at Rippon Lea mansion by Sir Rupert Clarke. But it sold poorly, partly because Nelson's thought it could get $45 a copy from the wealthy people who were assumed to be the main market: not so. Other reactions were amusingly mixed. Mark Thomas in the *Canberra Times* decided the book gave an 'honest insight into what made Australia tick', but one customer at Webber's Bookshop in Melbourne returned his copy with the angry comment that 'the author must be a communist'.

As a result of all this activity, I was able to save enough money to look for a better house, assisted by selling the cottage at Main Ridge for $90 000. My mother had built a small house next to Dina's family in Mount Eliza, and I stayed there for a time while awaiting settlement. One day early in 1986, after swimming at Moondah Beach, I decided to return home along a delightful clifftop road called Earimil Drive. At number 8, I glimpsed an auctioneer's board. Behind a huge cypress tree, which spanned the entire 80-foot frontage, was a charming old brick cottage with a galvanised-iron roof and wraparound verandah. Although sagging and decrepit with age, it had a magical atmosphere, its half-acre planted with fragrant old-fashioned roses and overgrown trees.

I felt I could never afford to buy such a property but decided to attend the auction. Few people turned up, and even these I may have deterred by gazing meaningfully at a wall of handmade bricks that was leaning outwards and seemed likely to topple at any time. Not often have I been so nervous as when the bidding started, nor as stunned when it was knocked down to me for only $157 000.

I moved in at the beginning of May 1986 and discovered that I was the owner of Mount Eliza's oldest surviving house, built by captain Edward Lintot in the 1840s, when he grazed sheep on a large freehold acreage running up to the Nepean Highway. He and his servants had quarried clay on the slopes and made bricks that turned a wonderful orange shade when subjected to primitive wood-fired kilns. To make mortar, they crushed and burned seashells, the remnants of which could be uncovered by scraping between the bricks with a fingernail. After 140 years of storms from the bay, the bricks and mortar had begun to soften and needed to be protected by heavy layers of oil paint. It was the slow collapse of the pliable bricks that had caused that wall to lean outwards, as well as opening 2-inch cracks in the internal plasterwork. And so, with the enthusiasm of new ownership, I bought large quantities of filler, paint and other essentials, and in my spare hours set to work stopping up the holes. Some of the internal walls were so bad that I simply built ceiling-high bookshelves to cover the worst openings. Still, within a few months the house had been transformed—although the mouldy bathroom outside the back door remained a problem.

Early in this resettlement program, I had a call from Meg Fraser, the general books editor of Reader's Digest. They wanted me to prepare a lavishly illustrated book to be called *The Exploration of Australia*, dealing with the subject from ancient times to the era of satellite mapping. I had barely touched the fringes of the topic in earlier books and was immediately enthused, especially when the digest offered to pay me $35 000 for 120 000 words. As I received the instalments, the money enabled me to pay off my remaining debts.

My working hours were now more profitable but even more onerous. Every morning, seven days a week, I crawled out of bed at 5 a.m. and began work on the Reader's Digest book. I went back to the explorers' original journals and diaries, in the form of photocopies, comparing what they had written with modern survey maps. By lunchtime, my brain would be reeling with overloads of new information, so for a few hours I would turn my attention to plastering and painting the house. Late afternoon and early evening were devoted to work on the current volumes of *HRV*, after which early nights were essential. No wonder I didn't need a TV, record player or any books beyond those about the subjects I was working on.

Through this intense method of working, I finished the exploration book in double-quick time. Reader's Digest took a gamble and decided to print 60 000, about 50 000 of which were sold by mail order. For some reason, most newspapers were reluctant to review the digest's books; even so, the remaining copies trickled out through booksellers at various prices. It is one of the most satisfying books I have ever done, and certainly the biggest-selling.

~

While my work on the *HRV* was ostensibly a part-time pursuit, it nonetheless stretched across the entirety of the 1980s, and well beyond. To begin with, it was during 1980 that the difficult first volume, entitled *Beginnings of Permanent Government*, mostly took shape. MUP had applied to be licensed as the publisher of the series, but the government rejected this approach from a proven professional publishing house and entrusted the task to the Victorian Government Printing Office (VGPO), which had to grapple with the conservatism of ageing employees in secure public service jobs. This resulted in quotations that were double those which I obtained from commercial book printers—remarkably, even at those rates, the VGPO couldn't break even.

On 28 October 1981, the first volume was ready to be announced by the state governor, Sir Henry Winneke. The final sheets had been hastily printed and included with a few leather-bound copies on which the glue was still damp when the first of them were delivered to Government House—five minutes before Winneke was to give his address on the importance of making accurate history available to the public at an affordable price. Nonetheless, considering that *HRV* consisted mainly of antique documents (albeit with modern commentary), the VGPO did well to sell its initial print run of 4000 copies.

Academic historians, who apart from Alan Shaw and Geoffrey Blainey had been largely ignored in setting up the project, were not slow to go on the attack. In his *Age* review, Dr Lloyd Robson criticised our attempts to make the documents comprehensible to the general public, instead of publishing them with ancient spellings and annotating them with endless footnotes. Robert Sharman, the WA state librarian, similarly ignored our oft-repeated statement that we would publish *all* available documents, claiming in the journal *Archives and Manuscripts* that the editor 'seems to have chosen the documents in order to suit the whim of the moment'.

Harry Nunn reached compulsory retiring age in 1981. His replacement was Chris Hurley, whose career path after university had woven through several federal government departments, including the Australian Archives. For a time he interfered little with the *HRV* project. However, in mid-1981 he arbitrarily removed our two expert typists from the publications staff and put them into a general typing pool. From then on, manuscripts had to be prepared by whatever typist might be available. One employee summed it up in their letter of resignation: 'The standard of typescript coming from the pool is not suitable for printers' copy ... It is inconsistent, done on several different machines, and full of errors.' Our two specially trained typists naturally resigned as well. Why should such efficient people put up with faulty theories of personnel management?

Coming on board now was Ian MacFarlane, a former journalist who had worked for some years as publications officer for the Public Service Board. Ian was pretty well accustomed to the subterranean ways of the bureaucracy and stuck loyally to the task of producing *HRV*. It was largely Ian's doggedness that made it possible for my part-time arrangement to last as long as ten years. Somehow, he coped with every attempt by senior public servants to sabotage the project and prove that it either couldn't or shouldn't be done.

With the publications staff reduced from four to one-and-a-half people, Hurley was able to strike another shrewd blow. He evicted Publications from the quiet private area of the repository allocated by Harry Nunn, and forced Ian MacFarlane to sit in a corner of the open-plan general office, where interruptions and annoyances were frequent. At lunchtime, Ian even had to act as telephone switchboard operator.

Volumes 2A and 2B of *HRV*, dealing with the Aboriginal people of Port Phillip, rolled off the presses on schedule in 1982 and 1983, respectively. By this time, reviewers were beginning to realise that the project was bringing together a vast hoard of unpublished material that had been scattered among many different files, assembling it in a way most useful to individual researchers. In volume 3, dealing with the first years of European settlement in Melbourne, we made a special effort to include all of the relevant government documents and illustrations, for it was to be published at the same time as Victoria's sesquicentenary celebrations. The result was a volume of more than 650 pages, with many colour illustrations on fold-out inserts. Even the VGPO excelled itself on this one, publishing the book towards the end of 1984 for less than $30 a copy.

However, Dr Robson again succeeded in an *Age* review in damning the project with faint praise: 'Although the series may succeed in irritating some historians, no doubt there are many others overjoyed with the material now at the disposal of students ...' Robson and others still couldn't see the impossibility of imposing theoretical requirements on torn and tattered documents we had barely saved from destruction. Even worse was Chris McConville, who opined in the February–March 1985 issue of *Australian Book Review* that the *HRV* project was 'a scandal ... a lavish, unimaginative, unsourced publicity stunt'.

Ian MacFarlane and I pressed on with volume 4, another large production of more than 600 pages dealing with communications, trade and transport, and published at the end of 1985. It gave the first detailed history of early Victorian shipping, customs, immigration and postal services. Family historians in particular appreciated its complete listings of the sponsored immigrants who had settled in Port Phillip. By this time, too, it was noticeable that many thesis writers and historians were beginning to use *HRV* as primary source material.

By 1986, John Cain junior's Labor government was starting to suspect that something was seriously wrong with the management and procedures of the PRO. Outside consultants were employed to investigate public complaints and make recommendations. Unfortunately, they knew little about archival procedures or scholarly publishing. Even more unfortunately, *HRV* came under their close scrutiny. This led to long delays in the publication of volume 5, entitled *Surveyors' Problems and Achievements*, which was further hindered by the insistence of the Public Records Advisory Council that a subcommittee should be set up to 'assist' the editors in their work.

Ian and I were facing enough problems as it was. When we got into the bowels of the old Survey and Lands Department, we found that the records were in an even worse state than we had feared. Surveyors' field books had simply been stacked without lists or labels into one underground vault—no-one alive could tell us which field books had been kept by which surveyors. The correspondence was a similar jumble, kept in no coherent order, and often mixed in with hundreds of boxes of general land records. Luckily, the original survey maps, many beautifully executed in ink and watercolours, had been well sorted and preserved by Bob Spreadborough, and could readily be copied. With all these difficulties, the survey volume did not appear until 1988, but it did manage to show readers more of the historical treasures that lay, mouldering away, in forgotten archives.

Meanwhile, the inefficiencies of the VGPO were also being investigated by a firm of management consultants. Its 1987 report, leaked to the *Sun News-Pictorial* and published in January 1988, determined that management had been unable to overcome many entrenched practices. In addition, the VGPO, like the PRO, was part of the Department of Property and Services (DPS), which had effectively been taken over by a politicised group of varying capacities. And so the bureaucratic infighting began in earnest. In early 1989, hundreds of memos and meetings later, the DPS's corporate services director refused to produce any further volumes of *HRV*, thus breaking the compact which the VGPO and PRO had made with book purchasers to complete the whole Foundation Series.

Ian MacFarlane and I had continued to transcribe records—doing it ourselves, since all of our remaining typists had now been taken away—and prepare the volume 6 manuscript, to be entitled *The Crown, the Land and the Squatter*. A new director, Brian Wilder, had taken over at MUP and offered to complete the series as long as MUP received a subsidy of $20 000 for each of the remaining volumes. But the new director-general of DPS, Michael Blamey, in consultation with the minister, RW 'Bunna' Walsh, decided to ignore MUP's offer, instead cancelling the clearly annoying *HRV* project out of hand and giving me notice of dismissal. Hurley made no further protest, accepting the apparent fait accompli. Learning about all this on 28 February 1989, I decided I had nothing to lose by going public about some of the many attempts the public service had made to kill the publication of its historical documents.

First of all I wrote to the new department chiefs, complaining that MUP's offer had been ignored and that no other government department in the democratic world would 'summarily close down a project of cultural, educational and historical importance, without consulting the foundation editor'. I also offered to pay the $20 000 fee required by MUP out of my own salary, and to continue to edit the series for practically nothing. I had realised that it would have been easy for these officials to ignore and simply file my letter, so I took the precaution of sending copies to the premier and the state governor, whom I knew were enthusiastic about the publication of early government records. This all had the effect of stopping the officials in their tracks and forcing them to reverse the shutdown. In April, detailed negotiations with MUP began, and for a time it seemed that the department would find the $20 000 subsidy required. Six months later, Blamey wrote to me stating that every attempt had been made to find the money in the departmental budget, but without success—my contract as editor would not be renewed after November.

It was time to take even stronger action. A petition calling for the continuation of *HRV* was signed by 90 per cent of PRO staff. Next, I circulated a list of suggested parliamentary questions among Opposition members, who discovered for the first time that up to $300 000 would have to be refunded to *HRV* subscribers who had been promised the full set of volumes. And I gave the full facts to John Lahey of the *Age*, who on 17 October published a long article outlining the DPS's dog-in-the-manger attitude. A flurry of correspondence followed in the *Age*, with prominent historians calling for the continuation of this 'great boon to scholars'. Some *HRV* subscribers, including Supreme Court judges, even phoned the PRO, offering donations if a fund could be established to save the project. McPherson's, the book printing firm, said they would produce the remaining volumes at cost price as long as the VGPO handed over all necessary materials. These remarkably generous and unprecedented offers were bandied around until eventually McPherson's gave up in despair.

On 20 October, the *Age* published a strong leading article saying that the government was showing 'extraordinary shortsightedness' in halting the series. The editor, Creighton Burns, followed this with a phone call to John Cain, warning him that the *Age* would continue to publish similar editorials and articles until the battle was won. The premier then instructed minister Walsh to reverse the department's decision. Attempting to turn around this political disaster, Walsh issued a press release stating that the history of Victoria should be made readily available to the people of the state.

I was not finished, however. On 26 October I wrote to the auditor-general, Chesleigh 'Ches' Baragwanath, pointing out that the VGPO had failed to follow normal commercial practice by not depreciating its unsold book stocks each financial year. The auditor-general's subsequent investigation showed that the VGPO had accumulated losses of $7.2 million on its total operations. Next, I distributed to interested MPs a document showing how the government could save many millions of dollars each year by abolishing the entire DPS, along with its minister and hangers-on, and transferring its few essential functions to other departments. The DPS in fact was only a supervisory department that had been permitted to set up its own top-heavy executive structure over operational bodies like the PRO; altogether, the department employed 2400 public servants, many of whom were obviously unnecessary and grossly overpaid. I circulated this damning document to all interested MPs.

One early result of my new occupation as a lobbyist was that the VGPO lost its stranglehold over government printing business—it would later be split up into specialised units. By mid-January 1991, after Joan Kirner had taken over from John Cain as premier, she had learned enough about all the bureaucratic hijinks to authorise the abolition of the DPS.

In July 1991, volume 6 of *HRV* was launched by Victorian governor Davis McCaughey to widespread plaudits, although there were still some dissenting voices: Don Watson, for one, complained that we hadn't made the story of Victorian squatters more exciting. Volume 7, entirely edited by Ian MacFarlane, would be published by MUP in 1998, at last completing the Foundation Series, apart from a volume comprising a cumulated index and supplementary documents that had been discovered. The project would take more than twenty years to complete, largely because of the extraordinary interference experienced by its editors.

~

In the early spring of 1987, I found myself ready for new activities. The back of the house in Mount Eliza was a crumbling wreck, besides which I was fed up with having to go outside in all weather to use the primitive toilet and bathroom. I decided on a major renovation and borrowed $30 000 to finance an extension. In this way I became what is known as an owner-builder. Two years later, as the boom of the 1980s neared its peak, I offered the house to an agent, who sold it within twenty-four hours for just over $380 000. Immediately on taking possession, the new owner cut down the magnificent old cypress in front, to allow a better view across the bay, and resold the house for $450 000. It was a fittingly ironic point in the life of the one-time idealist who had written *The Land Boomers*.

I moved to a cheaper but more modern house in Mornington, with a verandah from which you could catch glimpses of the bay.

My books and files were now so extensive that they filled most of the rooms. Towards the end of 1993, my two older sons would build a spacious second-storey extension. One of the most satisfying aspects of life for a parent is to see their offspring practising advanced skills which they themselves are too old to master. Adding a new storey to an existing house can be the most complex possible undertaking in the field of domestic architecture. The potential complications were huge, yet within eight weeks of the submission of plans to the local council, we had the job ready for painting and carpeting. When we stood back and admired the result, I felt as proud as any creator can be. The rebuilt house had a large sunny balcony level with the tops of the gum trees on my neighbours' properties. This gave a feeling of being in the bush, while through the trees you could see all the way from Arthurs Seat, around the bay, to the faint outlines of Melbourne's skyscrapers. It seemed a neat compromise between country and urban living.

Meanwhile, in some ways the politicians and bureaucrats had done me a favour by making my *HRV* position untenable. I was able to concentrate once more on the real business in my working life: sorting out the tangled skeins of past events and laying them down in fresh versions of history. I felt enormous relief, and a new surge of creativity.

The first product was an analysis of all the available trustworthy material on the fate of Victoria's Aboriginal people before the gold rush. The remorseless expansion of white settlement had practically obliterated the land's original inhabitants, but no-one quite knew how it had happened. The generally accepted version was that brutal squatters and their convict servants had simply massacred the several thousand Indigenous people who wandered across the fertile grasslands, now dominated by sheep and cattle grazing. But there seemed to be something wrong with this story. Police, magistrates and Aboriginal 'protectors' had been instructed to report every murder that occurred or was even rumoured. At most, these could account for only a few hundred killings. As I read through thousands of pages of handwritten contemporary reports, however, the real story started to emerge. By and large, the genocide of full-blood Aboriginal people had been caused not by squatters' guns but by disease, a change from hunting to charity handouts, and loss of tribal pride. It still amounted to genocide, but it was somewhat subtler in its execution than outright murder.

I wrote up the results of this research in a book called *Who Killed the Koories?* On Bill Green's advice, I gave the manuscript to John Timlin, who ran a small literary agency. John cleverly played one publisher against another to win what seemed to me a large advance on future royalties, eventually paid by Louise Adler, then the publisher at William Heinemann Australia. The 5000 hardback copies, released in 1990, eventually sold out—the book would be reprinted as a paperback early in 1994 under a new title, *Black Land, White Land.* And yet, although the hardback retailed at nearly $35, I doubt if Heinemann ever made a profit, while I remained rather conscience-stricken about profiting from the story of those long-dead Aboriginal people.

It is intriguing to look back on reviews of *Who Killed the Koories?* The reviewers were confronted with first-hand evidence from contemporary reports by generally objective and sympathetic observers who actually lived with the tribes. Tim Rowse, in *Australian Book Review*, thought I needed a better 'moral–historical thesis' to enable me to pass judgement on the worth of the source material. The Aboriginal activists whom I met in Melbourne liked the book's attempt to reach a balanced historical viewpoint, and promised they would do all they could to assist its sale.

I was now approached by Roy Farrell, whom I had replaced as manager of the Melbourne University bookshop nearly a quarter-century earlier. He had opened a bookshop in Mornington, in partnership with his wife Elizabeth, also an experienced bookseller, and was now intent on fulfilling a longstanding dream of becoming a specialised publisher. He asked me whether I had any suggestions.

During the early 1970s, while researching material for *Life in the Country*, I had come across a remarkable memoir of the gold-rush and land-boom eras called *Forty Years in the Wilderness*. Written by John Chandler, it described the incredible hardships he'd experienced as a boy and then as a young man struggling for survival. In his old age Chandler became a religious fanatic, but through the judicious editing of his more outlandish passages, we were able to produce what still seems a rare and enthralling narrative of life at the lower levels of society. Some of Chandler's descendants were still alive at this time, and the information they provided on family and company history added considerably to the book's value. The Farrells' Loch Haven Books produced the work in 1990 in a paperback edition of 2000 copies, which sold very well, and in a hardback edition of 1000 copies, which did not do so well.

The Farrells then agreed to sink some of their capital into the lavish production of *Old Melbourne Town: Before the Gold Rush*, a 500-page epic I had written, supplemented by colour plates of contemporary paintings. It covered many forgotten but remarkable aspects of life in the city, including the story of the Batman family, and Melbourne's first great land boom and bust of the 1840s. It was an instant success, reaching the bestseller list at A&R in Melbourne in 1991, and one week even scrambling into the *Bulletin*'s top ten—I was delighted that the Farrells' gamble had paid off. We published a sequel in 1993 entitled *Melbourne After the Gold Rush*, which included hundreds of rarely seen paintings and sketches, mainly from the State Library's La Trobe Collection and the Parliamentary Library.

~

In the early 1990s, my mother began to show the effects of a stressful life of more than eighty years, including sixty years of heavy cigarette smoking, being admitted on several occasions to Hastings Hospital on the Mornington Peninsula. In February 1992 I made a quick trip to France to see James, and did my best to make my way around

Paris and the south of the country. When I got to England, however, I received an urgent message saying that I should return home as quickly as possible: my mother was back in hospital and frailer than ever. On 14 March, while Dina and I were holding her hands, a faint smile came over her face and she stopped breathing. It took us a minute or two to realise that she had died.

Dorothy left behind a mountain of press cuttings and other material. There were also a couple of boxes of family memoirs into which I had seen her dipping from time to time, during attempts to write the story of her journalist father, Monty Grover. Some months after she died I decided to have a look through these documents, and I was delighted to find a bundle of Monty's own biographical writing describing his early days working for Melbourne and Sydney newspapers. Most of it appeared to have been written about the time of World War I, possibly when he relinquished editorship of the Sydney *Sun* to concentrate on building up the *Sunday Sun*. To any journalist, writer or historian, the manuscripts were a goldmine of first-hand information about the days when the main outlet for literary endeavour lay in printed newspapers and journals. So I decided to pull together twenty-five chapters of Monty's press reminiscences, to which I added his amusing *Bulletin* satire 'The Last Day: A Sub-Editor's Dream'. Monty did not include anything about his own family history, but I had already spent a good deal of time tracking down his military and convict ancestors in Britain and Australia, and I wrote an introductory essay showing how a man like Monty and his newspapers could only have been produced in the context of Australia's peculiar history. The result was *Hold Page One: Memoirs of Monty Grover, Editor*, published by Loch Haven Books. The book was largely ignored by contemporary metropolitan newspapers, but provincial papers, where many old-time journalists still possessed a sense of the continuity of history, gave it a better run.

One collection in the PRO which attracted my attention was the Crown Law Department's archived case files of capital offences—that is, serious crimes that had attracted the death penalty before it was abolished in 1975. Nearly 200 people had been judicially executed in Victoria for murders and serious sexual offences since 1842. Among those hanged were five women, and since the hanging of women arouses particular horror, it seemed to me that it would be of greater impact to deal only with their cases. The result was a small volume entitled *The Woman as Murderer: Five Who Paid with Their Lives*. To my amazement, the transcripts of evidence showed that only one of them, Jean Lee, should have been hanged, even if we still believed in capital punishment for premeditated murder. I published 1000 hardbacks in 1994, and the volume attracted favourable reviews from the *Age*, among other papers, and rapidly sold out. The *Herald Sun* reprinted several chapters in full, and the Australian Institute of Criminology listed the book's complete details on its website.

Computer desktop technology had now reached the point where all typesetting and images could be processed electronically on storage discs, with a large reduction in cost. This led me to develop a more ambitious project. The immigration files of the PRO and various state libraries provided copious information on the hardships endured by early immigrants to Australia, yet no historian had utilised this material to any extent. With the assistance of many of the pioneers' descendants, I developed a large-format paperback titled *Perilous Voyages to the New Land* that included many old woodcuts and photographs. I typeset the work using the latest Macintosh computers and software, and it was printed in Melbourne in 1995. I assumed the market would accommodate around 1000 copies, but I received about 1500 direct-mail orders. This success led to the production in 1997 of 2000 copies of an even more elaborate hardback edition containing large colour plates depicting sailing ships and seaports of the era, which retailed for almost twice as much as the first edition.

For many years I had been collecting photographs and information on the Great Depression years. I could remember some of my own experiences as a child, but in later life I had become dissatisfied with the somewhat bloodless accounts of the period written mostly by academics. In 1995 I sat down to sort out the mass of material, to see if I could produce a more realistic book. It occurred to me that many people still living would have clear memories of their experiences of the 1930s, so I wrote to hundreds and received excellent replies from individuals as diverse as BA Santamaria, Jim Cairns and Dame Elisabeth Murdoch. One Melbourne man even told me how he had helped the secret White Army set up a radio network to counter the anticipated communist revolution. These memoirs formed about a third of the book and balanced my own interpretation of events. The result was *The Human Face of the Great Depression*, published in 1996 in hardback and soon sold out. For the first time since *The Land Boomers*, I received hundreds of deeply affecting letters from readers whose lives had been twisted out of shape by their family experiences. A large-format paperback edition followed, by which time I was glad to have the professional distribution services of Dennis and Lee Jones to handle bookshop sales.

About this time I was selected by the Australia Council as the last recipient of its Emeritus Award, given to writers with a long history of contributing to the literary scene. One of Paul Keating's final acts as prime minister was to present the award at a function at the Forum Theatre in Melbourne. At sixty-seven, I felt this was a fittingly ironic conclusion to my writing years.

And then, once again, fate stepped in. Having met the solicitor Bill Slater when he was attorney-general during my *Age* reporting days, for years I had been tracking the progress of his law firm Slater & Gordon, mainly through newspaper reports of its efforts to win compensation for industrial victims. Occasionally I had thought of trying to write the firm's history, but I would back off because I believed that solicitors would never give me access to their clients' files. So it was a complete surprise when, in 1996, MUP publisher Teresa Pitt asked if I would be interested in writing the history of 'a radical law firm'.

'What, Slater & Gordon?' I blurted. 'Yes, but only if I can have complete access to their files.'

In that strange manner developed my last major work, *That Disreputable Firm: The Inside Story of Slater & Gordon*—the oddball title evolved from a comment made by premier Jeff Kennett under parliamentary privilege that Slater & Gordon was indeed disreputable. The book took two years to complete and was published in 1998 as a hardback selling at $39.95; today it commands much higher prices on the antiquarian book market. The work showed me how essential it is to have law firms which are not part of the establishment but genuinely believe in using lawful methods to win justice for helpless people damaged by free enterprise and governmental systems.

I almost produced one more book. Penguin Books had taken over Lloyd O'Neil's publication rights to my 1985 work *Australia: Spirit of a Nation*. In 1999 Penguin proposed an updated edition with a new introduction, to be published in conjunction with the centenary celebration of Federation. This seemed a great idea, and I enthusiastically concentrated on writing about historically important developments that had taken place during the fifteen-odd years since the first edition. I also wrote new material emphasising that the pressing social problems of Aboriginal people would never be solved unless those people were better assisted to live with the dominant white civilisation.

Several months after I submitted the revised material, in May 2000, I received a letter from the publishers stating 'It's your book and you can say whatever you like', but also that Penguin had to 'ensure that the company does not attract unsought controversy or adverse media comment'. I replied that the publishers' comments 'looked perilously like censorship'.

That venture, apart from a daily diary and this autobiography, was practically the end of my writing career.

PART IV

LAST EFFORTS

CHAPTER 10

All Dreams Must Fade

As THE 1990s drew to a close, Mornington began to expand rapidly. No longer was it a peaceful little fishing village. When plans for a large new supermarket were announced, I decided it was time to move somewhere quieter. I was able to sell my house for $410 000, determined to retire at age seventy and live off the capital gain. I then drove all over southern Victoria, within a radius of 200 kilometres from Melbourne, searching for a suitable property. I was shown a startling number of broken-down, filthy farmhouses in equally appalling surroundings. I was just about to give up when Steve Paragreen, an estate agent at Foster in South Gippsland, showed me a wonderful old homestead called Fernhyll that was set on 90 undulating acres in the foothills of the magical Strzelecki Ranges. So began a fascinating new life.

I do not propose to write too much here about Fernhyll, as the history of the old dairy and the surrounding district is contained in my 2004 publication *Living in the Clouds*. But what I did not write much about in that book was the local characters. They reminded me so much of the Western District people I had known in the 1930s and 1940s that I immediately felt at home. Most of the local inhabitants had come from poverty-stricken backgrounds and had comparatively little formal education or advanced work experience. Nevertheless, they often possessed deep wells of common sense and practical capabilities.

My century-old homestead, built up from the much smaller original dwelling, had many of the obvious drawbacks—poor water supply, rusted iron roof, leaking ceiling, primitive bathroom, poor sewerage and so on—so I had to find local tradesmen to make the most urgent alterations. Their ultra-casual attitudes startled me at first. They might say they would come on a particular day, then turn up days later without warning or apology. Later, I would find out they had been called on to get an old mate out of trouble: to fix a busted truck or water pump or leaking pipe. As a newcomer, I was a long way down their list of priorities. But after a year or two of working alongside them as far as I was able, they would go to great lengths to assist me.

Absentee owners often found it hard to get tradespeople, no matter how much they were able to pay. If a task was left partly done and the weekender ventured to complain, he might be told that the contractor was 'waiting on delivery of a truckload of stump holes'. By the time the owner realised that this was typical way-out humour, the worker had called out 'See you later' and gone on to another job.

Without ever trying to analyse themselves, the tradesmen preserved old bush traditions such as fierce independence, a sardonic attitude to misfortune, dislike of authority, and rat cunning. So when urban politicians and lawyers began legal action against the dangers of passive smoking, the local pubs refused to employ anyone who wasn't already a smoker. Once you established mateship qualifications, some locals began to tell you awful stories of their rough upbringing, including cases of incest, mental illness, domestic violence, even murders disguised as 'accidents'. On the other hand, they all showed remarkable stoicism in the face of illness or financial hardship. There was also a surprising amount of artistic talent hidden in the backwoods, in the form of music, painting, pottery and sculpture.

During my years at Fernhyll, I planted innumerable native trees with the help of Greening Australia—the property was ideal for reforestation, joining up the neighbours' mountain ash planting to other remnants of natural bush. But by 2008, when I was nearly eighty, the more routine tasks of felling and burning trees and branches, along with the constant mowing of several acres around the house for protection against bushfires, were beginning to take their toll. My medical problems were becoming quite severe, too. So I was forced to put my beloved Fernhyll on the market. Impressed by the ambience of seaside Inverloch in south-western Gippsland, I rented a cottage there for a few months and then bought a modern four-bedroom house. Here, I spend my time reading, swimming and reviving past endeavours, and here, with reasonable luck, I will lay me down to sleep.

~

As the years pass and physical strength declines, the joys of life are taken from you one by one. But even as hair and beard turn grey, there are some benefits of ageing that help to compensate for the inevitable. One becomes calmer and more philosophical, accepting the passage of time, and realising that everything important in your life has either been done or will never be done. There is a certain relief in being able to meander along, achieving small victories here and there. One of my favourite poems, 'The Red Mountain', by Francis Maguire, says it best:

> *Now I am a member Of mild events Never given*
> *To bloody ascents.*
> *Yet there was the mountain Sheer rock and height:*
> *And oh, how the summit Was bright, was bright.*

After dying, you may be lucky enough to live on for a few more years in the memories of those who knew you, perhaps even loved you. Then, inevitably, you must join the billions of forgotten people on whose shoulders stand the new generations, your known and unknown descendants.

Postscript

Michael Cannon died peacefully on 24 February 2022. His one regret was to not see this book published, although the thought kept him going for quite a while. He rests in the tranquil Foster Cemetery, Gippsland, near his beloved Fernhyll.

Index

abortion law, 197–8
Adam, FJ 'Bluey', 124
Adams, Arthur (author), 102
Adams, Arthur (poet), 95
Adler, Louise, 227
adolescence
  burst appendix, 52–4
  camping, 59–61
  cycling adventures, 58, 75–7
  dreams, 47
  fatherly advice, 46
  first love, 56–7
  helping in the printery, 44–5
  scouting, 47–51, 59–60
  secondary school, 52–4, 61–2, 63–5
  sexual arousal, 55–6
advertising career, 152–4
Age (Melbourne)
  campaign to save *Historical Records of Victoria*, 223–4
  caption writing, 135
  editorials from gold-rush era, 204
  employment as journalist, 126, 128–32, 135
  general reporting, 130–2
  history of, 126–7
  'inside' articles, 189
  Junior Age supplement, 92–3
  production, 127
  scoop on Heard Island rescue, 130–1
Age Literary Supplement, book reviews, 206
ageing, benefits of, 237
alcohol abuse, 128, 129
Alexandra Palace, London, 121
A.M. (Australian Monthly), 167
Amalgamated Wireless Australasia, 88
Amazing Stories (magazine), 142
An Australian Camera 1851–1914 (Cannon), 207–8
Angus & Robertson, 202, 203
Ansett, Reginald, 158
Antarctica, Heard Island rescue scoop, 130–1
Anthony, Hal, 125, 134
Anzac Day services, 30
Archives Authority, NSW, 213
Argus (Melbourne), 75, 90–1, 151, 189
Atlas Publications, 139, 141
Attiwill, Keith, 143
Auld, Elizabeth, 144
Austin, Harold, 126, 132, 135
Australasian Post, 91
Australasian Sketcher (facsimile edition), 199
Australia, HMAS, 130–1
Australia: A History in Photographs (Cannon), 215
Australia Council grants, 208, 231
Australia in Asia (Barton), 191
Australia Party, 190, 191
Australia: Spirit of a Nation (Cannon), 215–16
Australian (newspaper), 184
Australian Council of Trade Unions (ACTU), 129, 195
Australian Fashion News, 150–2
The Australian Thunderer (ed. Cannon), 204
Australian Wool Bureau, 156–7
Avalon residence, Sydney, 170, 181

Baden-Powell, Robert, 48, 50
Baillieu, WL, 179, 182
Baillieu family, 183
Ball, Macmahon, 178
Ballyhoo (magazine), 142
Baragwanath, Chesleigh 'Ches', 224
Barbara Ramsden Award, 205
Barton, Gordon Page, 190, 191–2, 194, 195, 197, 199, 201, 202, 203
Barton, Yvonne, 191
Bate, Weston, 185
Batt, Leon, 96
Baume, Eric, 120, 171
BBC Television, 121
Bea (aunt), 89
Bean, Charles, 62
Beasley, 'Stabber Jack', 117, 119
Beaumaris residence, 154
Beaven, Sue, 205
Beckett, Ray 'Gander', 170
Beckett, Richard, 201
Bednall, Bill, 158
Beitzel, Harry, 193
Bellew, Jack, 92, 139, 141, 143, 145
Bellew, Peter, 92
Bent, Thomas, 179
birth, 3
Black Land, White Land (Cannon), 227
Blainey, Geoffrey, 183, 208, 213, 219
Blair, Harold, 97
Blamely, Michael, 222–3
Boles, Bernard, 194, 201
Bolte Liberal government (Vic), 189
books
  Australia: A History in Photographs, 215
  Australia: Spirit of a Nation, 215–16
  An Australian Camera 1851–1914, 207–8
  The Australian Thunderer, 204
  Australiana facsimile reprints, 199–200, 209
  Black Land, White Land, 227
  The Exploration of Australia, 218–19
  Famous News Pages in Modern Australian History, 207
  Hold Page One: Memoirs of Monty Grover, Editor, 229
  The Human Face of the Great Depression, 231
  Land Boom and Bust, 206
  The Land Boomers, 183–5, 205–6
  Life in the Country, 209
  Living in the Clouds, 235
  Lola Montez: The Tragic Story of a 'Liberated Woman', 206–7
  The Long Last Summer, 216–17
  Melbourne After the Gold Rush, 227
  Old Melbourne Town: Before the Gold Rush, 227
  Perilous Voyages to the New Land, 230
  That Damned Democrat, 213–14
  That Disreputable Firm: The Inside Story of Slater & Gordon, 232
  Vagabond Country, 214
  Vagabond Papers, 189
  'Victorian Age' trilogy, 205, 209
  Who Killed the Koories? 227
  Who's Master, Who's Man? 205
  The Woman as Murderer: Five Who Paid with Their Lives, 230
Boy Scout movement, 47–8
Brain, Hugh, 182
Brass, Douglas, 174
Brennan, Niall, 193, 201
Brighton residence, Melbourne, 181, 189
Brighton Rock (film), 110
British Empire, loyalty to, 44
Brodney, Spencer, 183
Brodzky, Horace, 183
Brodzky, Maurice, 183
Bromwich, John, 95
Browne, Frank, 171
Bulletin (Sydney), 51, 58, 95–6, 184
Burgess, John, 186
Burns, Creighton, 62, 224
bushfires, 37–8

cadet training, 73–5
Cain, John (Jr), 224
Cain, John (Sr), 128
Cain Labor government (Vic), 221
Cairns, Jim, 198, 231
California News-Sheet (company journal), 108
California Productions, 108
Calwell, Arthur, 117, 135, 167, 174
Campbell, Frank, 183
Campbell, Harold 'Ham', 126
Camperdown, 52, 61–2
Cannon (nee Booth), Agnes Marie (grandmother), 4–5
Cannon, Arthur (father)
  assistance with typesetting business, 139–40
  atheism, 23
  birth, 4–5
  character and personality, 15, 89, 107
  Cobden Times ownership, 5–6, 8, 16, 45
  death, 149

first marriage, 5, 83, 87, 106
as Freemason, 23–4
as ham radio enthusiast, 17
Morse code proficiency, 45, 49
politics, 11, 23, 45
post-war employment, 88
relationship with son, 46, 61, 80, 83–4, 107, 139–40
second marriage, 149
war service, 45, 55, 80, 83
Cannon, Dina (sister), 17, 18–19, 62, 65, 88, 168, 181, 217
Cannon (nee Grover, later Parker), Dorothy 'Dolly' (mother)
appeal for polio sufferers, 36–7
atheism, 23
caring for grandson Paul, 161, 165, 179
character and personality, 38, 88, 90
death, 228–9
family background, 4
history of J.C. Williamson Theatres, 180
journalism career, 5, 16, 37–8, 45, 75, 88, 180
marriage to Arthur Cannon, 5, 83, 87, 106
MBE, 180
politics, 23
public relations career, 107
relationship with Malcolm Parker, 106–7
relocation to Camperdown, 61–2
relocation to Melbourne, 75
Cannon, Henry John (grandfather), 4–5
Cannon, James (son), 181, 182, 209, 226, 228
Cannon, Jill (sister), 8, 36, 38, 62, 65, 88
Cannon (nee Pearce), Kerry Ann (wife). *See* Pearce, Kerry Ann
Cannon, Patrick (son), 181, 182, 209
Cannon, Paul (son), 150, 160, 161, 165, 170, 179, 182, 226
Cannon, Sarah 'Za' (daughter), 181, 182, 209
Cannon (nee Ussher), Susan (wife). *See* Ussher, Susan
Carroll, Vic, 184
censorship laws, 142–3, 158, 167, 171, 201
Chaffey, Bob, 76
Chaffey family, 76
Chambers, Reg, 99
Chandler, John, 227
Chifley, Ben, 119–20, 121, 128, 134
Chifley Labor government, 119
childhood
accidents and injuries, 6–9
Anzac Day services, 30
birth of siblings, 8, 18–19
cinema, 28–9
diet, 21
earliest memories, 3
fantasies, 26–8
football, 30–1
kaleidoscopic nature of, 24–34
mischief, 13–15, 19–20, 22–3
poliomyelitis epidemic, 36–7
primary school, 9–10, 12–14
seaside visits, 31–4
Sunday school, 23
children, 181, 182, 209
Children's Encyclopaedia (Mee), 11–12
Childs, Kevin, 201
Christie, John, 117
cinema, 28–9
Clark, Manning, 155, 205
Clarke, Rupert, 217
Clinch, Lindsay, 170
Clothing News (journal), 150
Cobden, Victoria
Aboriginal people, 35–6
earliest memories of, 3
electricity, 8
during Great Depression, 10–11
history of, 5
hotels, 34–5
residences and way of life, 6–7, 16–18
rubbish tip, 35–6
Cobden Times, 5–6, 16, 45
Cobden Times printery, 6–7, 16, 17, 18, 44–6
Coburg Courier (suburban newspaper), 110
Colac, Victoria, 16
Colombo, Sri Lanka, 114
Commonwealth Literary Fund grant, 205
contraception, 20
convict ancestor, 4
Costigan, Michael, 194, 201
Cousland, Lyle, 169
Cramer, Debby, 216
Crawford, John, 95
Crew, John, 190, 191, 196–7, 198, 199
Cronan, John, 102
Crystal, Fred, 142, 143
Cuthill, WJ, 213
cycling, 58, 75–7, 88, 89, 115–16

Daily Mirror group, 120, 128
Daily Mirror (Sydney), 168

Daily Telegraph (Sydney), 96, 131, 167, 206
Darwin, Northern Territory, 104–5
Davies, Jim, 129
Davis Cup history, 95
Deamer, Syd, 178
defamation law, 184
democracy, 101
dentistry, 21–2
Department of Property and Services (DPS), 222, 224, 225
diet
  at boarding school, 72
  in childhood, 21
  in post-war years, 89
Digest of World Reading, 98–9
donkey engines, 7, 9, 18, 39, 44
Douglas, Irvine, 115, 118, 119, 171
Doyle, Ted, 91
Drysdale, Henry, 108, 109, 126, 132–3, 136, 140
Drysdale, Russell, 172
Duman, Lloyd, 97
Dunn, Ray, 157
Dusseldorp, GJ, 171

East Brighton residence, 189, 208
education
  boarding school. *See* Geelong College
  primary school, 9–10, 12–14
  secondary school, 52, 61–2, 63–4
  self-education, 100
Eichmann, Adolf, 114
Eidlitz, Frank, 144
elections, 45, 174
Ellery Queen's Mystery Magazine, 141
Empire Air Training Scheme, 45
Encel, Sol, 201
Enticott, Graham, 199
existentialism, 111
The Exploration of Australia (Cannon), 218–19

Fairfax, Warwick, 174
family background, 3–6
Family Circle (magazine), 143, 144–5
Famous News Pages in Modern Australian History (Cannon comp.), 207
Fanning, Larry, 134
Farrell, Elizabeth, 227, 228
Farrell, George, 190
Farrell, Roy, 186, 227, 228
Farrell, Tom, 91
Fashion News, 152, 156, 165–6, 175, 177, 178, 181, 185
Fashion Pictorial, 185
Fashionweek, 177
Faust, Beatrice, 201
Fenton, Jane, 215
Ferguson, George, 202
Fernhyll homestead, 235, 236–7
film industry, articles on, 92–3, 94, 115
Film User (trade journal), 115
Financial Review, 184
Fink, Theodore, 179
Fink family, 183
firearms, 29, 41, 74–5
Fitchett brothers, 157
Fitzgerald, Alan, 194, 201
Fitzgerald, Margaret, 172
Fitzgerald, Tom, 172, 178, 190, 203
Floyd, AE, 110
Fly Paper (Scouts magazine), 50–1, 58
Focus (journal), 110–11
football, 30–1
Footscray Advertiser, 137
Forbes, Alison, 205
Forty Years in the Wilderness (Chandler), 227
Foster, Alfred, 62
Fraser, Meg, 218
Frognall, Mont Albert, 87
fruit picking, 75–7
Fullagar, Wilfred, 132, 133

Gardner, Ava, 156
Geelong College
  cadet training, 73–5, 82
  church services, 69–70
  classes, 70–1
  dormitory life, 68–9, 77
  evening study, 70–1
  hobby work-rooms, 78
  initiation, 67–8
  leave, 79–80
  meals, 72
  parental visits, 80
  scholarship to, 64–5
  unhappiness at, 77, 79, 80, 81–3
  uniform, 66–8
  violation of rules and traditions, 81–4
The Ghan, 103–4
Gill, ST, 215
Gillard, Judith, 212
gold rush, 4
Goode, John, 195
Gordon, Mac, 92
Gordon & Gotch, 142, 155, 157, 158
Gown of the Year contest, 185

Graham, Billy, 156
Grearson, David, 216
Great Depression, 3, 10, 231
Green, Alan, 171
Green, Bill, 193, 194, 201, 202, 227
Greer, Germaine, 201
Grover (nee Goldberg), Ada (grandmother), 4, 5, 6
Grover (nee Varley), Regina, 5
Grover, Harry Ehret (great grandfather), 4
Grover, Montague (grandfather), 4, 5–6, 18, 62–3, 97, 109, 229
Gunn, William, 156
Gurney, Alex, 14–15

Haeberle, Ron, 198
Haigh, John, 116
Hamer, Rupert 'Dick', 209
Hamer government (Vic), 210
Hardy, Frank, 108–9, 128
Harney, Bill, 105
Hawke, Bob, 195
Haye, Valerie, 216
Heard Island, Antarctica, 130–1
Henderson, Rupert, 119
Hepworth, John, 201
Herald (Melbourne), 93, 98, 99, 127, 130, 132, 151, 178, 181, 184
Herald & Weekly Times Ltd, 97
Herald group, 144
Heritage Publications, 204, 207
hiking, 78–9
Hill, Beryl, 183
Hince, Kenneth, 132–3
Historical Records of Australia, 210–13
Historical Records Victoria (HRV)
  cancellation of project, 223
  editor-in-chief of, 219
  editor-in-chief of project, 213
  Foundation Series, 211, 225
  locating documents, 211–12
  opposition to publication, 222
  preparing materials, 212–13, 222
  production difficulties, 220
  proposal for, 213
  public campaign to continue project, 223–5
  volume 1, 219–20
  volumes 2A and 2B, 220–1
  volume 3, 221
  volume 4, 221
  volume 5, 222
  volume 6, 222–3, 225
  volume 7, 225
hitchhiking around Australia, 103–6
Hogben, Brian, 174
Hold Page One: Memoirs of Monty Grover, Editor (Cannon), 229
Holeproof house journal, 99–100
Hollway, Tom, 97
Homewood, Helen, 193
homosexuality, 69, 118
How Television Works (booklet), 153
The Human Face of the Great Depression (Cannon), 231
Humphries, Barry, 201
Hurley, Chris, 220, 223
Hyland House, 214

Inverloch residence, 237
IPEC Australia, 190, 195
Irving, Freda, 193

Jackson, Michael, 154–5
James, Gwynydd Francis, 178, 210
James, John Stanley, 188
J.C. Williamson Theatres, 180
Jenkins, Ida Elizabeth, 144
Johnston, George, 91, 96, 106
Joinson, Don, 156–7, 165–6, 177
Jones, Barry, 201
journalism career
  associate editor of *Sunday Mirror*, 168–76
  cadetship at the *Herald*, 98, 99
  company magazines, 99–100, 108
  copyboy at the *Argus*, 90–2
  freelancing, 92–7, 98–100, 102, 110–11
  journalist at the *Age*, 126, 128–32, 135
  in London, 117–19, 120–1
  managing editor of *Truth*, 169
  wrongful dismissal, 174–6

Kaye, William, 198
Keating, Paul, 231
Kelly, Ned, 199
Kerr, Laurie, 91
Kinglake, 90
Kirner, Joan, 225
Kneale, Bruce, 91
Knight, Al, 214
Knox, Errol, 91
Knox, Peter, 91
Knox, Robert, 97

Lahey, John, 223
Land Boom and Bust (Cannon), 206

The Land Boomers (Cannon), 183–5, 205–6
Larkins, Ralph, 176
'The Last Day: A Sub-Editor's Dream' (M. Grover), 229
lead poisoning, 138
Lean, Bill, 174, 176
Lee, George, 99
Lee, Jean, 230
Leonard, Reg, 98
Leser, Bernie, 108, 177
Leunig, Mike, 201
libel case, 157
libel law, 184
Life (magazine), 198
Life in the Country (Cannon), 209
linotypes, 98, 136, 137, 151, 152, 155
Lintot, Edward, 217
Living in the Clouds (Cannon), 235
Loch Haven Books, 227
Lola Montez: The Tragic Story of a 'Liberated Woman' (Cannon), 206–7
London, England
  Australia House, 117–18
  boarding house life, 116–17
  cycling in countryside, 115
  job hunting, 114–15
  post-war rationing, 116
  romantic liaisons, 116–17
Lone Hand (magazine), 109
The Long Last Summer (Cannon), 216–17
Lonsdale, William, 211, 212, 213
Lovett, Harry, 194

MacCallum, Mungo, 201
MacFarlane, Ian, 220, 221, 222, 225
Macmillan, Jocelyn, 213
Main Ridge residences, Mornington Peninsula, 208–9, 217
male deodorants, 166–7
Maller, Alan, 152, 155, 158, 165, 175, 177, 185
Mappin, Tam, 134
marbles, 12–13
marriages
  first marriage, 145–6
  second marriage, 181, 209
Martin, David, 158, 193
Mataranka, Northern Territory, 104
McCaughey, Davis, 225
McConville, Chris, 221
McGuinness, Bruce, 201
McGuire, Peter, 4
McKay, Claude, 96
McLaren, John, 193
McLean, Ian, 212
McNeece, Marjorie, 144, 145
Mee, Arthur, 11
Melbourne, 58
Melbourne After the Gold Rush (Cannon), 227
Melbourne Bulletin, 5
Melbourne Public Library (later State Library Victoria), 100
Melbourne Punch, 5
Melbourne Times, 132–3
Melbourne University bookshop, manager of, 186–8
Melbourne University Press
  assistant director of, 188
  and *Historical Records of Victoria*, 219, 223, 225
Melbourne University Press book printery, 188
Mendelsohn, Oscar, 110
Menzies, Robert, 42, 121, 135, 156, 174
Menzies government, 126, 158, 190, 205
Meudell, GD, 178, 183
The Migrant Experience (SBS TV series), 214
Mingay, Oswald 'Ossie', 95, 138
Mollie Bryon's Offbeats, 97
Monk, Albert, 129
'Montague Grover. He Brightened the Inky Way', 62–3
Montez, Lola, 206–7
Montmorency residence (Melbourne), 149–50, 154
Mooltan (P&O liner), 117–18
Morning Post (Melbourne), 5, 88
Mornington residence, 225–6, 235
Morongo Girls' College, 65
Morrison, Guy, 171
motor cars, 140–1
motorcycling, 140
Mott family, 110
Mount Buffalo, 78–9, 147
Mount Eliza residence, Mornington Peninsula, 217–18, 225
Munro, James, 179
Munster, George, 172, 190, 201
Murdoch, Elisabeth, 169, 231
Murdoch, Keith, 62, 93, 97–8, 126, 128, 173, 178
Murdoch, Patricia, 172
Murdoch, Rupert, 168–9, 172–6, 178, 185–6, 206

Murdoch, Walter, 171, 184
Murray Town, South Australia, 103
music scene, articles on, 96–7

Nation (journal), 172, 203
'Melbourne Spy' column, 178
Nation Review, 203
National Times, 206, 216
Neill, Edwin, 127
New Idea (magazine), 94, 158
New Statesman, 194
Newman, Keith, 170, 172
Newsday, 155–8
Newsday Publications, 154–8
Nichols, Syd, 94
Norton, John, 170, 213–14
nuclear energy and weapons, 118–20
Nunn, Harry, 178, 210, 212, 213, 220

Oakley, Barry, 201
O'Hearn, Dinny, 216
Old Melbourne Town: Before the Gold Rush (Cannon), 227
Oldham, GC, 130, 131
Oliphant, Mark, 118–19, 120
O'Neill, Frank, 170
opera, 97
Orcades (passenger liner), 121, 124
Ormonde (steamer), 112–14, 121
O'Shea, Clarrie, 129
O'Sullivan, Jack, 128
Oz (magazine), 202

Pacini, John, 194
Packer, Frank, 132, 143, 167, 170, 176
Packer, Kerry, 203
Parker, Hilda, 106–7
Parker, Malcolm (stepfather), 106–7, 108, 179–80
Pearce, Kerry Ann, 109, 168, 181, 209. *See also* Kerry Cannon
Pearce, TA 'Jim', 109
Pearl, Cyril, 144, 167, 168–70, 172–3, 174, 176, 193, 201, 208
Pearl, Irma, 208
Penton, Brian, 96
Perilous Voyages to the New Land (Cannon), 230
Perkin, Graham, 127
Pertinent (journal), 96
Peter Isaacson printery, 177, 192, 196–7, 199, 203
Peterborough, Victoria, 32–3
photography, 78

Pitt, Teresa, 231
Plummer, Jack, 171, 173
pocket-money, 19–20
poliomyelitis epidemic, 36–7
Port Campbell, Victoria, 32, 33–4
Port Said, Egypt, 114
Portnoy's Complaint obscenity trial, 201
Price News (journal), 139
printing presses, 7, 9, 18, 44, 136, 137, 151, 155
Public Records Advisory Council, 222
Public Records Office (PRO), Victoria
problems at, 221
publications officer, 210–13
support for *Historical Records of Victoria*, 223, 224
publishing career
Australian Fashion News, 150–2
Australiana facsimile reprints, 204
commercial typesetting business, 136–8, 139, 141
equipment purchased from *Argus* and *Truth*, 151
Family Circle (magazine), 143, 144–5
Heritage Publications, 204, 207
managing editor of Atlas Publications, 141–5
Newsday Publications, 154–8
takeover of *Radio Times* plant, 128–32
Teleview (magazine), 134–6
Puckapunyal Army base, 74

Quist, Adrian, 95

RAAF, 45
Radio & Electrical Retailers' Association, 138
Radio Times (Melbourne), 108–10, 111, 121, 124, 126, 132–4, 135–8, 153
Rapke, Trevor, 199
Rasmussen, Ted, 91
Reader's Digest, 218
Realist Film Makers, 93
Red Lion Hotel, Lonsdale St, 4
Red Ragger ('newspaper'), 63–4
Refshauge, Bill, 124
research projects
fate of Victoria's Aboriginal people, 226–7
general survey of nineteenth century, 204–5
Great Depression, 230–1
immigrants' stories, 230
John Norton, 213–14

land boom of nineteenth century, 178–9, 182–3
Lola Montez, 206–7
state executions, 229–30.
See also Historical Records of Victoria (HRV)
Reynolds, Patricia, 199, 207
Richardson, Hal, 104
Riches, Norah, 177
Riddell, Elizabeth, 170
Ridgeway, Percy, 109
Robie, David, 198, 200
Robinson, 'Robby', 141, 150, 152
Robson, Lloyd, 219, 221
Rolland, F.W., 101
romantic liaisons, 79–80, 116–17, 121–2, 166, 170, 172
See also marriages
Ross, John, 186, 215
Roth, Philip, 201
Rowse, Tim, 227
royal tours, Duke of Gloucester, 15–16
Royal Women's Hospital, 124–5
rule of law, 113–14
Russo, Peter, 171–2
Ryan, Peter, 139, 141, 152–3, 170, 178, 182, 183, 184, 186, 206, 214
Rylah, Arthur, 198

Salter, Denbeigh, 194
Santamaria, BA, 158, 231
Sawer, Geoffrey, 201
Sayers, Stuart, 206
Sayers, Ted, 194
Schepsi, Joseph, 97
science fiction magazines, 26–7, 142
Science Fiction Monthly (magazine), 142
Scott, Eric, 143
scouting, 47–51, 59–60
Seager, Helen, 91
seaside visits, 31–4
serial killers, 116, 117
Serventy, Vincent, 201
Sharman, Robert, 219–20
Shaw, Alan, 213, 219
Shell, advertising for, 153
Sheppard, Alex, 171, 184
Shillito, Thomas, 199
shooting, 29, 41
Sinclair, Keith, 132
Skalkor, Theo, 203
Slater, Bill, 128, 231
Slater & Gordon, 128, 231–2
Slessor, Ken, 173
smallpox, 118
Smith, Ian, 173
Smith's Weekly, 96
South Yarra residence, 75, 88–9
Southdown Press, 157–8
Spalding, Alan, 134
spiritualism, 7–8, 100
sport, 12
Sports Novels (magazine), 95
Spowers, Allan, 91
Spreadborough, Bob, 222
Squire (magazine), 139, 142–3
stammering, 64, 77, 78, 80, 97, 133
Star (Melbourne), 167
Steed, John, 194–5
Stokes, Cathie, 177
Stokes, George, 144
Stone, Julius, 113–14
Strzelecki Ranges, 235–7
sugar consumption, 19, 21
Suich, Max, 206
Sun (Sydney), 116, 127
Sun (Sydney), 5
Sun News-Pictorial, 97, 207
Sunday Herald, 115, 119
Sunday Mirror (Sydney), 119, 168–76, 190
Sunday newspapers, legalisation of publication in Victoria, 189
Sunday Observer
battle for free speech, 199
closure, 203
comic strips, 194
dummy run, 192, 196
editor-in-chief of, 190–1, 199, 200
exclusive stories, 197–8
first issue, 196–7
owner's plans for, 191–2, 194, 200
plant, 206
staff, 192–4
Sunday Post (Melbourne), 189–90
Sunday Review, 200–1
Sunday school, 23
Sunday Telegraph (Sydney), 167, 168, 170, 206
Sun-Herald (Sydney), 168
Sun-News-Pictorial (Melbourne), 5
surgical operations, closed-circuit TV transmission, 124–5
Survey and Lands Department, 222
swaggies, 19
Sydney, in early post-war years, 93–4
Sydney Morning Herald, 94, 95, 114, 117–19, 174, 214

Syme, David, 127
Syme, Oswald, 127

Tait, Frank, 180
Tait, Viola, 180
Teleview (magazine), 134–5, 138
television, 111, 121, 124–6, 134, 136, 153–4
Tempo (magazine), 96–7
Testro, Ron, 91
Textile Council of Australia newsletter, 186
That Damned Democrat (Cannon), 213–14
That Disreputable Firm: The Inside Story of Slater & Gordon (Cannon), 232
theft, 90
Thomas, Mark, 217
Thompson, Duncan, 131–2
Thomson, Donald, 148–9
Thorn, Arthur, 95
The Time is Now Ripe (M. Grover), 63–4
Timlin, John, 227
Tomorrow (journal), 92
Trades Hall reporting, 128–9
Tree, Ernest, 138–9
Tribune (communist newspaper), 108
Truth, 213–14
Truth (Melbourne), 142–3, 151, 169, 194
Tuddenham, Des, 193
Turnbull, Clive, 93, 193
Turnbull, Noel, 195
TV Week (magazine), 158
typesetting, for *Cobden Times*, 7, 8, 44, 46
typesetting business, 136–8, 139

Udovikoff, Serge, 130–1
Unwin, Terry, 186
Ussher, Susan, 145–50, 158–6. *See also* Susan Cannon
Utting, Jeff, 169, 173

Vagabond Country (Cannon), 214
Vagabond Papers (ed. Cannon), 189
Victorian Authorised Newsagents Association (VANA), 195
The Victorian Gold Fields 1852–3 (Gill), 215
Victorian Government Printing Office (VGPO), 219, 222, 224, 225
Vietnam War, 190, 198
Vogue (magazine), 108, 166, 177
Volunteer Air Observers Corps, 57–8
Volunteer Defence Corps, 49–50

Wainer, Bertram, 197, 198
Walkley, Bill, 171
Walkley Awards, 171
Walsh, Kerry, 193
Walsh, Richard, 142, 202–3
Walsh, RW 'Bunna', 223, 224
Walters, Wes, 143
Ward, Russell, 216
Warnecke, 'George', 143, 144
Warrandyte residence, 179, 181
Watson, Don, 225
Watson, James 'King', 206
Watsonia Army Camp, 74
Wells, HG, 71, 90, 101, 183
Western District, Victoria, visits to homesteads and mansions, 38–42
Western Mail, 94
White, Osmar 'Ossie', 98
Whitington, Don, 193
Whitlam government, 206, 208
Who Killed the Koories? (Cannon), 227
Who's Master, Who's Man? (Cannon), 205
Wilder, Brian, 222–3
Wilson, David, 201
Winneke, Henry, 219
The Woman as Murderer: Five Who Paid with Their Lives (Cannon), 230
Woman's Day (magazine), 144, 167–8, 181
Women's Weekly (magazine), 143, 144
Woods, Walter, 185
World (Sydney), 92
World War II
  bombing of Darwin, 105
  effects of Pacific War, 57
  loyalty to British Empire, 44
  outbreak, 42
  'phony war', 43
  Volunteer Defence Corps, 49–50
  wartime shortages, 57–8
Wren, John, 91, 109, 128
The Writer (magazine), 102

Yaffa Syndicate, 141
Yarra River, kayaking, 89
Young, Alan, 195

THE MIEGUNYAH PRESS

This book was designed and
typeset by Cannon Typesetting
The text was set in 11½ point Adobe Caslon Pro
with 15½ points of leading
The text was printed on 80gsm
This book was edited by Paul Smitz

THE
MIEGUNYAH
PRESS